Youth Technoculture: From Aesthetics to Politics

Youth in a Globalizing World

Series Editors

Vincenzo Cicchelli (*Ceped, Université Paris Descartes/IRD*)
Sylvie Octobre (*DEPS-Ministère de la culture and
Centre Max Weber-ENS Lyon/CNRS, France*)

Editorial Board

Valentina Cuzzocrea (*University of Cagliari, Italy*)
Ratiba Hadj-Moussa (*York University, Canada*)
Claudia Jacinto (*PREJET-Instituto de Desarrollo Económico y Social, Argentina*)
Jeylan Mortimer (*University of Minnesota, United States of America*)
Andrea Pirni (*Unversità di Genova, Italy*)
Dan Woodman (*University of Melbourne, Australia*)
Chin-Chin Yi (*Academic Sinica, Taiwan*)

VOLUME 13

The titles published in this series are listed at *brill.com/ygw*

Youth Technoculture: From Aesthetics to Politics

By

Sylvie Octobre

Translated from French by

Sarah-Louise Raillard

BRILL

LEIDEN | BOSTON

Originally published in French under the title *Les techno-cultures juveniles. Du culturel au politique*. Copyright © L'Harmattan, 2018. www.harmattan.fr

Cover illustration: Image by Gerd Altmann from Pixabay.

The Library of Congress Cataloging-in-Publication Data is available online at http://catalog.loc.gov

Typeface for the Latin, Greek, and Cyrillic scripts: "Brill". See and download: brill.com/brill-typeface.

ISSN 2212-9383
ISBN 978-90-04-44736-3 (hardback)
ISBN 978-90-04-44753-0 (e-book)

Copyright 2021 by Koninklijke Brill NV, Leiden, The Netherlands.
Koninklijke Brill NV incorporates the imprints Brill, Brill Hes & De Graaf, Brill Nijhoff, Brill Rodopi, Brill Sense, Hotei Publishing, mentis Verlag, Verlag Ferdinand Schöningh and Wilhelm Fink Verlag.
All rights reserved. No part of this publication may be reproduced, translated, stored in a retrieval system, or transmitted in any form or by any means, electronic, mechanical, photocopying, recording or otherwise, without prior written permission from the publisher. Requests for re-use and/or translations must be addressed to Koninklijke Brill NV via brill.com or copyright.com.

This book is printed on acid-free paper and produced in a sustainable manner.

Contents

Foreword: Understanding Our Global Cultural World IX
  Modesto Gayo

Introduction: From Mediaculture to Technoculture 1
  1   After Mediacultures   4
  2   Technocultural Mutations and Social Mutations   6
  3   Going beyond Moral Panic   9
  4   The New Barbarians   12

1 **Culture in a Technological World**
  Major Fears Resurface   14
  1   The Fear of Technocultural Mutations   14
      1.1   *Convergence,* Mon Amour   15
      1.2   *Globalizing Hyperculture*   16
      1.3   *From Works of Art to Cultural Contents*   19
  2   The End of Culture?   22
      2.1   *The Destructive Power of Technological Hegemony?*   22
      2.2   *The Loss of the Tangible*   25
      2.3   *Behind Technological Change, Cultural Shifts*   27
  3   The World of Machines   29
      3.1   *Computational Dynamics*   29
      3.2   *The Past Predicts the Future; or, Birds of a Feather Stick Together*   31
      3.3   *The Cultural Promise of Big Data*   33

2 **The Cult of Participation**   37
  1   The Pro-am: A Form of Commitment in the Technocultural Regime   37
      1.1   *The Roots of The Pro-am: The Poacher*   37
      1.2   *The Pro-am Revolution*   41
  2   Collective Intelligence and Community   42
      2.1   *What Is Collective Intelligence?*   43
      2.2   *Collective Intelligence and Cultural Expertise*   45
  3   The Culture of Doing   47
      3.1   *Compensatory Skills*   48
      3.2   *Creative Remixing*   48
  4   A New Ecology of Attention   51
      4.1   *In Search of Lost Attention Spans*   51

- 4.2 *In Praise of Free-Floating Attention and the Illusion of Multitasking* 53
- 4.3 *Hyper Attention: An Autopsy* 55

3 The Impact of Youth Technoculture on Cultural Myths 59
1. Expressiveness 59
   - 1.1 *Expressive Individualism* 59
   - 1.2 *The Rise of Experimentation* 61
2. Emotions First and Foremost 63
   - 2.1 *Peak Experiences* 63
   - 2.2 *Presentification* 65
3. Mobility as Value 66
   - 3.1 *The Call to Mobility* 67
   - 3.2 *Aesthetico-cultural Cosmopolitanism* 68
   - 3.3 *A New Criterion for Ranking* 71
4. Additive Comprehension 74
   - 4.1 *Putting Together the Collaborative Transmedia Puzzle* 74
   - 4.2 *The Reputation Filter* 76

4 How Technoculture Shapes Youth Norms 81
1. Autonomy, an Ambiguous Standard 81
   - 1.1 *Cultural Consumption: The First Steps towards Autonomy* 81
   - 1.2 *Private and Public Autonomy* 84
   - 1.3 *The Framework of Cultural Autonomy and Its Inner Tensions* 86
2. Norms of Engagement, Relation and Selection 89
   - 2.1 *The Importance of Choice* 89
   - 2.2 *From Relationships to the Proximity Effect* 91
   - 2.3 *What Engagement Signifies* 94
3. The Vices and Virtues of Eclecticism 96
   - 3.1 *Revisiting Youth Omnivorism* 96
   - 3.2 *The Challenge of Eclecticism* 98

5 Technoculture, Education and Self-Education 100
1. Is Technoculture an Alternative Form of Education? 100
   - 1.1 *A "real-world" Education* 101
   - 1.2 *The Return of Aesthetics* 104
   - 1.3 *Modes of Learning and Affinity Spaces* 108
2. The Challenge of Transliteracy 110
   - 2.1 *Literacy, Media Literacy and Digital Literacy* 110

        2.2   *The Components of Transliteracy*   111
        2.3   *A Weapon against Bullshit*   112
    3   Mediation and Remediation   115
        3.1   *A New Organizing Principle for Knowledge?*   115
        3.2   *Self-Organization and Remediation*   116

6   **Technological and Cultural Fault Lines**   119
    1   Technocultural Fault Lines   120
        1.1   *The Access Divide*   120
        1.2   *The Usage Divide*   121
        1.3   *The Transferability Divide*   123
        1.4   *The Reflexive Capacity Divide*   124
    2   A Universe Where Important Inequalities Persist   130
        2.1   *An Argument against "the tribalization of youth culture"*   131
        2.2   *Factoring in Gender*   132
        2.3   *Cumulative Inequalities?*   135

7   **The Political and Ethical Implications of Youth Technoculture**   139
    1   Technoculture Is (Inherently) Political   140
        1.1   *Becoming a Political Actor in the Era of Technoculture*   140
        1.2   *Towards a Technocultural Public and Political Space*   142
        1.3   *The Technocultural Regime Threatened by Rumors*   145
        1.4   *Far from the Technocultural Crowd*   147
    2   Political Activism and Technoculture   151
        2.1   *Political and Cultural Media Activism*   152
        2.2   *Political and Cultural Hacktivism*   154
    3   Democracy and Technoculture   157
        3.1   *Democracy and Polyphonic Regimes of Truth*   158
        3.2   *Knowledge Societies and Cognitive Bubbles*   160
        3.3   *Neo-democracy or Democracy Threatened by Technoculture*   163

Conclusion: Resisting the Appeal of Worst-Case Scenarios   170
1   A Twofold Movement of Creativity and Diversity   171
2   Reconfiguring Public Space   174
3   Rejecting Pessimism   176

Bibliography   179
Index   203

Foreword: Understanding Our Global Cultural World

Modesto Gayo

The book *Youth Technoculture. From Aesthetics to Politics* is an invitation to travel through time, changing in the same turn the traditional national space for a global landscape. In other words, the ontologies of time and physical distances experience a radical change that makes the foreseeable societies substantially different from those human beings have known up to these days. This does not mean that those humans are going to be substituted by cyborgs, or that flying cars will soon be the usual way of urban transportation, but more realistically that notions such as 'locality', 'belonging' and 'inequality' are going through an irreversible process of unprecedented redefinition. Technologies have always been essential elements in any account of History, difficult to be conceived as mere tools or lacking of any epistemological depth. Precisely what the term 'technoculture' is meant for, offering to electronic advances and computer techniques a cultural dimension which demonstrates that virtual reality and digital devices are much more significant than spectacular fireworks of an eventual empty contemporary hour.

Therefore, we should not be misled by the term "techno", assuming that it simply refers to technology (internet, apps, complex softwares, amongst others), or pointing out what has happened to youngsters of the already old beginning of the xxith century, when changes have been in some ways speeding up beyond any expectation. In this vein, 'techno' could be equated with notions such as 'neo', the adaptable 'contemporary', or even the extremely flexible and very often stretched out 'modern'. That means that it is not a fashion, something hot today and fading away tomorrow, but a new whole and hegemonic era that opens a myriad of new alternatives and opportunities regarding economic development, occupations and models of work, family, communications, transportation, ways of leisure, and, no doubt, distinctive forms of culture and social cleavages in the making. This turn also shuts down possibilities of being, probably many of them for good, and for that reason throws some ideas and those who bear them into the past, sometimes in the present itself as an old toy or a book never open again. This has already produced the contents of memories of the time before "techno", setting the basis for emergent narratives of nostalgia. Taking all this into account, technoculture cannot be reduced to a new culture, but above all it becomes constitutive of a transformative temporality which has come to a definitive existence in the last few years, and even more in those to come, but, needless to say, it has a long tail into the past of the last two centuries if someone wants to trace it or follow its steps backwards.

If this book is about a culture which contributes decisively to define a new civilizatory step for society, studying technoculture should not pay the main focus on analyzing patterns of practice or looking at types and intensity of use of tech devices. More than anything, what is at stake is a profound transformation of views and meanings. Perhaps even more than a cultural revolution, the book is a portrait of a cultural substitution which is coming in place while it is written, and ever faster: more bytes (from giga to tera to peta), more access to the Web, more Facebook friends, more videos in Youtube, more in millions, billions and trillions; from survey samples to big data; the Humanity caught up in multiple cages of servers, powerful and fragile contents which include financial numbers and emotions without any discrimination, and which will be soon in the next few decades a deposit of memories of death, past lives registered in real time outnumbering the users and breaking the ice of those glaziers of history for genealogists, historians, anthropologists, and all kind of social and not social scientists, but also for art experts of new media, public administrators, private investigators, crime analysts, amongst many others, and above all for the sake of meeting the expectations and questions of indagatory and curious minds of all kind, silently produced by the new tech, digital and virtual, a brand new scenario of human information and interaction, a new theatre of live, with all the laughs and sadness of existence.

If traditional notions of distance and duration become outdated, the idea of 'youth' has also been reached by the dynamics of this society in technological turmoil. In a World in which youngsters are vectors of change, looking at them is very much an opportunity to put attention to constantly renovating innovative trends. However, this time, different to the Sixties and Seventies, October makes clear that they are not much involved in or fighting for new ideologies, but incorporating technologies, in principle politically neutral, that have radical consequences for our reality, silently putting a revolution in place that makes Twentieth century embodied practices and meanings rapidly fading away. Probably the real liquidity of our times, being not much the lack of traditional identities, but how many things we can do per hour, or how far my collaborators can be. In that vein, the barbarians are not anymore those living undress in Amazonia or central Australia, but those who resist to be involved in the digital world, those without the skills and/or the will to take part in social networking via Facebook, Instagram, TikTok, individuals imbued by nostalgias of lost ways of life, still echoing in human minds, calling for alternatives that seem to disappear drowned in the current waters of pentabytes dominated by Google and the e-trade of Amazon.

Rituals are here at stake, and this book brings to the fore not only a radical transition in society, but the way technoculture practices are increasingly becoming a ritualization of an ever coming new world of wonders. However, these rituals are not well-known religions, or the prototypical ceremonies organised by the State, but an everyday life consolidation of practices of communication, information collection and production which calls for an individual that admires technological achievements and is constantly plugged in the virtual space. Most of the contents are profane, but, surprisingly for many, it has turned out being a territory of sacred notions (friendship, wisdom, love and so on) and also sacred rituals in formation (community's recognition, educational titles, gaming championships, amongst others in increasing numbers). In that sense, it should not strike us if we are witnessing the shaping up of new forms of religious belief, mixing up science and traditional after death or transcendental orientations. The digital world is produced by and large by computer engineering, but the new beliefs are not digital, but totally on- and off-line in their effects.

One of the main consequences has to do with family dynamics, and particularly processes of learning concerning cultural capital transmission. One might be unfair simplistically contending that Pierre Bourdieu's famous thesis about habitus production is not right anymore, but history has shown us that parents' ability to shape up their offspring's cultural orientations is also a restricted picture of an account that needs to conceive children as a more autonomous agent. This also affects any critique about the school institution. *La République* has been significantly overtaken by currents of globalization and digitalization. Today, the school is a limited referent for any understanding of teaching and learning processes.

There is so much to say about a book which introduces the reader to an emergent new world, not necessarily a brave one. We are not still in the limits of our civilization in a way that mirrors the first Foundation of Asimov, but we are far off from the Twentieth century in many senses. This book is very well written, thoughtful in contents, dynamic and precise in making a portrait of our present. It softens fears while face them directly, fearlessly. It opens a door for what is coming, a future unimagined by science fiction, but somehow beyond it.

INTRODUCTION

From Mediaculture to Technoculture

Equipped with all sorts of new gadgets like smartphones and wireless headphones, today's youth is plugged in at all times. The younger generations have developed their own vocabulary, sprinkling words such as *geek, like, fake, mods* and *gaming* into their daily conversations. From their earliest childhoods, today's young people are accustomed to screens, be they tablets, smartphones or laptops, spending significant hours each week on these devices. As they grow up, they will use these tools to communicate and have fun, of course, but they will also grow to rely on them for their education (for instance, to read textbooks or complete video assignments). As devices grow increasingly versatile, it becomes nearly impossible to distinguish the different kinds of "screen time" that individuals engage in, to pinpoint what constitutes "reading" or "learning," — especially given that these various dimensions are collapsed or combined in a number of various practices — or to untangle the various forms of technological savvy at play.

Today's youth has received a number of strange epithets: from the alphabetical Generation X and Generation Y — perhaps evoking the image of headphones plugged into one's ears with the wire connecting back to the phone (Dagnaud, 2013) — and Generation Z, to Digital Natives, Generation C (for communication), Generation Alpha and a host of other pithy names, and finally the App Generation (Gardner and Davis, 2014). These cohorts are thus the first to be described by a specific cultural behavior (such as communication or creation) a technological medium (the digital sphere) or an attitude (the "why" of Generation Y). The media has increasingly subdivided these generations into more and more micro-generations whose technological habits ostensibly become their identity markers (Cocquebert, 2019): hence Generation Facebook and Generation Instagram, for instance. Their predecessors were, on the contrary, defined by contemporary political events (the Vietnam War, the Algerian War for Independence, etc.), economic crises (the 1970s energy crisis), social movements (flower power, May 68) or epidemics (the AIDS generation) (Donnat and Levy, 2007). To a greater degree than any of the generations that preceded them, today's youth are also cause for moral panic: digital generations are described as apathetic, uninterested in work, fickle and ultimately superficial. In fact, all sorts of social ills appear to have been visited upon today's youth. They are linked to the collapse of sociocultural transmission and the institutions trusted to conduct those processes — school and the family — with, on the one hand the "crisis of masculinity" and the forms of authority supposedly associated with the former, and on the other, the rhetoric surrounding the "loss of culture" that is constantly deployed by reactionary thinkers, as well as the breakdown of the social fabric due to technology (a common image has nerds holed up in their rooms or asocial individuals devoted to spending their entire lives virtually and online). These themes are so widespread that a popular work by David Buckingham was provocatively titled *After the Death of Childhood* (Buckingham, 2000); Michel Desmurget similarly called his book *La fabrique du crétin digital. Les dangers des écrans pour nos enfants* [The creation of digital morons. The dangers of screens for our children] (Desmurget, 2019).

It is undeniable that technoculture is an integral part of youth today. From their earliest age, children now learn how to use tablets, at first to watch movies and television. Kids can be seen walking around with headphones, reading online, writing blogs or contributing to opensource projects; some of them even create and produce music online. Cell phones have become the main cultural hub in our new multimedia ecology. In fact, digital technologies have granted the humble cell phone extensive powers over content, from creation (or co-creation) to mediation (in particular through recommendations and dissemination) and finally reception (for example, in creating music playlists). The rise of technoculture has also heralded a new era on the heels of the era of mediaculture (Macé et Maigret, 2005);[1] one where interacting with machines does not only entail gaining access to cultural contents, but also acting upon and interacting with them.

But beyond these admittedly noteworthy technological developments, what is particularly striking is how new technocultural behaviors have been used to justify critical interpretations of today's youth, an attitude that is utterly in thrall to a "minimal" or even metaphorical use of the generational concept. The concept of a generation, which was originally meant to be a tool used to analyze transformations in the past (Mannheim, 1952), in this case becomes an interpretative framework to understand society and its

---

[1] The term mediaculture was coined by Eric Macé and Eric Maigret with a view to transcending the highly entrenched dichotomy between media and culture; or as it is seen in France, the chasm between what is popular and lowbrow on the one hand, and what is artistic and highbrow on the other. Their intention was to highlight the number of hybrid forms that today have eliminated this long-standing distinction (mass culture, pop culture, pop art, subcultures, countercultures, fan cultures, cyber-culture, publics and counterpublics, etc.). The authors therefore felt it was imperative to analyze the cultures produced by the media as points of intersection for practices of constructing meaning, thus breaking down the silos between the studies of media, culture and representation more broadly.

various power struggles, both now and in the future. In order to comprehend this use of the concept, we can look at recent history, recalling that the May 68 generation in Europe gave rise to the illusion that there ever existed a homogenous generation composed of free and revolutionary individuals who were highly engaged in culture. This illusion became the benchmark against which subsequent generations were measured, thus producing the generational matrix of media representation and marketing strategies — the latter especially so, given that generational identities became an important tool to capture market attention as purchasing power rapidly increased. The illusion of a homogenous generation was based on an "immediate" analysis; the May 68 generation was discussed "in the heat of the moment," as Philippe Beneton and Jean Touchard have observed (Beneton and Touchard, 1970). This double interpretive matrix has in turn given rise to successive media generations, which each time represent a new but surprisingly unchallenged narrative about the individuals at hand, one with major sociopolitical repercussions. For instance, the contemporary myth of the "entrepreneurship" generation which touts freedom and creativity, the desire to be one's own boss and the widespread use of digital technologies cleverly glosses over the growing Uberization of society — illustrated by the emergence of individuals belonging to the "slash generation," allegedly choosing a lifestyle that entails the combining a variety of small jobs — and the price paid by young people due to contracting labor markets throughout Europe. Among such generational illusions, we shall take a closer look at the so-called digital natives (Prensky, 2001), the almost omniscient beings who were born with a tablet in their hand and an obsession for pop culture, which in turn has propagated their mythical representation (Kirschner and De Bruyckere, 2017). Is surfing the internet equivalent to mastering digital technologies? Is this the purview of digital "natives" and to *what* are such individuals truly "native"?

The concept of a generation cannot in fact be dissociated from the issue of intergenerational linkages, be they similarities, solidarities or cleavages. Generational clash is a widely accepted fallacy. In reality, solidarity, especially within family units, has never been stronger, given the need to face economic difficulties. In France, private financial solidarity accounts for 10% of the nation's wealth; 80% of young people between 18 and 24 years old receive financial assistance from their parents and 60% of them consider this financial assistance to be essential (Castell, Portela, and Rivalin, 2016). Autonomy, which is generally considered to be characteristic of aging, has thus been radically altered. While it may be delayed financially, autonomy now emerges in the cultural sphere very early on, with children being empowered to make their own musical or televisual choices, and with the influence of obligatory constraints such as school and one's family being counteracted — and at times outweighed — by the growing influence of the media and one's peers. Although the latter are often seen as more liberating influences, they in fact merely serve to produce other forms of normativity. In the cultural domain, autonomy has undergone a number of important shifts with the advent of technoculture, which has exploded the number of possibilities with regard to previous cultural media forms, by adding the ability to act upon cultural contents through creation, modification and diffusion.

1 After Mediacultures

The media — and then multimedia — context of cultural industries and the rise of popularization through cultural massification, which has overtaken entire swathes of the cultural landscape, highlights the precocious development of the "cultural consumer" as an occupation. This phenomenon redesigns the spheres of socialization in which young people move (family, school, work, (un)institutionalized free time) and develops its own norms, skills and constraints (informational, reflexive, interpersonal, reputational, etc.) with the same vigor as the more traditional roles attributed through education or lineage (Sirota, 2006; Octobre and Sirota, 2013).

With the rise of digital media and the growing importance of cultural industries, new forms of cultural consumption have appeared that have further altered the occupation of the cultural consumer. On the one hand, the digital revolution has significantly increased the number of contents and products available, even created new cultural forms such as the webtoon[2], and multiply and individualize forms of consumption and reception; it has likewise transformed the respective place of different activities in the lives of children and young people. Cultural consumption has become all encompassing, seeping into all spheres of life, especially as consumption becomes more and more polymorphic, customized and divisible into bite-size chunks (Octobre, 2011 and 2014b). We have entered the era of hyper-choice (Durand, 2016). To measure the amplitude of this transformation: each minute, 300 hours of video are uploaded to YouTube. This hyper-choice is accompanied by the accelerated acquisition of legitimacy by cultural products (TV shows in particular) which had hitherto been seen as popular — in the low-brow sense — a process that produces a large number of cultural resources that are not organized into any formal or informal cultural or educational program.

---

2 It is a digital comic, originated in South Korea and increasingly popular around the world.

On the other hand, technoculture is reshaping cultural amateurism by increasing the ability of individuals to act upon contents, ranging from video game mods[3] to musical sampling[4] and the creation of different videos (memes,[5] tutorials,[6] vlogs,[7] etc.). Consumption has thus become an action in of itself, and the distinctions between consumption and practice are slowly disappearing. As a result, technoculture is redefining different cultural spaces and the relationships between them, changing how time, split between family constraints and school obligations, is experienced by young people (Zaffran, 2010), and how contents (in particular through hybridization), representations, skills, mythologies and even ideologies are shaped. For example, Wattpad,[8] a platform for literary writing, allows conversations to occur on a permanent basis between readers and writers, given that chapters are posted progressively and that subsequent chapters take into account reader reactions.

Finally, technoculture has marked the definitive entry of youth culture into the sphere of cultural globalization, belying fears surrounding the eradication of local cultures (Martel, 2010) and instead promoting the rise of different hybrid forms (Pieterse, 2009) — a phenomenon which has been accompanied by a certain degree of cultural resistance and a number of conservative policies (including the French law on the cultural exception), but which has also, on the contrary, helped certain local cultures to flourish (Castells, 2013; Tomlinson, 1999).

It is therefore not just youth cultural media that is the target of current transformations — that is, content which comes predominantly from existing

---

3 Mods are player-driven alterations made to an existing video game, or the creation of a new game using a graft-like process.
4 Musical samples are taken from longer pieces (soundtracks, songs, etc.) and used to create something new in a different context.
5 Memes are elements or visual phenomena that are repeated, tweaked and disseminated many times on the Internet.
6 How-to guides, while originally technical in nature, have expanded in scope. How-to tutorials can now be found on subjects as varied as hair and makeup, tuning, video games, creative hobbies, gardening, etc.
7 Vlog is a contraction of the two words "video blog". Vlogs are used to publish videos, often commented by viewers.
8 Wattpad is an open access website where users can, for free, write and share stories, poems, fan fiction, novels and articles in all genres, either posting them on the website or making them available on a mobile application where they can be downloaded and read later without an internet connection. Both published and unknown authors can be found on the site. Most contributions take the form of serial novels, with short chapters of about 2,000 words each. Readers are encouraged to post their comments on authors, books or even individual paragraphs.

cultural industries — but also *how* this content is used, thanks to digital technologies that put the world in the palm of one's hand, at little economic or (apparent) human cost. It has become quite easy to compose entire cultural universes for oneself by combining products that have been excised from their initial centers of production, or have been user-generated thanks to cooperation between amateurs on the fringes of traditional institutions of transmission and endorsement. Technoculture thus refers to a set of contents, operational modes, techniques of self-creation and self-representation, skills (how to do things, but also how to be and present oneself in public), norms and ideologies. Young people have all become the curators of their own cultural repertoires, designed to "authentically" show the world who they are. Technocultural participation thus becomes another kind of identity marker, given that the cultural resources we choose to consume are supposed to describe who we are. In short, technoculture acts as the conduit for a twofold phenomenon: the technologization of individual and social relationships to culture, in tandem with the culturalization of those relationships to technology. We shall investigate the technocultural regime in depth in this volume.

2 Technocultural Mutations and Social Mutations

Cultural consumers in the technocultural regime are endowed with a unique set of tools, timelines, skills and constraints, which are simultaneously informational, reflexive and relational (Octobre, 2017). Technoculture is therefore an ideal vantage point from which to observe a number of social mutations: mutations in educational systems, in the representation of youth, in linkages between work (or school) and leisure, in the construction of identities (Arleo and Delalande, 2011; Cook, 2004). In those realms, young people are seen either as spearheading progress (through an implicit connection between generational renewal and technological innovation) or as the reef upon which the "laws" of sociology flounder (young people are supposed to defy the weight of the social stratification of practices with their freedom to choose). Youth technoculture has also simultaneously given rise to new fault lines — in particular around the issues of gender and social usage — and new forms of cultural creativity, stemming from the concept of networks. The younger generations have thus become the subject of many different studies and been interpreted variously as the actors of so-called "interpretive reproduction" (Corsaro, 2003); the source of shifting age group markers (de Singly, 2006); the cause for the diversification of transmission modalities (Pasquier, 2005); the focus of family dynamics (Attias-Donfut, Lapierre, and Ségalen, 2002; Ségalen, 2011); and the agents of their own (cultural) transformation (Octobre, 2010). They can also be analyzed in light of the mutations they have undergone in the age of globalization, both in terms of the cosmopolitanization of imaginaries (Cicchelli and Octobre, 2018a) and the creation of new tensions which reveal themselves in the culturalization of minorities and their "small differences," thus fueling the resurgence of xenophobic tendencies (Appadurai, 2006).

Our analysis of youth technoculture draws on and further develops observations made by the sociology of culture and the arts, as well as by pedagogical science, psychology, philosophy, information and communications science, ergonomics, and neuroscience. Given that it is obviously impossible to cover all of these topics in a single volume, we shall focus on the contribution of social and human science to the matter at hand. We must nevertheless be willing start from scratch, abandoning a number of central concepts used to analyze cultural leisure activities and which were implicitly designed with adults in mind, and in the context of a labor value model that is inherently national.

The same limitations apply to the definition of leisure originally proposed by Joffre Dumazedier (1988) and whose pertinence becomes questionable when discussing youth in the media age (Yonnet, 1999). In fact, challenging the relevance of the criterion of *freeness* — as in the concept of "free time" — we instead prefer the notion of use or exchange value. Investment in amateur communities usually leads to symbolic benefits — in particular, recognition amongst one's peers — and sometimes material ones, such as winning prizes and games. It is overly simplistic to define leisure by its allegedly hedonistic nature, given that this characteristic is not the sole purview of leisure activities and can in fact be applied to other spheres of life (for instance, when good students claim to like school). The individual nature of leisure activities likewise seems insufficient to describe what young people do in their free time today. In fact, their leisure activities are far from being devoid of familial burdens and constraints. Family structures are often decisive for early enrollment in artistic or athletic training, as well as for determining the degree of childhood exposure to cultural institutions such as museums, libraries, and theaters. But the same can also be said for (multi)media consumption habits, which have become a source of constant negotiation between parents and children, in particular when it comes to regulating how much time should be spent in front of a screen. The vast number of publications that demonize the effects of screen time, leading to diminished creativity, sleep disorders, and the emergence of violent behaviors (Math, Desor, and Witkowski, 2015; Duch, Fisher, Ensari, and Harrington, 2013) attests to the high degree of visibility this issue has attracted in the educational sphere, and to the role that parents play in shaping the leisure activities of their children, at least until adolescence (Bach, Houdé, Léna, and Tisseron, 2013). What about the supposedly emancipatory nature of leisure activities? The consumption patterns and cultural practices of young people do not necessarily free them from the daily grind — as evidenced by the number of young people who watch television every day but claim to be able to take it or leave it, or by those who compulsively but randomly surf the web. And yet some forms of youth consumption do contribute to self-development and the process of growing up, in particular digital and expressive practices. And what should we make of the argument that leisure activities are dictated by passion (Bromberger, 1998)? This argument, according to which leisure activities are defined by their potential for intense attachment, exclusivity, rarity, or sacrifice, does not seem like it can easily be applied to young people today. In some of the surveys published, a large number of young people state that they have hobbies without evincing any trace of sacrifice associated with the idea of passion, even when declaring great attachment to certain activities (Octobre, 2014a).

To these facets of leisure, which have already been studied by a number of researchers, we can add those that stem from the global context engendered by cultural industries. This context is rarely studied, except from the angle of production (for instance, with regard to quota policies or financial support). The analysis of youth cultural imaginaries in an era of global cultural contents is likewise rarely discussed in a world where culture is nevertheless inherent to globalization. Arjun Appadurai thus argues that within the different flows of globalizations — what he calls *scapes* — there are three which are related to culture and media (Appadurai, 1996). Without a doubt, these three scapes are the ones with which young people are the most involved, both because they are mobile and exist in the midst of global cultural and informational flows, but also because today's youth is one of the most multicultural populations to have ever existed, the result of successive waves of migration.

By leaving behind a certain number of traditional concepts in cultural sociology and by taking into account the new global context, we can adopt a more "open" and non-normative attitude towards technoculture and examine cultural behaviors in the broader scheme of lifestyles and outlooks on the world. We must therefore turn our gaze to the various forms of "miniscule knowledge" (Pasquier, 2002) that young people accumulate thanks to technoculture: sets of references that stem from potentially globalized contents that allow them to construct their identities, to have access to behavioral and interpersonal models, and to experiment by proxy (which belongs to the realm of social skills, or literally, "knowing-how-to-be"). Youth now also have the skills (the know-how) necessary to access, produce and disseminate cultural contents. In both cases, young people can produce mobilizable resources that serve to define themselves with regard to others (which is a form of knowing how to present oneself).

3   Going beyond Moral Panic

Attempting to understand youth technoculture means that we must absolutely distance ourselves, to the extent possible, from the moral panicking that has become a widespread media staple: every day, we are allegedly threatened by cyberbullying, online predators, internet addiction, rampant pornography, etc. While these concerns are not always entirely unfounded, such phenomena are thankfully much rarer than popular media coverage would suggest. Behind these worries, which are often manipulated for the sake of ratings, another fear lurks in the shadows: the fear of change, which each generation faces when it is confronted with its successors. These fears, expressed by parents, educators, and employers alike, have encouraged the proliferation of "therapeutic" tomes aimed at mitigating the panic (Palfrey and Gasser, 2008). The movie *The Barbarian Invasions*[9] illustrated this phenomenon clearly: every generation views its successors as barbarians, accusing them of frittering away the cultural legacy with which they have been entrusted. This has especially been the case for generations which displayed significant political engagement, including during the second half of the 20th century. Over the years, young people have been accused of losing sight of everything — and especially of themselves — first because of television, then video games, and now the internet. Much declinist lamenting has occurred, with many pundits deploring the loss of value, cultural quality, and even moral sense. But beyond what these kinds of discourse say about who is making them, they also raise questions about the socialization of the younger generations. The technocultural habits of today's youth are the subject of endless commentary, with the result that they seem central to what constitutes a generation. Such commentary has often implicitly associated the

---

[9] *The Barbarian Invasions* (French: *Les Invasions barbares*) is a 2003 Canadian-French sex comedy-drama film written and directed by Denys Arcand. It was the first Canadian film to win the Academy Award for Best Foreign Language Film, at the 76th Academy Awards in 2004. It also won awards at the 2003 Cannes Film Festival, six Genie Awards, including Best Motion Picture, and three César Awards, including Best Film. The film is a sequel to Arcand's 1986 *The Decline of the American Empire*, and continues the story of Rémy, a womanizing history professor of the Flower Power generation who is now terminally ill with cancer. Rémy is faced with his heirs (his daughter and son), whose life-choices he considers as opposite to his own (hence tarring them with the brush "barbarians"). The sequel also incorporates a response to the September 11 attacks of 2001.

"novelty" of certain technological phenomena with the younger generations, as though new advances did not affect older generations at all. In reality, the internet is global: the fact that young people are among its most frequent users has unfortunately lead to the hasty pronouncement of generalized diagnoses establishing linkages between youth, culture, and the digital age.

This moral panic has emerged against a rather paradoxical backdrop. On the one hand, cultural practices, uses, and tastes, as well as consumption choices and the ability to create cultural content, are often believed to exist in the realm of autonomy and self-actualization. In that regard, every individual is an entrepreneur of their own life, and every life is a project (Martuccelli, 2010). The "active" nature of technoculture is thus supposed to reveal "authentic" abilities by embodying the "free" space of personal taste preferences. On the other hand, however, growing aversion to potential risks — risk of harassment, risk of being exposed to dangerous content or predators — has led to the desire to protect youth spaces, including by controlling the access of young people to technoculture and monitoring their use. Just look at how many conflicts have arisen between parents and children regarding the amount of time spent on a tablet or smartphone!

Contemporary moral panic has also fed off of the fears produced by major transformations in the social structures and spaces that shape youth and childhood in France. These fears are demographic in nature. While youth is measured by its relative weight in a given society, in Europe and in most Western nations, the youth population is diminishing. Although today's children are largely the result of planning (Léridon, 1998), due to a drop in fertility and a rise in the average age at first birth, they have often become the central focus of fears concerning their ability to integrate into society and to shoulder the intergenerational solidarity that is expected of them. These fears are also pedagogical: younger generations have been shaped by highly specific educational systems where the role played by motherhood has profoundly shifted, due to an increase in working mothers, the rise of women's emancipation, increased wages for female employees, higher educational achievement among women, greater access to birth control, and the diffusion of feminist ideas (Afsa Essafi and Buffeteau, 2006; Damon, 2013). In addition, the parental couple no longer represents permanent stability, given widespread divorce, decreased marriage rates and the rise of civil partnerships, cohabitation, and single parenthood. The conditions of intergenerational transmission have thus been profoundly altered, on both ends of the spectrum. In families possessing new relational dynamics, the goal of "good parenting" is to help children self-actualize, to develop their skills (by, for instance, having them play a musical instrument because this helps to learn discipline, which can be applied to academic studies), while still allowing them to discover themselves (the goal ostensibly being that parental injunctions should not unduly influence the development of personal taste preferences). Such "good parenting" also includes the psychologization of family relations and paying greater attention to proper development, in both the biological and psychological sense. The latter has in fact become a new responsibility for good parenting at the micro level and for a "good society" at the macro level. Cultural consumption is largely touted as a source of important psychological benefits. Debates surrounding gendered toys and cultural activities likewise attest to the growing awareness paid to the socially constructed nature of differences in taste, as well as the important ramifications of the former. The fact that some children prefer to play video games (a generally male activity) rather than read (a primarily female activity) is the result of socialization processes that are highly differentiated by gender — processes which are often followed unconsciously but which nonetheless deeply affect the development of both girls and boys (Zegai, 2010). Family interactions and their effects in terms of transmission have also been closely studied: while cultural transmission still remains largely the purview of mothers, fathers have claimed an increasingly important role in cultural education. Gender stereotypes have shifted somewhat and led to blurred boundaries, especially among the more educated and urban segments of the population.

These transformations have also reinforced the primacy of education in determining leisure activities (Morch and Andersen, 2006), since both the "self-actualization" and free time of young people prioritizes cultural consumption, in terms of both uses and practices. Extracurricular activities are also used to occupy the free time of children when they cannot be supervised by either their parents or their teachers, in particular in urban environments where spending prolonged time in public spaces is seen as dangerous (Garcia Canclini, 2004 and 2013). Similarly, extracurricular activities are also touted as a means to acquire skills that will be useful in other spheres of life: discipline, agility, self-control, etc. The stated goal of promoting creativity and personal development is sometimes only a façade. Children study music — the instrument doesn't matter — because learning music teaches concentration and bodily control. Moreover, technological devices used in the family sphere often serve pedagogical aims that correspond to different outlooks on the world: for example, working-class families were, in France, among the first to equip their children with computers, in the hopes of promoting their empowerment and success in the modern workplace, whereas more privileged families tend to "protect" childhood and prolong it as much as possible (Octobre, 2004).

This logic can likewise be applied to the relationship between education and culture. Legitimate culture — i.e., knowledge of the fine arts, classical music and literature — has become less and less academically "profitable" as mathematics have become the dominant criterion for selection (Coulangeon, 2013). But this does not mean that the academy has opened its doors to newer cultural forms: young adult literature and graphic novels have barely made onto a handful of syllabi, while television shows are not generally included in film studies curricula. The more technological a cultural product or practice is, the more likely it is to be excluded from educational programs — just look at video games, for instance. At the same time, however, "popular" media forms have become increasingly legitimate in the cultural sphere: celebrities such as David Bowie and Tim Burton have been the subject of exhibits in major museums around the world. Through this process of international legitimization, the products of global cultural industries are slowly making their way into schools around the world.

4   The New Barbarians

These transformations have thus engendered a new bout of moral panicking, a phenomenon that has routinely resurfaced throughout the history of media, from the invention of the printing press to the rise of radio and television to today's video games and the internet. Moral panic of any stripe makes it difficult to conduct an objective investigation of the effects of technoculture in terms that go beyond the framing ideas of loss (of cultural values), danger (the corruption of behaviors, such as when video games are blamed for "making kids violent"), or pathology (as seen when the concepts of addiction and harassment are mobilized to talk about youth behavior and technoculture).

   The objective of this volume is, on the contrary, to analyze youth technoculture in the digital age by highlighting the characteristic traits of its relationship to culture — not by systematically comparing it against the relationship to culture that previous generations espoused, but rather by arguing that mutations are in fact elements of continuity. The focus of this text is French society, which means that our analysis is conducted against the backdrop of a decreasing youth population, rising tensions with regard to social integration, and a glut of cultural contents and facilities. In many regards, France's situation is unique, especially with regard to the central role played by the education system in the process of cultural transmission (Lamont and Thevenot, 2000; Octobre and Dallaire, 2017). It should moreover be noted that inequalities in France play out against a Jacobin and republican backdrop: multicultural issues are relatively minor in importance, whereas issues related to social status and educational achievements are essential. More recently, reflections on generational belonging and gender have also risen to the fore. Rather than being mutually exclusive, such factors behind difference and cultural inequality tend to cumulate and overlap, thus justifying an intersectional approach. Finally, the French context is characterized by an ambiguous relationship to cultural alterity, as it is simultaneously composed of a great degree of openness to foreign cultural production (e.g., manga, indie cinema and world literature... including anglo-american products), and a genuine resistance to anything that may be construed as Americanization, thus leading to strong efforts to defend national cultural products, including by drawing on the concept of cultural exception.[10]

Diving into the cultural universe of young people therefore means examining the significant transformations provoked by globalized technoculture with regard to systems of cultural value, as well as the effects of these new and widely shared cultural imaginaries on youth relationships to culture and on the development of youth culture itself. How does the digital world connect to the pre-digital world (the world of analog media and national cultural institutions, which embody the world of objects, conversation, long time and cultural heritage)? Are the skills derived from the technico-cultural world merely technical, and what is the role played by cultural competencies in the digital revolution? Examining the cultural universe of children and adolescents today also entails understanding how identities are shaped and reshaped, processes which inform and reveal a value system, a conception of individuality and a set of interpersonal norms.

Ultimately, diving into the cultural universe of children and young people is a way to answer the numerous questions raised regarding changes to the socio-political fabric of contemporary society, a fabric which is becoming increasingly cultural in nature. Democracy states that all citizens are equal; as a result, defending cultural diversity presupposes that all cultures should be treated equally. Democracy likewise recognizes the right of all individuals to express themselves and promote their own culture(s). Finally, democracy has engendered a unique relationship to the authority of creators and experts, and to the contradictory debate of ideas. Western democracies have in fact become cultural democracies.

---

10 This concept was introduced by France in international free trade negotiations at the World Trade Organization in 1993. The concept of the cultural exception is used to argue that cultural products should be treated differently than other commercial products. The relevant provisions aimed to ensure that States would remain sovereign in choosing to limit the free trade of cultural products on the global markets, with a view to supporting and promoting their own artists, who represent and disseminate their national culture.

CHAPTER 1

Culture in a Technological World

Major Fears Resurface

Youth culture is closely linked to technological transformations, especially given that technological innovation has been fueled by cultural contents. This phenomenon is not entirely new, however. Young people have always been the most eager and precocious to adopt new technologies. This thirst for technological innovation has important repercussions, shaping cultural uses and formats.

Nevertheless, the digital revolution has wrought at least two fundamental changes: on the one hand, it has significantly increased the availability of cultural contents and the diversity of consumption modes that are possible, while on the other hand, it has encouraged the hybridization and interactivity of cultural products, prompting consumers to participate in their creation, reception and circulation. In this chapter, we shall therefore discuss the major fears associated with technoculture, not in order to endorse their lamentations, but because a critical reading of these moral panics shall enable us in turn to more calmly — and more objectively — describe the technocultural regime and its impact. These moral panics are often couched in definitive and universalist terms: the end of culture, the failure of cultural transmission, the blurring of distinctions between high art and popular entertainment, even the peril of dehumanization through the standardization of our cultural tastes and desires ... But what is really happening in today's cultural landscape, and of what are these Cassandras the symptom?

1 The Fear of Technocultural Mutations

There are three major cultural mutations brought about by the technological revolution and the rise of digital culture: accrued individualization, increased globalization, and changes to the value chain that stretches between cultural content and its endorsement by public institutions and/or private producers. These transformations are so many sources of hand-wringing and concern.

1.1 *Convergence,* Mon Amour

The first major concern — individualization — is often decried as engendering the commodification of culture and accelerating the shift towards ever more individualized forms of consumption, changes which are seen as either embodying or at least foreshadowing the dangers of neo-capitalism. Convergence is seen as the armed branch of commodification, a development even more dangerous because it hides under the guise of technological progress.

In fact, convergence heralds the advent of a technocultural age in which fixed devices that are each dedicated to a specific function have been replaced by mobile, multifunctional devices that seamlessly combine elements of entertainment, culture, and communication. Web 2.0 is collaborative and participatory; it has transformed how people access cultural content and routinely juxtaposes cultural products stemming from official production centers with user-generated content. In France, the main cultural hub is now the cellular phone (ARCEP, 2012). The cloud and big data are disrupting cultural channels: mediation increasingly occurs thanks to quantitative (and sometimes even binary) ratings (Beaudoin and Pasquier, 2014), or thanks to the use of algorithms. The 2013 report entitled "Internet: Prospective 2030" published by *France Stratégie* (a ministerial forecasting agency)[1] stated the following:

> These changes mean that users, and the objects to which they connect in mass numbers, will increasingly contribute to digital traffic and available content. But the active role of users goes beyond the production of content. They can potentially become producers and distributors of more and more sophisticated applications. From this perspective, crowdsourcing can be seen as taking things a step further: users can come together without knowing each other to collaborate on tasks of all kinds.
> FRANCE STRATÉGIE, 2013: 3

Ours is an age when the individualization of uses and desires is driving the constant refashioning of the economic chains of cultural production, creating a myriad niche markets, some of which even operate at a financial loss (as has been the case for Netflix until 2020).

---

[1] *France Stratégie* is a forecasting and research institution that examines public policies and proposals under the aegis of the Prime Minister. As a site for debate and dialogue, *France Stratégie* works with social partners and civil society to enrich its analyses and nuance its research. The organism takes into account the territorial dimension of European and international issues in its work.

The digitalization of content and the convergence of media platforms have contributed to both the increased speed with which devices and formats are updated, and the development of multifunctional devices which are themselves the source of convergence. It is not uncommon for individuals today to possess an MP3 player as well as a smartphone and a computer on which they can also listen to music. Moreover, significant improvements in the quality of household devices — from the audio cassette to the CD, from VHS to DVD formats, from cathode televisions to plasma screens, and from physical collections to downloading and streaming — and the appearance of on-demand consumption (video on-demand, streaming and of course downloading) have transformed the demand for consumption into the demand for "consumption experiences" which are highly customizable for each individual (like automobile tuning)[2] and have a strong emotional component. The skillfully timed distribution of cultural products — whether by creating anticipation or flooding the market — has also become an important element of consumer attachment to favorite products. In fact, emotional exchanges are at the heart of social media networks, composed of friends, likes, and followers. This demand for experiences is often considered to be a pillar of capitalism, a means of selling mental real estate, as described by Patric Lelay, the then-president of TF1 (France's main television channel, which was privatized in the mid-1980s). The demand for experiences is also viewed as a form of cultural commodification that atomizes hierarchies as well as the groups that have traditionally recognized the former (communities, sub-cultures and experts). In her work on "emotional capitalism," Eva Illouz (2006) describes the advent of *homo sentimentalis* in the modern world, illustrating how emotional capitalism feeds on these sentimental dynamics.

1.2   Globalizing Hyperculture

The second major source of fear is globalization, a phenomenon that is inseparable from the meteoric rise of digital cultural industries. When young people chat, upload videos, post messages on blogs or social networks, when they download content or share their favorite tunes, they often do so in complete ignorance of national borders and continental limits. Despite being surrounded by products, networks and know-how that stem from international flows, young people today remain deeply marked, in terms of what they appropriate as well as what they produce, by local culture and language, by community-based

---

2 Originally, tuning referred to modifications and improvements that were made to factory-standard automobiles to personalize them. By extension, tuning has come to designate any activity that personalizes an object through modifications.

preferences and geo-historically rooted social constraints — what Robertson has termed *glocalization* (1995). This is why, as Motti Regev (2013) has pointed out in the case of rock music, cultural flows have increasingly become hybrid, combining transnational elements with specific and culturally rooted elements.

The circulation of products, ideas, representations, and imaginaries across borders is an ancient one, laying at the heart of all cultural creation (Amselle, 2001). Thanks to the rise of cultural and digital industries, however, it has exploded in both speed and scope. Music, film, and television, as well as YouTube videos and social media posts are some of the most globalized elements of this circulation, but literature has not been immune either, as evidenced by the immense success of the *Harry Potter, Hunger Games, Twilight,* and *Fifty Shades of Grey* series.

The globalization of culture entails the development of shared norms as well as modes of listening and interpreting; it also means growing interconnectedness between cultures and communities, with social networks speeding up what travel used to accomplish with regard to inter-knowledge; it also means the creation of more shared cultural references. For instance, many individuals will recognize New York's yellow cabs before even setting foot in the city, thanks to their consumption of movies and television shows set in the city (Cicchelli and Octobre, 2018a). This transformation has been colossal in terms of language. At the outset, it promoted the spread of "international English". In addition, dating back to the 1970s (in other words, the generation most often associated with the parents of today's children), young people began to massively favor English-language music. The proliferation of cultural products and the subsequent shift to digital technologies ushered in a new era of linguistic availability: young people today can access their favorite shows in their original language just a few hours after the latter are initially posted on the web or broadcast on cable. Immigrant communities can therefore remain connected to the culture(s) and language(s) of their home countries whereas choosing original language (even if not mastered) is also more and more common among young amateurs without migration background as part of an "authentic experience". There are a growing number of shared and global cultural references, including iconic cultural symbols, which are often used as shorthand to denote cultural localization as part as a cultural mapping of the world: the Pyramids for Egypt, the Christ the Redeemer for Rio, the Statue of Liberty for New York, the Great Wall for China, the Kinkaku-ji for Japan, the Maj Mahal for India, the Wailing Wall for Jerusalem, the Kaaba for Mecca, the Hagia Sophia for Istanbul, the Coliseum for Rome, the Eiffel Tower for Paris, etc.

This global culture has been criticized for a number of reasons. First of all, it is accused of stereotyping and reifying cultures by creating a sort of global mosaic: the local or specific character of any given local culture is often painted in broad, exaggerated brushstrokes in order to be easily identifiable over time. These stereotypes can apply equally to niche productions on Native American reservations and to the vast number of films portraying France as little more than berets, baguettes and sidewalk cafés — including French films looking precisely to appeal to foreign markets. In the world's cultural mosaic, each culture is called upon to "be itself" so that it can be easily spotted and described. Young people play an important role in this mosaic, as they are particularly involved in global cultural competition (Bajoit and Franssen, 1995).

Embodying — or even pretending to embody — a kind of local authenticity has become a marketing strategy in globalized cultural markets, a way to promote a brand amidst tough global competition. Major international brands are well aware of this, given that they conduct different market positioning studies for specific products in different geographical regions, despite the fact that the products sold are almost identical across the globe. In fact, even the most standardized products must be localized in order to reach their public. The products of globalized cultural industries are therefore locally reappropriated and hybridized. George Ritzer (1993), coining the term McDonaldization, has analyzed how this phenomenon can lead to criticisms of cultural globalization as simultaneously begetting the lowest common denominator of cultural diversity *and* promoting the productive hybridization and cross-fertilization of cultural forms. Hybridization is necessary in order to "decide — and to learn how — to co-exist, not just at the local or national level, but at the global level, to accommodate differences that are essentially cultural and constantly resurfacing" (Tardif and Farchy, 2006: 20). Depending on whether one adopts an essentialist or constructive definition of "culture," the concept of cultural globalization can be described as either the homogenization of cultural goods consumed by the "planetary village," or the creation of a universal grammar broadcast far and wide by powerful information and communication technologies.

Technoculture is in reality "glocal" (Robertson, 1995): it can establish linkages between every corner of the world, producing a twofold and sometimes paradoxical process of cultural globalization and its counterpart, hyper-localization, born of growing identity-based claims that reverberate throughout network culture. As a result, technoculture can give rise to a myriad of cultural forms, ranging from resistance against the fear of cultural homogenization, to global-local hybridizations and even local appropriations of international forms (Pieterse, 2009; Tomlinson, 2003). In all of these different situations, technoculture is the preferred context to express tensions between the local and the global, the universal and the particular (Cicchelli, 2018).

1.3 *From Works of Art to Cultural Contents*

The third big fear concerns the disappearance of works of art, now ostensibly replaced with mere "cultural content". In the United States, as well as in France and most of Europe, most young people are equipped with smartphones, listen to music online, steam television shows and movies, engage in P2P computing and take selfies that they upload onto social networks. Multimedia and digital cultural industries are the first point of contact that most young people have with culture; as a result, cultural contents have by and large replaced artworks in their world. They are overwhelmingly more likely to listen to recorded music or watch videos, shows and movies then they are to go to a museum and contemplate artworks, to attend theater productions or to visit cultural heritage sites (regardless of whether these visits take place in person or virtually). The shift from in-person encounters with artworks to the consumption of cultural contents has significantly and irreversibly transformed value systems and altered expectations amidst "traditional" cultural sectors, in particular because the industrial, competitive and events-based production and diffusion of contents today has permeated the artistic sphere. Major cultural institutions have, as a result, started to adopt the logic of cultural seasons, creating programming and events to market their collections. In this context, digital technologies are often seen as tools that can attract young people to traditional cultural institutions: more and more virtual visits are possible — and not just at large museums with issues of overcrowding, such as the Louvre, the Tate Modern, or the Guggenheim, where virtual visitors now outnumber in-person visitors.

Technocultural industries are not merely the operators of this shift from artworks to cultural contents: they are also responsible for producing new ways of organizing time. The transition away from the timelines of traditional production cycles is a significant one. In the past, the day when a new record, book, or exposition was scheduled to come out was a momentous occasion that inherently attracted social and cultural visibility; as the volume and speed of production have increased, however, it has become increasingly difficult, albeit essential, to find new ways to promote and popularize works in a rapidly changing landscape. Today, streaming and illegal downloads on the Internet have reconfigured timelines of reception, while digital formats have influenced a number of stylistic elements such as length, size, and sequencing. In particular, digital media has also changed how young people watch television shows: when a popular show has a new season or episode, young people often get together to watch it as quickly as possible online, even if this means losing sleep. Technoculture has therefore ushered in a labile and interstitial temporality, reconfiguring individual units of time according to the reality that how time is used is increasingly dissociated from the demands of linearity and single-tasking (that is, doing one thing at a time, from beginning to end). Moreover, individuals are now much less beholden to the broadcasting schedules of private companies or state conglomerates, given that they can consume whatever they want whenever they want online, from streaming video to virtual museum visits. This new temporality blurs the distinction between personal and professional time, between work and school and extracurricular activities, in turn encouraging the desynchronization of different social groups (perhaps even abolishing the concept of "publics"?), and the proliferation of communities with different patterns. As a result, personal time management strategies have developed in tandem with the increasing fragmentation of cultural time. The fact that our cultural landscape now moves quickly — almost impatiently — has significant effects on our general relationship to time: we curse at our computers when an application doesn't open quickly enough, we feel surprisingly bored when watching a classic film that seems to move so slowly, we get annoyed when we have to wait in a long line at the supermarket, etc. Such anecdotes are supported by data: a number of surveys conducted in France, often by companies that claim to want to help us "save time," confirm these suspicions. According to a poll conducted by an online bank without any brick-and-mortar branches, 82% of French people self-report "being more impatient than before". Another study performed in 2018 for the website of the newspaper *Le Monde* estimated that after five seconds of attention span, three potential readers out of ten visiting the site would leave. The website has adapted as a result: loading time has gone down from eight to two seconds, and views have increased significantly (Belot, 2019). Our patience can now be measured in mere seconds. Of course, mutations born of technoculture are not limited to this realm; in reality, all of our cultural and social activities have been deeply affected by the transformation of our relationship to time.

With regard to both artworks and timelines, the contemporary technocultural regime has been vehemently criticized: it has been accused of imperiling "real" culture; of catering to the lowest common denominator; and of being in thrall to market demands. By recycling legitimate values (e.g., Mozart is transformed into the star of a pop-rock comedy musical), the technoculture regime shapes new cultural values that pay no heed to traditional cultural hierarchies and their respective temporalities. The historic sedimentation that is necessary for cultural heritage to be recognized and the annual rhythm of cultural seasons have been replaced by uninterrupted cultural flows and rapid turnover among stars. For instance, Daft Punk[3] belongs to the musical hall of fame for

---

3   French electronic music group which has enjoyed worldwide success.

young people today, and *World of Warcraft*[4] is an integral part of multimedia imaginaries. But this technocultural regime is not one of unified control. As Henry Jenkins has explained, so-called mass culture — which enjoys a complex relationship to popular culture — has become the most widespread form of culture, shared in by the greatest number of people while still remaining outside of the control of high-brow cultural industries (Jenkins, 2006). Nonetheless, even if these technocultural industries play a structural role in shaping the cultural offer, these have likewise made room for the emergence of user-generated content (which has possibly its most massive incarnation in YouTube).

Technoculture is also transforming cultural objects: not only is it increasing the abundance with which the younger generations grow up, it also promotes hybridization between culture and communication. Social networks illustrate this perfectly, as social media posts often claim a cultural alibi (the appearance of a new CD/trailer/movie/interview, which users can often comment), thus reinforcing the weight of marketing logic but also promoting permeability and hybridization between cultural categories. Cultural omnivorism, which is often highlighted as a youth trait (Peterson, 1991; Peterson and Kern, 1996; Peterson and Simkus, 1996) entails the co-existence of individual choices that can be wildly heterogenous in terms of cultural legitimacy; it can be considered as a knock-on effect of the cultural possibilities offered by digital networks and the circulation of the cultural contents they encourage. The fact that individuals can now watch a digital screening of a live event, consult a fan blog and create new content by recombining different elements in new ways thus facilitates hybridization, permeability and the blurring of lines between traditionally separate cultural categories.

A final point: technoculture has begun to restructure the cultural chain. Objects such as tablets and smartphones are no longer limited to one function, nor can functions only be accessed from unique, purpose-built objects — as was the older relationship, for instance, between radio receivers and radio programs, television sets and TV shows, or movie theaters and cinema. In the span of ten years, the number of young people in France who use a computer every day has increased eleven-fold; many young people today possess multiple technological devices such as smartphones, laptops and tablets, all of which are connected to the Internet. The fact that so much of their daily life takes place within various digital networks (wikis, mods,[5] etc.) has led to the rise

---

4 A massively multiplayer online role-playing game set in a fantasy medieval universe.
5 Collaborative web sites and online games that can be modified by each user on their own computer.

of new voices and gatekeepers (e.g., webmasters) that pass judgment on the quality of cultural content, entirely sidestepping the traditional institutions of cultural transmission. These gatekeepers help to shape new forms of cultural mediation that are inherently tied to both their production (which is sometimes user-generated) and their reception (given that some of the gatekeepers of these new styles are amateurs rather than professionals). In this new world, community managers[6] and other webmasters play the role formerly assumed by institutions of transmission: they select, structure and refine data to build forms of knowledge that can be communicated, shared, exploited and even transformed. As culture is now a product that can potentially be produced everywhere, it can also be disseminated through a much greater variety of channels than those offered by traditional cultural institutions of transmission.

2   The End of Culture?

These transformations are often accused of killing off "real" culture, whose quality is vouchsafed by traditional institutions and which requires an unmediated and in-person encounter with artworks in the present moment. Christopher Lasch explains:

> The new media merely universalize the influence of the market, reducing ideas to commodities. Just as they transform the selection and certification of political leadership by substituting their own judgments of newsworthiness for popular accountability, so they transform the certification of literary or artistic excellence. Their insatiable appetite for novelty (that is, for old formulas in new packages), their reliance on immediate recognition of the product, and their need for "annual ideological revolutions," as Debray puts it, make "visibility" the sole test of intellectual merit
> LASCH, 1981: 20

Let us examine this notion in greater detail.

2.1   *The Destructive Power of Technological Hegemony?*
Youth technoculture is often called upon to respond to criticisms of its destructive hegemony, already presumed to be a characteristic of mass culture

---

6   This term, which became popular with the advent of Web 2.0, refers to any person who builds and manages online communities for a company, brand, cause, celebrity, group, or institution.

but now deemed exponentially more dangerous due to the invasive nature of the Internet and technocultural objects. Christopher Lasch thus expresses the fear of seeing high art and mass culture collapse into homogeneity, leading to the alienation of the public. The issue is ultimately not one of lost quality, but diversity: the diversity of works, forms of expression, and kinds of reception. As Richard Mémeteau has clearly argued, "the problem with Britney Spears is not that she's a bad singer, it's on the contrary that she manages to tug at the world's heartstrings through artifice" (Mémeteau, 2014: 10) — but also that she eradicates the popular and local cultures that ostensibly pre-dated her. The argument for authenticity is thus combined with a defense of local productions and ultimately supersedes any criticisms of poor quality. Such forms of disapproval also reveal nostalgia for a time when culture and collective political demands went hand-in-hand, as culture was a vector of communication both within and between peoples. The transition from counterculture to youth culture can thus be seen as sounding the death knell of its collective political dimension, as well as the authentic dimension of culture.

Such lamentations require a few points of clarification, first and foremost with regard to youth technophilia. The attraction of young people to novelty and the use of educational strategies in the family sphere means that technological devices can acquire two different meanings. On the one hand, they are used for recreation, with audiovisual and then digital devices being ushered into the child's bedroom according to the argument that every age has the "right" to enjoy its "own" culture. On the other, technological devices are also pedagogical, with certain tools being considered as necessary for functioning in modernity. In France, in the 2000s, the first children to have personal computers largely came from the working classes, given that their parents were eager to familiarize them with new technological tools that seemed essential for the future. Two different visions of youth are thus encapsulated in the use of digital devices: youth is seen both as a time where constraints are lifted and pleasures are permitted (distraction), *and* as a period of time where it is important to integrate behaviors and skills that will be useful in the future (education). In both of these registers, technocultural tools and objects play a major role. In most cases, however, the aim is a kind of technophilia of use. We must therefore distinguish with regard to this technophilia what: a) stems from habituation — being born or raised with access to certain technological devices, which are used on a daily basis (this applies to any generation that grows up with a technology that is new only to previous generations); b) what relates to competencies — i.e., going beyond mere passive use, including by developing a understanding of technological frameworks, a situation that is much rarer than habituation and c) what stems from an even rarer form of reflexive knowledge concerning uses — and which, amongst younger generations, often takes the guise of critical distance and even subversion. These three registers of technophilia are often conflated when speaking of the so-called "digital natives". We shall return to this topic later.

Adopting this critical stance means that it is also necessary to address shifting cultural agendas and the relative weight granted to different cultural activities and forms of consumption. Namely, does going digital spell the end of culture? It is undeniable that the advent of digital technologies and their unprecedented speed has led to the reconfiguration of cultural agendas and values. The time spent by young people engaging in cultural consumption has become increasingly dense, as multi-tasking has become the norm and the boundaries between different cultural disciplines have faded, as have traditional classifications of legitimacy (Coulangeon, 2011; Glévarec and Pinet, 2009). As a result, new technologies have eliminated the linearity of cultural time and dependency on the usual channels of distribution. Technoculture has favored the individualized proliferation and deprogramming of cultural time, which has in turn influenced how tastes are shaped and cultural contents are received. When individuals can consume whatever they want whenever they want, they have a very different experience than when previous generations had to patiently wait for their favorite TV show to air, or a cultural event to come to town. Steaming, downloading, on-demand capabilities and peer-to-peer exchanges[7] allow young people — by far the most likely to engage in such activities — to emancipate their modes of consumption from the many competing matrices of both public and private programming, often going beyond national borders (and sidestepping issues such as distribution rights, media chronology, etc.). Being able to watch, read or listen to (almost) everything they want to, whenever and wherever they want (or almost), in whatever modality they choose and regardless of the ethno-national origin of the production in question (with a few exceptions); being able to transform and even create cultural products that they can disseminate through social media; being able to exchange knowledge and interact with fans and other individuals in far-away countries who are similarly devoted to the same passion: this is what technoculture promises youth (and all of us, in fact). For instance, *Game of Thrones* was watched by young people all around the world just moments after it officially aired on HBO, thanks to illegal downloads and the work of amateurs who quickly produced subtitles and helped to distribute these pirated versions

---

7   A kind of distributed network where equipotent individuals are both server and client and which can be used to share files under the guise of communication or planned distribution.

worldwide. In fact, the pirating of some episodes only made certain viewers more attached to the show.

In addition, technoculture abolishes some of the distinctions between different cultural sectors, thanks to transmedia cultural linkages and genre crossovers which encourage eclecticism and permeability between cultural categories, as well as the development of aesthetic and emotion-based marketing which is invasive and troublingly persuasive. The *Harry Potter* franchise perfectly illustrates this phenomenon: the original idea has been extrapolated from novels to movies, video games, blogs, websites and countless forms of merchandise. Even more incredible: the Hogwarts School now exists as an online community where you can take lessons towards your degree in wizardry. *Harry Potter* has in fact become a transmedia cultural "world" unto itself, a universe where young people can participate, contribute, join fan clubs, write fanzines and spin-offs, and more.[8] Globalized cultural technologies are therefore at the root of many, many transformations. But are the youth cultures born in this landscape truly less "cultural" than those produced by their predecessors? What criteria can justify this interpretation?

2.2   *The Loss of the Tangible*

The emergence of technoculture has also led to the rise of a new fear: a lack of physical materiality. This fear is often expressed in the many sectors that have been deeply affected by technological advances. In the field of finance and economics, for example, the creation and success of Bitcoin — a decentralized cryptocurrency that is not indexed to any material counterpart, unlike traditional forms of money backed by gold deposits — has become the subject of wild speculation, as evidenced by the title of an issue of the French publication *Libération*: "*La monnaie qui rend fou*" [*Money Madness*] (Alix, 2017). The main hook was the following: "Exclusively electronic and controlled by no central banking authorities, the digital currency has seen its value multiple 10-fold in just a few months, leaping past the 10,000 dollar-mark. When will it crash?" All of the ingredients for panic are there: a lack of tangibility that makes control impossible and the end of equilibrium likely, coupled with the specter of a world in thrall to a new form of excess, this one without a material standard for reference.

---

8   Spin-offs are narratives derived from a primary source material; for example, when a supporting character from a series (be it literary or televisual) becomes the main character in a new series. Spin-offs can also take the form of sequels and prequels, for example recounting the childhood of a major (adult) character in a hit show.

It is true that our new technocultural world is largely dematerialized, with contents being able to circulate (almost) instantaneously and (almost) regardless of national borders. The technocultural revolution has broken the traditional associations between practices and platforms: a computer can now be used to listen to music, to watch a movie, to write, draw, compose music, conduct research, or chat with friends. But ultimately, computer ownership — and even frequent use of the former — does not shed much light on the truly revolutionary ways in which new technologies are exploited. The same observation can be made regarding cell phones, which are of course used to make calls, but also to take photos, to listen to music and to surf the Web. The digitalization of cultural content has moreover ushered in a new era, where individuals live in a world with fewer and fewer physical objects: think about the progressive disappearance of vinyl records, CDs, DVDs, or even books … This double transformation of usages has thus blurred traditional boundaries: whether these were between different practices (the example of blogging comes to mind), between personal and familial space (watching a movie or show forbidden by one's parents on a personal computer, for instance), between the public and private spheres, between activities that were considered to be the purview of "boys" or "girls," between the working class and the elite. In this regard, the Internet (in all its various incarnations, on computers, smartphones or tablets) is not just a form of media: it is hypermedia, as it combines the capacities of all the media platforms that preceded it (sound, image, text) and adds to these the ability for individualization with regard to both content and forms of reception — something that was rarely if ever possible with older forms of media. The feeling of being overwhelmed, both by new technologies and their pedagogical implications, can give rise to renewed moral panic,[9] as well as difficulties when attempting to describe the hybridization of uses — which always change faster and more fluidly than observers can take note of them — a phenomenon already noted by Claude Grignon and Jean-Claude Passeron (Grignon and Passeron, 1989) with regard to popular culture.

By losing their materiality, cultural contents become deterritorialized — at least on the surface — and subject to increasing hybridization. The recent Chinese-American movie *The Great Wall*[10] thus combined all the trappings of

---

9 As Olivier Donnat has pointed out, the new forms of moral panic have moved away from television, which has become banal, and focus now on the newer screens in our lives (as evidenced by the decrease in individuals in France who express concern regarding television) (Donnat, 2009: 73).

10 A 2016 Chinese-American (30%/70%) movie, directed by Zhang Yimou (one of the most famous Chinese directors) which stars American Matt Damon and Chinese star Jing Tian.

an American blockbuster — a strong protagonist, numerous action sequences, an emphasis on courage and heroism — with references to Chinese culture (including heavy symbolism around the Great Wall[11] and images of a fictitious wall), ultimately presenting a kind of Asian soft power. The worldwide success of the film, which was shot in both English and Chinese, is indicative of important shifts in the geopolitical and geo-cultural equilibrium, as well as of the new hybrid forms being creating in this climate. The same occurred with the global success of *Hallyu* (the South Korean wave): South Korea, formerly marginal in the realm of global cultural exchange, has now become a leading nation in the TV, film and most of all music industries, attracting audiences all over the world, be they part of the Korean diaspora or foreign publics seduced by the high quality of Korean hybrid products. How has pop culture from a minor player on the international stage become a semi-global phenomenon? It should be noted that K pop's international rise intersects with the history of colonial modernization or post-cold war politics in East Asia, with the rise of cultural cosmopolitanism in Western countries, and with the new capacity of social media to give birth to a digital youth culture.

2.3 *Behind Technological Change, Cultural Shifts*

The digital revolution has injected technology into every debate and sometimes — perhaps often? — leads us to forget that the changes wrought by new technologies are inherently cultural ones. Different forms of media and multimedia (including both their content and their modes of operation) in fact constitute cultural biotopes: that is, ergonomic, ecological and ethical environments that shape how we see, think and interact with the world, in turn producing different representations of culture and youth. To understand the changes afoot, we must therefore not just examine technological innovations, but also seek to grasp the socio-cultural transformations that they have unleashed.

The movie is loosely based on Chinese mythology, combined with science fiction classics portraying alien invasions. This was the most expensive film to ever be shot in China.

11   The reason Zhang Yimou, a famous Chinese director, was immediately interested by this Hollywood project was because, as he clearly explains, "this was a feature film about the history and culture of China that was entirely shot in China. The cultural elements really resonated with me, I think. It's a fascinating story that is full of emotions and interesting themes". He adds: "The Great Wall is mentioned in our national anthem, it symbolizes the same thing in the hearts of every Chinese person — our people, our country and our history. We also use the symbol to express spiritual concepts. For all of us in China, the Great Wall is the symbol of the national Chinese spirit. It represents our traditions and our soul." (Hondebeyrie, 2017).

Cultural mutations, both sociologically and anthropologically speaking, are those that concern how we view collectivity, as well as how we relate to art and the new youth mythologies. Is technoculture a form of cultural mutation in that sense? Technoculture associates cultural contents, attitudes and representations, but these associations occur without mediation by a collective group or institution (which have been relegated to the background), both because they do not target the collective public (the audience for a Facebook page is quite unlike the audience at a concert, for example, given that it is partially or wholly lacking in simultaneity, co-presence, and intersubjectivity) and because community ties have, in some cases, become ephemeral (e.g., the weak ties of social networks). Take, for example, the culture geek: a term applied to those who are fans of video games, science fiction, and computer programming, and who are always on the hunt for technocultural novelty. The world of the culture geek is self-constructed, without any reference to outside institutions (their logic, norms, and ways of thinking) or outside actors.[12]

In doing so, young people institute a new relationship to art that transforms how works are received: the art of re-appropriating the creations of others now takes centerstage in technocultural productions. From Eminem to John Snow, Psy to Lara Croft, Princess Mononoke to Devdas, pop culture heroes now become the subject of collages and parodies (both individual and collective) that incorporate this skill set. Convergence is also exploited for its remix[13] possibilities; mods, for example, but also the creation of digital movies that reuse the products, images and platforms of commercial culture. Technoculture seems more like a generalized practice of tinkering than a fully integrated cultural or technological agenda. Technoculture feeds off of the myriad individual contributions that are local, circumstantial and iterative, as well as user-generated content that establishes hierarchies and priorities, passes and publishes judgment on aesthetic quality, and plays with existing media, including by perpetuating hoaxes[14] and posting spoilers.[15] YouTube has thus become the first "hit-making machine" (Carpentier, 2013).

---

12   There are sites devoted to curating culture for this international community (e.g., https://www.culturegeek.eu, https://london.culturegeek.com). The culture geek community also has its own TV shows (for example, http://www.bfmtv.com/mediaplayer/replay/culture-geek/), newspapers (https://www.journaldugeek.com/category/culture-geek/), and its Twitter feed (https://twitter.com/culturegeek?lang=en).
13   A remix originally referred to a song or piece of music that was altered from its original state; remixes can now be made in all sorts of cultural spheres beyond music.
14   A hoax is a prank that is often conducted with malicious intent.
15   A spoiler is a document or other form of medium that reveals some of part of the future plot in a book, movie, or game and thus "spoils" the pleasure and surprise of discovering this in one's own time.

3 The World of Machines

For a cultural discussion to truly take place, we must become aware of the vast transformations that have occurred in the world of machines. The digitalization of our societies has been a rapid process, one that is in fact still ramping up. This process has bred a society obsessed with numbers and quantification. Just a handful of figures can prove this. Every day, 3.3 billion searches are made amongst the 30 trillion pages indexed by Google; more than 350 million photos are uploaded and 4.5 billion new *likes* flow into Facebook per day. "If we digitized all forms of communication and written texts from the dawn of humanity until 2003, we would need 5 billion gigabits of storage. Today, we generate this volume of digital information in two days!" (Cardon, 2015: 23).

The ancient fear of man being supplanted by machine has resurfaced, as the machines around us have become more and more (and perhaps overly?) intelligent. At the Sci-Fi Film Festival in London, where participants compete for prizes by creating sci-fi shorts in under 48 hours, one 2016 winner was written by an A. I. named Benjamin. By pilfering snippets of dialogue from other films, "Benjamin" wrote a script and Oscar Sharp made a 9-minute short out of this material. The short film was deemed surrealistic but ultimately, not innovative enough. In the creative domain, at least, our replacements are not quite ready yet, it seems. Nevertheless, today's machines are transforming our relationship to culture, in particular thanks to the barrage of recommendations they propose to help us navigate the world of consumer hyper-choice. While it was long seen as a form of progress and increased consumer freedom, hyper-choice has now also become a psychological and emotional burden (Schwartz, 2004). How can we make a choice when we are unable — for financial reasons as well as lack of time — to sample the plethora of options available to us?

3.1 *Computational Dynamics*

Increasingly efficient machines are everywhere. Translation software, though largely imperfect for the most part, allows us to understand foreign languages almost immediately when we consult sites on the internet; the option to translate a page often comes up automatically, based on our previous search history. Dictation software recognizes our voice, transcribing our words and obeying our commands. Other kinds of programs measure our food intake, our health metrics or our physical activity levels, often recommending behavioral changes as a result. The algorithms used by Google, Apple, Facebook, and Amazon shape our behaviors, for instance by offering books that we had not even thought about reading yet. By observing global trends in terms of consumption and other behavioral patterns, such algorithms statistically "predict" the behavior of individuals. The dynamics at play are computational in nature: given a massive amount of data and content, the algorithms process, aggregate, and present information to provide analyses of our tastes and behaviors. These analyses in turn become the socio-cognitive and cultural frameworks adopted by our societies, used to measure, predict and evaluate our actions, choices and preferences. Metrics measuring audience size and popularity (Jouet, 2004), authority, and reputation, often with predictive elements, are proliferating and consequently shaping representations of who we are, ultimately creating "imagined communities" that stand in stark contrast to previous (local, national, etc.) communities (Anderson, 1983).

Do machines think for us? Chris Anderson, a Silicon Valley guru of sorts, declared the end of theory ten years ago: in other words, the end of the need for cultural, social or philosophical reflections on the ongoing transformations, given the rise of computational devices (Anderson, 2008). Despite the hyperbolic nature of this screed, it does draw our attention to the potential stakes of machine omnipotence. We do not exist in a sci-fi film and we are still far from being the victims of either malicious A. I.s like Hal 900 in *2001: A Space Odyssey* (1968) or benevolent ones like Annalee Call in *Alien Resurrection* (1997); nor have our forms of A.I. begun to travel down paths of human questioning, like David in the film *A.I. Artificial Intelligence* (2001). In fact, recent attempts to create an artificial intelligence capable of freely conversing on social networks ultimately failed: after a mere 16 hours of existence, Tay, an artificial intelligence chat bot created by Microsoft and deployed on Twitter, was shut down for having made racist and revisionist statements, backed into a corner by users testing its limits. Similarly, MIT studies on facial recognition software — which is currently being developed and refined — have found that the former is 99% successful when looking at white men, but markedly less successful when considering women or people with darker skin tones.[16] These studies provide fodder for the arguments made by Joy Buolamwi, a researcher at MIT and the founder of the Algorithmic Justice League,[17] who criticizes algorithms for their discriminatory flaws. She is not the first to accuse algorithms of racism: in 2015, Google was forced to apologize after one of its applications (Google Photos) mistook black persons for gorillas. As these examples illustrate, there are still quite a few obstacles before "the singularity," when humans will be replaced — and surpassed — by machines.

---

16 See http://gendershades.org/overview.html.
17 See https://www.ajlunited.org.

We shall not dwell in this volume on how algorithms are developed, nor analyze their already well-established pitfalls and dangers, such as the manipulation of reputations using false indexing (Cardon, 2012), or the difficulty of aggregating scores, signals, recommendations and digital trails of highly different natures (Pariser, 2011). We shall instead focus on the cultural and political implications of the allegedly neutral manipulations of big data, which is seen as existing outside of any pre-existing hypothesizes, interpretive frameworks, or representations of a desirable common good.

The computational models in question are quite different from the electoral polls that we are used to, or the metrics used to determine the effectiveness of public policies and which primarily analyze deviations with regard to a point representing an "average" individual as observed or projected. On the contrary, the crunching of big data is not deduced from any kind of desired outcome (be it institutional, commercial, or other), but presents itself as the ultimate product of participatory democracy: each micro-behavior can shed light on the trajectory of all. The illusion of big data is allowing us to believe that it expresses the truth of individual freedom and democratic equality since, unlike polls and their "average" individual, no one and nothing is there to tell us what is ideal and to define a common goal. As a result, no collective actions are undertaken to work towards this shared ideal, and no social or political reactions ask for accountability with regard to the success or failure of the goals established with a view to achieving this ideal. These two mechanisms, which have long constituted the primary operators of life in society, have thus lost their central role with the advent of big data, which is presented as merely the "neutral" and "objective" record of our actions in all their minuteness and diversity, no matter how insignificant or numerous they may be.

The distance is huge with the "old world" of cultural intentions. For example, when efforts are made to promote reading, it's because we as a society hope to develop individual reflection (which presumes stimulating emotions and thought without a "productive" goal in mind) and ultimately an informed citizenry. This also means targeting specific kinds of reading: literature and canonical texts are naturally preferred to romance novels, pornography, or cookbooks. None of these intentions and objectives enter into the algorithms that generate Amazon book recommendations based on previous purchases, however.

3.2 *The Past Predicts the Future; or, Birds of a Feather Stick Together*
When individual clicks, decisions, likes and dislikes are aggregated to predict future behaviors, they tend to lead us to what we already like, thus creating powerful waves of cultural homogeneity — quite in contrary to the libertarian ideals that fueled the early days of the internet (Hindman, 2009). When linked

to measures of reputation or authority, predictive tools powerfully confirm and reinforce our original choices: the suggestions and recommendations made by predictive algorithms are quite similar to what we, or our close friends and family, have read, watched, or listened to. In other words, our future web surfing activities are predicted by the past activities of people who resemble us, according to certain criteria which are in fact quite different from the traditional categories used in sociology — groupings used to inform or support various representations of the sociopolitical world, such as socio-professional categories, and whose tie to cultural *habitus* was demonstrated by Pierre Bourdieu through the statistical representation of taste preferences (Bourdieu, 1996: 21). "Algorithmic behaviorism," writes Dominique Cardon, "is all that remains of the *habitus* once we get rid of social structures" (Cardon, 2015: 71). This confirmation of resemblance happens despite (or because of) the proliferation of increasingly granular taste preference categories that are largely inaccessible to human minds but which nonetheless structure recommendation algorithms. Netflix has over 77,000 micro-categories organizing its offerings and which vary according to viewer profiles: for example, "post-apocalyptic comedies about friendship" (Madrigal, 2014). These categories — which clearly have little aesthetic, artistic or culture significance — only serve to segment the market into potential publics and marketing targets.

Moreover, when scores and rankings are aggregated (rather than recommendations), the pivotal role played by a small number of products in terms of authority and reputation is largely reinforced, given that scores are often lacking in the context and explanations that accompany recommendations. The democratic principle, according to which every score is equally valid, contradicts the notion of expertise, which says that the opinions of experts should count more than the opinions of regular people (who may or may not choose to follow the experts). By concentrating reputation and authority in a small number of sources, this phenomenon confirms the Pareto principle, according to which 20% of individuals hold 80% of the resources and value. With the internet, 10% of individuals, objects and information absorb 90% of our attention — across all sectors.

The long-tail effect of cultural consumption is its translation: in most cultural industries (books, films, recorded music), a small number of titles enjoy spectacular success, while a much larger number of titles struggle to stay afloat in their respective niches. The "Matthew Effect"[18] can easily be confirmed with

---

18 The Matthew Effect refers to the mechanisms by which the more privileged individuals in any given situation will tend to keep accruing privilege over others. The term was coined by American sociologist Robert K. Merton, who used it to illustrate how the most

regard to networked content as well: ultimately, this phenomenon increases inequalities, not around the media but by accelerating the concentration of value at the top of the pyramid. This effect, which has recently been described in terms of economic wealth (Piketty, 2013), is also prevalent in the art world. Each year, the *Kuntskompass* lists the 100 top-ranked contemporary living artists, using an algorithm similar to Google's "PageRank" that gives points to artists for museum exhibits, with the museums themselves being ranked in terms of reputation and prestige (Quemin, 2013). Facebook similarly reproduces inequalities between web users by favoring those who have ample sociocultural resources and large numbers of friends — which is logical, since the number of one's friends informs the number of potential posts, views and likes.

Finally, we must examine the radical behaviorism of such algorithms and the representation of the world that stems from this perspective. Computer engineers will often argue that they are merely using real individual behaviors to provide recommendations, whose legitimacy (and perhaps harmlessness) can be attributed to this strict compliance with past behaviors. The individual user, endowed with their particular social and cultural capital, is thus solely responsible for the recommendations that they receive. This has a trifold paradoxical effect. Can we still consider ourselves as free when a machine suggests something that we have not even thought about yet, including if this suggestion resembles a consumption choice we have made in the past? What remains of collective experience when individuals are never steered towards compromises, ideals or averages, but rather encouraged in the uniqueness of their individual choices and profile? And ultimately, how unique can individual tastes and recommendations be, given that they are calculated by aggregating countless similar profiles?

3.3 The Cultural Promise of Big Data

Big data has revealed a number of deep-seated changes in individual behavior. First of all, it suggests that individual behaviors align less and less with individual intentions, desires, and statements. Social networks have in fact created a space where individual opinions are rapidly and intensely produced, where desires and intentions "must" be expressed. The intensity and high frequency of these forms of expression are the lifeblood of social networks, composed of countless individual pages. According to some analysts, this phenomenon tends to widen the already existing gap between the multiplicity of desires and the "reality" of being (Rosa, 2010). Predictive algorithms are perhaps less

---

eminent scientists and well-known researchers will keep increasing in influence over their scholarly peers.

skilled at saying what internet users want to do, and more so at revealing what they do without explicitly stating it.

Big data also highlights the increasingly complicated relationship that young people have with different cultural universes. The proliferation of possible practices, linked notably to the hybridization of culture and communication (social networks being a striking example of the latter), the development of cultural consumption as a normal or even inherent part of youth, the diversification of modes of production, communities of diffusion and scales of judgment, as well as the augmentation of practices that exist at the crossroads of production and consumption ("consumer action") have all served to increase the complexity of individual cultural worlds. Consistent elements can be found, but they are more tenuous and multifactorial. By and large, young people are no longer strictly determined by the social class of their parents, nor do they have a clearly defined professional trajectory into the future, given that the latter is highly likely to change over time, as are increasingly flexible occupational categories and domestic arrangements (Pierru and Spire, 2008). We must therefore invent new common interpretative frameworks to describe a shared world — frameworks that reflect the importance of big data.

In addition, big data paves the way for new forms of production, especially in the realm of communications and information technology. Digital technology has, for example, deeply transformed journalism by rapidly linking events with the media buzz that they provoke, by quickly telling media houses what digital readers are most interested in (young people are legion amongst the former), by producing new vectors of information (for example, hashtags),[19] and by fundamentally changing how the cultural and political sphere operates. In the political domain, the transformations are striking: war rooms have popped up where campaign managers frenetically tweet every time their political leader makes a media appearance. The same thing has appeared with the rise of television singing competitions, where viewers can vote for the winner using their phones, and on musical sites which rank how often a song has been listened to.

These transformations challenge the traditional reflexivity of the social world (Strathern, 1997). The role played by quantification in youth culture today should be a sign of this, given that it automatically favors extreme and fringe behaviors, especially amongst those individuals who have the least access to psychological support in their environment. We should likewise be tipped off by the low degree of collective reflection on recommendation strategies that

---

19   The hashtag (#) is a metadata tag used on the Internet — and most notably on social media sites — which makes it possible to associate keywords with a content by preceding those words with the pound symbol.

merely prompt users to like what they previously liked, and are therefore in fact largely contradictory to any agenda of cultural emancipation. Ultimately, the twofold and often paradoxical promise of machines should also be viewed as a warning, since it purports to captivate the attention of all while increasing freedom of choice for every individual.

∴

In this context, the cultural behaviors of young people appear to follow three major pathways. First of all, the high degree of market segmentation as engendered by cultural industries, regardless of whether one looks at music, fashion, radio, or television, allows young people to differentiate themselves from older generations while nonetheless co-existing in a relatively un-socially stratified market. The ability to consume cultural products has become a generational marker which to a certain extent dilutes a number of social class markers and national borders. Almost everywhere in the world, children and adolescents can watch *Harry Potter* and *Twilight,* dance to songs by Psy and Shakira, listen to records made by David Guetta, watch the antics of programs like *Jackass* and play *World of Warcraft* or *The Sims*.

Secondly, in these cultural products, young people seem to find elements that help them to develop their own identities, curating their taste preferences and informing how they present themselves to the world. The major transformation wrought by cultural industries and their social repercussions can be summed up as follows: the aestheticization of identity by means of consumption (Lipovetsky and Serroy, 2013). Whereas once upon a time, individuals would cite their profession to describe themselves, or perhaps where they were born (if their accent hadn't already given it away), today, amidst the massification that creates fears of anonymity and uniformity, individuals openly state their likes and dislikes as so many shifting identity markers, sometimes used to transcend (or escape) their social origins. "Tell me what you like, I'll tell you who you are" appears to be the new motto, largely promoted by digital social networks, which log the changing history of our likes and dislikes, no matter how fleeting. While the debate regarding social mobility rages on, as academic meritocracy seems to crumble, and as the social ladder is increasingly seen — whether rightly or wrongly — as defective (Maurin, 2009), discourse on cultural identity has never been received more media attention. This is no random coincidence, but rather the result of the contradictory but also convergent forces at play in the wider world.

Finally, the relationship of young people to culture in the modern technological world operates under the aegis of abundance: the abundance of products on cultural markets, the abundance of information online and in networks, but also the abundance of public cultural offerings. In most countries, institutional policies have been developed to promote culture and the arts, using models that are either largely State-centralized (as in France), private (as in Great Britain and the United States) or both (as in Quebec). These policies combine content production with diffusion and cultural activities targeting amateurs. This abundance has been accompanied by an increasing demand for cultural offerings as a free public good, which has led to parallel developments in marketing: prepaid cards, subscription services, loyalty programs and free perks, especially in the domain of music and print media. This path has also been adopted by some governments: the French *Pass culture*, launched on the 1st of February 2019, is a free app that communicates the cultural and artistic opportunities available nearby to every young user of the app. It offers 500 euros to every 18-year-old individual living in France so they can buy cultural goods or services. Thanks to geolocation, young people can identify, choose and reserve a wide variety of cultural goods and proposals, from concert to theater tickets, books, artistic practice and video games.[20]

Technoculture can therefore be described by a number of its specific traits. It has given rise to a new form of cultural engagement that is based on participation and which gives a certain plasticity to variations in use that a device-based approach seems less likely to explain. In fact, "we cannot presume to understand the use or meaningful consequences of a technological device merely based on a thorough description of its existence and characteristics. It is the social meaning attributed to such devices that both grant them their value and inform their concrete uses" (Pasquier, Beaudoin and Legon, 2011: 88). If we look beyond the increasing homogeneity of access to technology, however, differences in the use of technology and modes of consumption reveal that the portrait of today's youth is one of variable geometry.

20   https://pass.culture.fr.

CHAPTER 2

The Cult of Participation

As described briefly above, youth culture today favors cultural engagement and promotes a new kind of amateur commitment, one where individuals can participate in the creation, mediation and even dissemination of cultural contents. For instance, diehard fans of certain TV shows subtitle new episodes the same night they are broadcast, while video game aficionados create in-game mods and a whole slew of amateur videographers post clips online that they created with professional (or semi-professional) tools. This new conception of amateurism heralds the advent of consumption-based activities (embodied by prosumers or pro-amateurs in English and *consom-acteurs* in French), which go hand-in-hand with the new emphasis placed on individual and collective creativity. While the latter is not as widespread in practice as we might be tempted to think, a number of possibilities for action are nonetheless accessible enough that society's relationship to cultural consumption has been dramatically altered, with younger generations exhibiting new forms of cultural engagement.

1 The Pro-am: A Form of Commitment in the Technocultural Regime

A consumer-actor who is involved in consumption, mediation and even co-creation can be better described as a "pro-am," or professional amateur. The pro-am's story is woven into the fabric of the techno-cultural revolution itself (Leadbeater and Miller, 2004; Turner, 2006).

1.1 *The Roots of The Pro-am: The Poacher*
In a starkly different context than that of our current technocultural landscape, Michel de Certeau had nonetheless already elaborated the concept of "cultural poaching" (de Certeau, 1980). Those engaged in cultural poaching develop new practices that creatively bridge the gap between two kinds of amateurs: those who create (such as artists and craftspersons) and those who appreciate (connoisseurs). In the realm of amateurism, these two attitudes can be combined, but in the art world they remain resolutely distinct, often embodied by the opposing figures of the artist and the critic (Jenkins, 1992; Flichy, 2010). In reality, the ancestors of today's professional amateurs are the tinkers, the gardeners

and the bakers — all devoted to "serious" leisure activities that develop forms of expertise and which can sometimes replace commercial services and goods.

Pro-ams are largely portrayed as enthusiastic about their passions both personally and collectively (Jenkins, 1992 and 2006; Le Guern, 2002; Flichy, 2010): they create and publish their own content, but evaluate and recommend the content of others (in turn even helping to erect new cultural values). Born and raised as part of the audience, pro-ams learn to spread their wings by acting directly upon cultural contents: fanzines and spinoffs prolong a character's story or depict new adventures, while memes and remixes appropriate and occasionally subvert existing contents. This tendency has only increased with the emergence of crowdfunding platforms, where some amateurs can find the means to achieve semi-professional status. Crowdfunding can help with recording albums, publishing books, and sending bands on tour: such was the case for the American musician Beck, who started his career by posting his videos online. A community of fans sprung up and helped to fund his first studio recording. This self-produced album was very successful, and piqued the interest of a major label, Universal. A few years later, after signing with Universal, Beck won a number of different awards judged by listeners and critics alike, including seven Grammys and a French *Victoire de la Musique*.[1]

In the literary sphere, self-publishing has also taken on entirely new proportions, revolutionizing the publishing industry in the process. Professional editors and agents are now constantly searching for tomorrow's new talent amidst the tidal wave of online content. On Wattpad, for instance, every month a total of 80 million of users post 665 million stories online, in 50 different languages (with 77% of the stories being in English). Wattpad offers possibilities for feedback, either constructive or personal, during the writing process, thanks to interactive margin commenting, which allows users to share their reactions with the writer(s). Readers can add comments and feedback to individual lines and paragraphs as they read, rather than after a chapter or story is finished. According to a recent study, Wattpad empowers adolescent writers, in so far as they learn and grow their craft with constructive feedback and criticism (Birch, 2016). As it is more democratic, the popularity of social writing challenges the role of cultural gatekeepers, such as publishers, as well as traditional notions of authorship. A double shift then occurs: established authority figures (such as famous authors or well-known publishers) intervene in the digital world,

---

[1] The *Victoires de la Musique* are the French equivalent of the American Grammy Awards and represent the pop music equivalent of the César awards for film and Molière awards for theater in France.

where emerging networks of influencers, such as budding authors and micro-celebrities, are also developed (Ramdarshan Bold, 2016).

This phenomenon is also wreaking havoc in the visual arts. With the development of technology for receiving, transmitting and recording images and video on mobile phones, a new field of exploration for image creation and screenwriting has opened up. The arrival of the latest generation of mobile phones (3G) has made it possible not only to watch movies, but also to shoot movies and send one's own creations to other phones or put them online on the internet. All throughout the world, festivals celebrating short films shot on cell phones are popping up: *Pocket film*[2] and the *Mobile film festival*[3] are two examples in France, but such festivals have also been established in Algeria, Australia, Belgium, Brazil, Denmark, Italy, Japan, the Netherlands, Portugal, Spain, Switzerland, Russia, Ukraine and the United Arab Emirates. And there are even film festivals for movies created solely from video game content[4] (e.g., the annual *Machinima Interactive Film Festival* in the United States).

Pro-ams are the children of technoculture, existing by and for mass cultural industries in the globalized and digital world; they exploit the different technological possibilities available to them in order to comment, co-create, reproduce and/or hybridize cultural contents. In so doing, pro-ams develop their own community of audience members, mediators and inter-mediators (in particular by giving their opinion and assessing quality), and producers, a community that is held together by shared emotions, sensations and passions. Pro-ams develop their expertise in three domains: art (by creating or interacting with artworks); knowledge (by analyzing and discussing cultural contents and modes of consumption); and the enrichment of public space (by offering their creations and analyses to a number of communities and audiences). By creating subtitles for television episodes, for instance, pro-ams seek to share something that they enjoy, in the process displaying a number of linguistic and technical skills. In reality, providing television subtitles is not merely a

---

2 The Pocket Films Festival, now six years old, was originally launched by the *Forum des images* in collaboration with the French telephone company SFR (its founding partner), and with the support of the *Centre national de la cinématographie* (National Center for Cinematography) and the *Société des auteurs, compositeurs et artistes* (SACD – the Authors Guild); the festival promotes video creation on cell phones. See https://www.mobilefilmfestival.com.
3 This festival focuses on one-minute films shot on cell phones. See https://www.mobilefilmfestival.com
4 *Machinima*, a word created by combining "machine," "cinema," and "animation," was invented by Anthony Bailey and Hugh Hancock in 1999. This term refers to a cinematographic genre and a film production method that uses sequences from video games saved from inside virtual spaces in real time, most often using the game's graphics engine.

question of translating, but also artistically and technically adapting a work in order to make it accessible to a new community.

Once again, the concept of proximity can help us to understand the transition that occurs between the poacher and the professional amateur: whereas distinct worlds might become closely related for the poacher, the professional amateur sees a complete interpenetration between the two. The pro-am swims between the world of art and the world of consumption, between creation and reception. This proximity requires significant fine-tuning to avoid being called a poseur (someone who will be mocked), an eccentric (someone who will be excluded), or a sell-out (someone who will be criticized for giving up their alleged freedom and autonomy, despite the reality that many more will remain unknown). Ultimately, the professional amateur seeks to find authenticity and originality in the no-man's land between distance and proximity.

Even though the cleavage between professionals and laypersons remains relevant today, the rise of professional amateurs shows just how labile the line between the two categories can be — as well as how each category can enrich the other. In the realm of astronomy, for example, the scientific historian John Dobson[5] reminds us that amateur astronomers have always contributed to major discoveries in the field thanks to their observations, which were historically confirmed or disproved by experts with more advanced tools and techniques. In the aesthetico-cultural realm, technical and scientific skills are deployed in the creation of digital products, video games, wikis and the like. Professional amateurs ultimately come to resemble experts. Their local reputation — that is, within their community of amateurs — is based on the experience and knowledge that they have acquired throughout their history as pro-ams. Such trajectories can include: following the evolution of a television show and its characters (either to provide commentary or create additional content such as fanzines and unofficial spinoffs on the internet); producing translations and subtitles in ultra-fast turnaround times; leading discussions on upcoming plot lines (discussions which are in turn closely followed by screenwriters); supporting the development of products that expand a character's storytelling potential (the creation of an online Hogwarts school, or the production of 375,000 *Potterfictions* (François, 2009)); or creating mods that become part of a "normal," albeit unpredictable, life for video games. Pro-ams even help with archiving and conservation in certain domains, like video games: without pro-ams actively working to screenshot and comment game sequences and provide tutorials, the actual traces of video-game playing would be lost, given that

---

5   www.space.com/scienceastronomy/astronomy/dobson_astronomer_000507.html.

institutions only tend to conserve tangible objects (consoles, game discs) that are then presented under glass cases like at Berlin's *Computerspiele Museum*.[6] But unlike with the work of experts, no institutions come to confirm the quality, position or authority of professional amateurs: these traits must always be assessed within the self-referential fan universe.

1.2   *The Pro-am Revolution*

There are countless examples of what pro-ams have created. A player of *The Sims* can create a family in the game, and watch those characters live out their daily lives, fall in love, get into arguments, get married, have children and even die. Before the online version of the game was released, game designers already offered a number of tools to let players create their own content: furniture, accessories, architecture, etc. In under a year, hundreds of independents creators on more than 200 fan sites had created more than one million new assets that were in turn made accessible to millions of gamers. More than 90% of the content of *The Sims* is provided by professional amateurs and it is estimated that 30,000 modifications developed by pro-ams are available online. Amongst the community of gamers, pro-ams are simultaneously players, creators and innovation stimulators. But professional amateurs cannot only be found in the technology sector: you can find pro-ams amongst the makeshift libraries erected by passionate readers in areas as diverse as a subway station in Chile, on a riverboat in Laos, in a Mongolian yurt, or on a horseback library in Indonesia. All of these examples attest to the same enthusiasm for creating and transmitting that characterize the professional amateur.

If it is fair to qualify the 20th century as the century of professionalism, across spheres as varied as culture, education, science and technology, where the objective was to define procedures, establish hierarchies and quality standards and elaborate regulatory modes and codes, while relegating amateurs to the shadows as (sometimes laughably) incomplete counterparts, it is quite possible that the 21st century will be the century of professional amateurism. As the tools available continue to multiply and become more accessible, as general education levels rise and as self-expression becomes a requirement according to the dominant way of thinking, the logic separating experts and amateurs has begun to crumble. In many cases, pro-ams adopt quasi professional quality standards when engaging in their various activities. Most of the time, they also develop strategies to enhance their knowledge, curiosity, and

---

6   Conference led by Carl Therrien, professor in the department of art history and cinematography studies of the University of Montreal, 6 February 2018, Paris-Sorbonne Nouvelle.

technical skills. They are often capable of expending significant effort, including by working within constraints and experiencing repetition, failure, competition and only occasional success. While the use of cultural resources to develop one's identity is predominant amongst professional amateurs, they also create a highly specific kind of cultural capital derived from their hobbies, knowledge and practical know-how that can form an alternative to "legitimate" cultural capital. For example, analyses on amateur film criticism online indicate that while hierarchies persist even amongst amateur critics — for example, between more subjective critiques and those who respect the criteria of cinephilia — "the amateurs who are the most invested in the critical exercise also come the closest to meeting the standards of professional criticism" (Pasquier, Beaudoin, and Legon, 2014: 23).

In this context, young people are not alienated by the new cultural landscape, but are in fact active participants in a world that is constantly shifting and recreating itself. They negotiate new strategies when faced with cultural globalization, reinterpreting who can be a creator and what intellectual property, expertise and its transmission will look like. Pro-am communities are not immune to the influence of either consumer or public culture, but they also influence both by means of their participation, helping to dismantle the programmatic constraints of cultural industries and institutions.

The figure of the professional amateur has also given rise to new forms of inequality, of course, given that transforming consumption into a productive activity associated with knowledge and autonomy is no easy task — and that not all forms of consumption are equally likely to produce active amateurs. In fact, there is little doubt that this kind of cultural activism largely develops amongst individuals with significant social and cultural capital, or amongst *marginaux sécants* ("intersectional outsiders"), to use the term coined by Haroun Jamous (1968) to describe individuals who travel on the outskirts of a variety of different worlds and thus have more varied resources than typical actors. The profiles of such individuals merely repeat, in a new context, the cultural inequalities of the pre-digital age.[7]

2   Collective Intelligence and Community

The figure of the professional amateur is closely linked to the notion of community: even if pro-ams may work alone, they are always operating in reference

---

7   We shall discuss this in greater detail in chapter 5.

to a community that establishes quality norms and criteria and organizes the processes of selection, assessment and validation. Examples include acting on a digital stage, sharing video creations and having one's games play-tested. The enthusiasm of pro-ams is derived from their interactions with likeminded individuals and groups, supporting the mythos of collective (amateur) intelligence in the digital age. This mythos forms part and parcel of the internet's origin story, based on a shared imaginary that operates as a kind of permanent reference point for the social practices of its most invested individuals (Turner, 2006). In general, we shall use the word *mythos* to refer to any of the implicit narratives of technoculture that inform its worldview, values, structure, and ideals.

2.1   What Is Collective Intelligence?

Collective intelligence refers to the open, intermittent, and iterative practice of processing information that is not necessarily exhaustive or complete, but rather scattered across a number of globalized and interdisciplinary fields. Henry Jenkins, an early champion of this perspective, defined participatory convergence as one of the pillars of convergence culture (Jenkins, 2006). The second pillar is that of collective intelligence, a concept developed by Pierre Lévy, which describes the collective direction taken by individual contributions; such collaborative mechanisms can be seen in the existence of Wikipedia, for example (1997).

In this perspective, everyone can contribute to varying degrees and with their own forms of expertise to the goal of furthering knowledge. Individuals can also decide on the intensity of their commitment, given that not all individuals are expected to participate equally. But the potential engagement of connected individuals who form, according to Pierre Lévy again, "smart masses" (1997), allows for new hierarchies to form in the realm of values, aesthetics and culture. Henry Jenkins has noted that on account of both the mode of production and the characteristics of their creators, these hierarchies tend to stray from "legitimate" values and instead gravitate towards popular culture, in the process forging new, community-specific codes of interpretation. We can thus maintain that convergence is not a technological phenomenon, as both multimedia producers and the technocultural pro-ams possess significant cultural dimensions (Beuscart, 2008: 33). While collective intelligence primarily operates in a horizontal manner, it is not devoid of hierarchy: it includes a kind of active peer review process that ensures the appropriateness of exchanges, even if "spoilers" in the realm of reality television and information diffusion can sometimes thwart such efforts (Jenkins, 2006).

Collective intelligence is therefore inseparable from the principle of collaboration. This form of collaboration is not spontaneous, as it is based on sequencing and the distribution of roles. It presumes forms of leadership, which generate tasks of varying priority in time and space. In other words, collective intelligence encourages project-based collaboration: individuals are mobilized according to their expertise on a given subject and exclusively within the context and timelines of a specific project, whose goals are explicitly stated as collective from the beginning. In project mode, roles are not set in stone — as they are in institutional processes — but on the contrary are defined in terms of local and circumstantial needs; such roles are therefore task-specific, reversible and interchangeable. This functioning is based on two elements: on the one hand, the fluidity of relationships and exchanges and on the other, the expectation of selfless contribution, which supports the requirement for fluidity and an endogenous manner of regulating goals and processes. We therefore shift from a perspective where what matters most is the possession of knowledge, to one where the process by which knowledge is codefined and coproduced through the accumulation of scattered contributions is key instead. As a result, the concept of authority is constantly challenged by the call for more explicative and egalitarian relations, whose legitimacy would instead reside in the power to convince. Whereas teachers have generally been presumed to possess knowledge, thanks to the authority their status confers — a classic example of the delegation of interpretation that is necessary in societies based on a belief in rationality — they now compete with the countless resources available on the Web (Wikipedia first and foremost), as well as the local knowledge claimed by the very communities they seek to address.

Practically speaking, these communities operate on multiple levels. They force us to enter fully into the documentation era, with actors developing a "compulsive need to document, in real time, what they are doing, what they think, what they plan to do, where they are located — and not necessarily with a view to future use of any kind. This need is projected onto other people and can translate into nagging and incessant requests for documentation from others" (Casati, 2013a: 149). Such communities are moreover large-scale consumers, exchangers and even producers of products, contents and cultural knowledge on the outskirts of cultural institutions, in particular because they rely heavily on the logic of documentation outlined above. The daily activity of Facebook users is documenting the self: users say where they are (when, of course, the system doesn't automatically use geolocation to find you), what they are doing, and what kind of mood they are in. Users can likewise see the same sort of documentation produced by their "friends," no matter how far-flung. These communities also help to popularize and disseminate knowledge, with Wikipedia, the free user-generated "non-expert encyclopedia" being the most famous example (Cardon and Levrel, 2009). Platforms like Wikipedia embody a kind of pedagogy that has little, if anything, to do with the traditional teacher/student relationship. The question that we must ask, however, is whether the collective creation of information, achieved through constant documentation, really amounts to shared knowledge.

2.2 Collective Intelligence and Cultural Expertise

The myth of collective intelligence raises two important questions. The first concerns the value chain of cultural production in a context where expert opinions are constantly being challenged by ordinary citizens — a phenomenon that can be observed in discussions on hot-button topics such as medically assisted reproduction, vaccines, genetically modified organisms (GMOs), and big data, but which also exists, albeit more subtly, in the cultural realm. In fact, cultural institutions, whose mission of transmission is crucial to their existence, are veering ever further from the aesthetic values of everyday consumption patterns; moreover, the cultural and political sway that such expertise had arbitrarily been granted has increasingly come under fire in the internet era, whose reigning ideology touts citizens as all equally capable. Capable of acting, of knowing, of questioning and of rejecting the so-called "official" versions and values. In addition, the fact that knowledge across all sectors has become increasingly specialized — and thus to a certain extent esoteric — as well as controlled by a handful of dedicated institutions adds fuel to the critical fire. In this context, the possibility of collective intelligence is seen as a means for individuals to wrest power back from institutions, with amateurs at times even supplanting professionals — a phenomenon which can be seen as justifying criticisms of the cult of amateurism in defense of professionals (Keen, 2008).

Collective intelligence is not the same thing as expertise; in some respects, it even runs counter to expertise, in particular because of the malleability of contents and transmission that it presupposes. The paradigm of expertise requires that there be a stable, constituted corpus of knowledge that individuals can master through a linear, logical and stratified progression specific to each discipline. Collective intelligence sidesteps all of these elements. In this regard, technology has proven to be an apt companion to the fluidity (or mobility) of contemporary societies, as well as their "reflexive turn" (Beck, 1998); collaborative platforms have exploited new possibilities for open, creative and horizontal action. Reflecting on collective intelligence means re-envisioning education and learning processes. Learning is not only a matter of gaining knowledge, it is also, and perhaps even more significantly, a matter of changing how we process information, as shown by the example of reading: reading is not just about being able to decipher alphabetic symbols, but rather about training parts of our brain to develop neurological and phonetic abilities. Do the internet and collective intelligence make us stupid (Carr, 2008 and 2010), do they prevent us from becoming intelligent (Casati, 2013b), or do they dramatically reconfigure learning processes? How do we share learning experiences that we have actually not had ourselves?

Secondly, which collectives are we targeting? Collective bodies have proliferated over the years, focusing on creative, democratic, anti-globalization and anti-consumerist issues. In these groups, Web users deploy their diverse individual forms of expertise in the service of shared goals (Lévy, 1997). The resulting knowledge communities escape the influence of neither consumer nor public culture, but they gradually change both of these thanks to public participation; for example, industry CEOs and institutional leaders can be swayed by public opinion. These communities are often tied to an imaginary of transnational mobility: they claim to reshape linkages beyond social and community-based forms of belonging (such as age, sex, class, family, etc.), promising new voluntary, ad hoc, and sometimes instrumental affiliations that are based on intellectual goals as well as shared emotions. This promise is particularly targeted at young people, who are more mobile than their elders, both geographically and socially speaking, since their life trajectories are poised to be much less linear than in the past.

The social impact of the changes affecting young people today is especially significant if we look at how the notion of collectivity is represented. Academia has been challenged, thanks to the emergence of new forms of learning, while cultural institutions have likewise been confronted with the proliferation of new production sites. Young people have seen the rise of user-generated content as well as the transformation of social ties, leading to the splintering off of a myriad amateurs' communities. The changes wrought have also included a growing distrust of representative bodies in politics (parties, trade unions) and the appearance of new, circumstantial forms of engagement in the service of various "causes" (be they natural disasters, epidemics, terrorist attacks, or foreign conflicts).

But sometimes, however, reality comes to disprove such promises: youth knowledge communities are not, in fact, as local and open in their recruitment as they might claim to be. While they can resemble rich islands of expertise (Allison-Bunnell and Thomson, 2007), these communities are — like islands — quite remote from each other and struggle to elaborate any kind of shared generational markers for all young people. These communities often lead to highly contrasting commentary, ranging from affiliation to rejection amongst young people themselves.

The myth of collective intelligence thus poses the question of how expression, politics and capitalism interact. Creative and artistic capitalism is a great fit for individuals who want to take over content creation, endorsement and dissemination within communities of amateurs who end up determining prescriptive guidelines for future consumers. The numerous and virulent controversies surrounding algorithms, controversies which often lament the loss of our freedom of choice and our right to be forgotten, may ultimately be concealing what commercial co-opting does to the creativity of professional amateurs. Christopher Poole, the creator of *4Chan*, was a major symbol of internet anonymity and a geek hero (given that he founded *4Chan*[8] in 2003 when he was only 15 years old and left his position as its administrator when he was 26). He now works … at Google. The opposition between the two worlds is thus illusory at best.

3   The Culture of Doing

The element of choice that ostensibly governs hobbies and leisure activities is based on the principle of pleasure. But such activities are not devoid of significant personal investment, whether we look at the author of a blog or the amateur musician who uses music software to create sampling-based tunes,[9] the fan of a television show that develops expertise regarding the object of his passion, the diehard reader who has learned to speedread, the gamer who creates mods for her favorite video games, or all the fans who create new scripts to expand the scope of their passion in fanzines, tutorials and the like. All of these individuals do, make, combine and adapt things. This culture of doing combines know-how (technical production skills), knowing-how-to-be (or the social awareness needed to belong to specific fan communities) and the capacity for dissemination (or the ability to ensure the publication and mediation of contents as well amateur self-portraits). These three skill sets are closely intertwined in the culture of doing.

---

8   *4Chan* is an English-language site where all users are anonymous, with some variation on the user's name and "anon". Users can exchange images across all genres. *4Chan* is known for its quasi-total freedom of expression, which gives rises to the best as well as the worst. Il currently boasts 2 billion posts.

9   Samples originally referred to devices that recorded sounds or musical segments and played them on a loop. As a result, the verb to sample has come to mean taking a piece of cultural content and reusing it in a new work.

3.1 Compensatory Skills

This culture of doing, which encompasses all forms of media in a collaborative and combinatory fashion, encourages a number of skills that young people can acquire through play, by listening to, participating in, and transforming the society around them. These skills are not trivial (Jenkins, 2006) given that they include: the ability to share information and value systems, comparing the latter and determining ethical stakes; to establish connections between scattered pieces of information; to express one's interpretations and emotions through the appropriation and recombination of cultural elements to create a personalized and individual form of culture; and finally, the ability to disseminate more broadly what is created within fan communities. These skills are acquired thanks to significant efforts deployed in the service of personal growth and learning (especially with regarding to information and communications technologies), driven solely by an attachment to the practice and pursuit of individual benefit.

And yet these skills all ostensibly emerge to compensate for other skills individuals may be lacking. Inferior in quality, these competencies are often at odds with the skills required by traditional learning environments, including schools. The emergence of youth technoculture has raised new issues for education, with educators debating the best pedagogical uses of technology. Many have wondered: do students learn better with or without technology? Attempts to incorporate technology in the classroom have produced political polemics regarding the use of tablets in place of textbooks and cultural debates surrounding the expansion of virtual museum visits in place of, or as a complement to, physical exposure to artworks (which would in turn affect how visitors are counted and what constitutes the museum-going public).

This question does not have a single answer, especially since research has shown that tools and devices must be understood in the context and environment of their use(s) (Charlier and Henri, 2010), thus prohibiting us from making any kind of hasty generalizations. More importantly, however, this question is not properly framed. Instead of focusing on the pedagogical uses of technology (how to educate students using technological applications and devices), we should perhaps look at the kinds of education that media and digital technologies support (what kind of education is produced by the use of technology) and at the transferability of skills acquired through such unorthodox educations with regard to traditional pedagogical models.

3.2 Creative Remixing

Steven Johnson (2005) has analyzed how "popular," industrial and media-based culture, despite being a frequent object of scorn, can in fact contribute to collective intelligence. He has also shown how the average quality of audiovisual mass culture products has gradually improved, acculturating young people to more complex scripts drawing on a more diverse pool of references and calling for more highly developed decoding skills. As a result, young people have also developed greater intelligence about what they consume, leading to demands for "quality". This is a far cry from the widespread notion that popular culture is necessarily functional (that is: always linked to a goal, be it leisure, entertainment, seduction or relaxation), with the parallel assumption that it was also devoid of any aesthetic power (Shusterman, 2007). This aesthetic lack justified historically the division between popular and learned pursuits. As Simon Frith (Frith, 1989) has noted, scholars have often argued that popular music is the purview of sociology, whereas classical music is the "natural" subject of musicology. Such an interpretation would mean paying very little attention indeed to the highly aesthetic and concrete experiences of young music listeners, including in a wide variety of settings that have nothing to do with learned tradition: on the subway, while doing homework, while running, etc. What can at first seem like a functional strategy — for instance, choosing to listen to a certain piece of music to match one's mood, or setting a romantic ambiance for a date — can also include elements of creativity and aestheticism. For example, listening to music in the car (Koops, 2014) or singing karaoke (Drew, 2001) develops a specific aesthetic criteriology among the young people who engage in those activities. The same division affects the production of films and television series, especially since the latter (long considered a secondary offshoot of the former, employing less-famous actors and directors and operating on a tighter budget with less visual innovation and less codification surrounding home viewing) is quickly becoming more experimental and prone to narrative risk-taking. For instance, television has invented and refined a number of techniques such as the cliffhanger, forking, and multiple narratives and the gradual development of increasingly ambivalent and complex characters, techniques that may affect our everyday behaviors (Jost, 2011, 2015, and 2018); it has also allowed for the emergence of new and perhaps "freer" viewing formats (i.e., ones that are not constrained by the schedules of movie theaters or broadcasts), as well as new experiential rituals of consumption.

Interest in the aesthetic component of popular media products and the experiences they procure leads us to the teachings of Dewey, Piaget, and Bruner, who all claimed that creativity had a central role to play in education. The rise of technoculture is therefore a good opportunity to revisit the question of creativity, as some recent studies in Great Britain (Jackson and Shaw, 2005) and Australia (Dawson and McWilliam, 2008) have done. An investigation into the relationship between imagination and creativity is also present in much of youth-directed discourse on globalization (Castronovo, 2007). As Arjun Appadurai has explained, "globalization is not simply the name for a new epoch in the history of capital or in the biography of the nation-state. It is marked by a new role for the imagination in social life" (Appadurai, 2000: 13). Charles Acland argues that Appadurai's mission was concentrating on human creativity and imagination, in the process demonstrating that the work of our imagination is never totally disciplined or totally free, but rather that it is a variable and contested space where individuals can establish linkages between the global and their own personal practices (Acland, 2003). Technoculture is adept at annexing both our practices and our imaginaries.

In order to better understand the kind of creativity we are talking about, we must distinguish between innovation (which is a kind of commercial creativity) and actual imagination, i.e. creative processes, which matter more than the final products they lead to (which may be of varying quality). By combining contents, ideas and elements of surprise (Lehrer, 2012), the goal is to make the familiar strange and the strange familiar. We can therefore argue that young people today are not so much trying to "become experts" — a label that they do not claim for themselves — as they are trying to elicit emotions, even in local and one-off situations. This represents a compromise between the position held by John Dewey (Dewey, 1934), who prioritized process over production, and that maintained by Gilles Deleuze (Deleuze, 1981), who valued Being over Becoming. This process is frequently called upon in various forms of media consumption, for instance when making playlists or any kind of amateur art. Video games also involve this specific creative process: while a standard quest is part of every video game narrative, players can also partially define their own side quests, behaving as cultural activators within the world of the video game.

This kind of youth creativity is manifest in remix culture. Young people are champions of the remix: they find familiar cultural elements or contents and recombine and reconfigure them to create something new. Sampling and remixing are at the heart of new youth creativity. Richard Memeteau explains: "Many people thought that the necessary standardization of mass art would inevitably lead to homogenization and the alienation of its audience. For these individuals, the 'pop' in pop culture heralded the imminent fulfilment of Léon Tolstoy's prophesy: 'where you want to have slaves, there you should have as much music as possible'. Wherever mass means are used, people shall be changed *en masse*" (2014: 9). He also reminds us that according to Henry Jenkins (Jenkins, 2006), we can distinguish two different phases, depending on the degree of youth creativity involved. During the first phase, mass culture slowly replaces popular culture with the creation of new publics; during the second, fans and groupies of all kinds start to reappropriate existing contents to create their own (pop) art. Technoculture clearly belongs to this second phase.

An important shift thus occurs: thanks to the digital age, the counterculture that was typical of the 1970s generation and which rejected artistic reappropriation or recycling has been replaced with a form of pop culture that not only tolerates but wholeheartedly embraces these processes as the basis for creativity. The notions of artistic authenticity and innovation were deeply important for counterculture and its modernist paradigm. Pop culture, on the other hand, is more suited to post-modernity, parody and collage (Guibert, 2004). The key element is the reappropriation and transformation of cultural contents; the authenticity of cultural works or cultural products does not matter as much as the authenticity of the emotions elicited. Heroes are often "recycled" and the very process of recycling is where creativity lies: Batman fights Superman, Neo/Jesus becomes the prophet of the Matrix/the world, Noah from the Bible becomes a science fiction film star ... The list of heroes is neither exhaustive nor exclusive, but on the contrary inclusive and collective. Creative pop culture "does not only reveal renewed faith in various myths. What it creates is also 'mythical' in a different sense: readers experience the solidarity of self-perpetuating beliefs" (Memeteau, 2014: 154).

4   A New Ecology of Attention

Collective intelligence, creative remixing and the cult of participation ... Despite such promising developments, countless voices denounce decreasing attention spans and the inability of young people to concentrate, supposedly due to their high consumption of digital media streams. This issue highlights the pre-existing distinction between the "public" (an audience that is attentive because its members all want to access certain content) and "the masses" (a versatile aggregate without its own specific desires).

4.1   *In Search of Lost Attention Spans*

The attention span of the masses is not a new concern. As early as 1902, Gabriel Tarde outlined the tenets of economic psychology, choosing to focus on the contemporary rise of "machinofacture" in the realm of industrial production. Gabriel Tarde describes how the alignment of attention spans gave way to a new economics of visibility under the aegis of glory, i.e., "the simultaneity and the convergence of attention and judgment around a single person or event that thus becomes glorious and noteworthy" (Tarde, 1902: 231). In 1969, Herbert Simon was the first to explicitly link economics and attention (the proceedings of the conference were published in 1971): "in an information-rich world, the wealth of information means a dearth of something else: a scarcity of whatever it is that information consumes. What information consumes is rather obvious: it consumes the attention of its recipients" (Simon, 1971: 8). This idea was further nuanced by Alvin Toffle's concept of "information overload" (Toffle, 1970), as well as by the psychological studies on the limits of our attentional resources led by Daniel Kahnman (Kahnman, 1973). Since then, publications have multiplied on the alienating effects of technology, especially with regard to the attention spans of young people. On both sides of the Atlantic, scholars have described an anthropological mutation (Crary, 2000; Stiegler, 2014), one that largely transcends traditional commercial exchanges and directly targets our desires and subjectivity in accordance with aims of market logic and capitalist profit. Many such scholars have expressed concern for our mental and cognitive capacities as a result.

In order to understand what is at stake here, we must distinguish between the collective attentional behaviors through which we tend to perceive the world and, on the other hand, joint attention (two people paying attention to a shared interest), a phenomenon implicated in education as well as in the development of skills and subjectivities that require physical (or at least virtual) co-presence. These forms of co-presence are established thanks to what specialists term affective and cognitive "tuning," processes that are essential albeit sometimes minor in degree. Although these two forms of attention are indeed different, Yves Citton argues that in the age of modernity, characterized by the increasing influence of fame and visibility in tandem with new media developments, every form of attention should be considered (at least virtually) as joint (Citton, 2017).

During the media era, the collective dimension was predominant. Mass media was based on the principle of radio broadcasting: namely, an uneven and asymmetrical exchange between an electrically connected broadcaster that disseminated attention (and could be cheaply reproduced) to collect the attention (scarce and costly) of individuals. With the rise of technoculture, we have moved from the model of collective attention (mass media) to the model of joint attention. Young people are now constantly engaged in affective tuning, which highlights the current primacy of communication over information (Bougnoux, 2001: 72–3). These efforts at affective tuning entail various strategies of improvisation, invention and tinkering.

Moreover, the economics of attention in the world of technoculture are tied to a need for fame and its inherently linked principle of value creation (by paying attention to something, individuals actively participate in determining the *value* of contents in circulation). But this process is also circular, with attention attracting more attention: celebrity feeds off itself, with fame becoming a good rather than a flow. This encourages opportunism (everything that emerges from anonymity is good) while generating fears that criticism is being forfeited. In the new economy, more than ever, "not everyone can attract the same amount of attention. Some of us are stars, but most [are] just fans" (Goldhaber, 1996).

4.2 In Praise of Free-Floating Attention and the Illusion of Multitasking

It is possible to make a theoretical distinction between two types of situations. The first situation resembles radio broadcasting: there is a single broadcasting device linked one-way to one or more receivers whose job is to transmit pre-determined pieces of existing information. In such cases, the information transmitted may or may not seem pertinent to listeners, and the latter may in fact have already acquired this information, including through networks. The second situation includes an interactive configuration where the goal is to co-create culture (contents, behavior, representations, etc.). In real life, most situations are a bit of both: MOOCs[10] and online tutorials, for instance, are based on collaboration between teachers and students. These examples shine a light on the assumptions at play, including their impact on how we judge skills and the importance of feedback and attention. The inherently asymmetrical nature of speaking does not mean we can dispense with maintaining attentional symmetry between speakers and listeners (even if this symmetry is diluted as the number of participants grows). The work of the mediator is thus to maintain a kind of attention that helps to create a situation of seemingly equal attention, often based on a strong emotional connection (Simondon, 2005).

In addition, a deeper analysis of the mechanisms of attention reveals that technocultural multitasking is little more than an illusion. In reality, we can only pay attention to one thing at a time, and that attention can only be divided asynchronously, by flitting from one object to another, rather than simultaneously, by truly focusing on multiple objects at once. Multitasking, which is common among young people today, is in fact based on the ability to optimally organize one's time and attention (Ophir, Nass, and Wagner, 2009). This entails the capacity for modulation: modulating the frequency with which one pays attention to a given object depending of the difficulty and level of attention required for comprehension, as well as the functioning of each task. Young people can calibrate the duration and quality of their attention spans

---

10   First available in 2006, MOOCs are massive open online courses, generally free online. As a supplement to traditional course materials such as text, audio and video, MOOCs also offer interactive forums where professors and students can exchange ideas.

in accordance with the degree of focus required by cultural objects, as well as the individual goals they may have. Strong, focused attention is sometimes necessary or at least ideal, but can also sometimes be sub-optimal, especially since concentration automatically comes with its own blind spots outside of the object of one's attention. One famous study illustrated this discussion on multitasking with brio: the invisible gorilla test,[11] conducted in 1999 by two researchers in cognitive psychology at Harvard University, Christopher Chabris and Daniel Simmons. This study, which won them the Nobel Prize in psychology in 2004, was conducted in the following manner. Participants were instructed to watch a short video where two groups were playing basketball, one dressed in white and the other in black. Participants were ordered to count the number of passes between the two teams. During this video, a person dressed as a gorilla strolled onto the screen, walking from left to right while thumping his chest. About half of all participants were so engrossed in their task (counting passes) that they did not report seeing the gorilla. This study illustrates the limits of our attention: when we are concentrating on one task, we have difficulty absorbing other information. Both Katherine Hayles (Hayles, 2012) and Yves Citton (Citton, 2017) have also maintained that certain kinds of "free-floating" attention, often described negatively as a loss of concentration abilities amongst young people, actually allow for more creative information processing. Free-floating attention is not necessarily less effective than its concentrated counterpart, given that it is by *not* concentrating one's attention on a single object that certain important details can be observed. Freudian psychoanalysis likewise revealed that it is easier to discover what the analysand desires to say if the analyst does not pay attention to what the former means. Paul North consequently argues that "attention and distraction are not opposites at all, but rather contraries, the one, distraction, consists in the other, attention, to the lowest degree. The age of distraction, it turns out, was always but the age of attention" (North, 2012: 5).

Cathy Davidson has also criticized the fact that undistracted attention is seen as the model of reference; according to her, assuming that laser-beam focus on a single task is the best model has naturally led to declinist arguments and creeping fears. Davidson refers to the concept of "partial attention" in order to describe how "we surf, looking in multiple directions at once, rather than being fully absorbed in one task only. Rather than think of continuous partial attention as a problem or a lack, we may need to reconsider it as a digital survival skill" (Davidson, 2011: 287). She goes on to highlight the different

---

11   The study video is available at: https://www.youtube.com/watch?v=vJG698U2Mvo.

forms of attention that have been rewarded throughout history: "the lesson of attention blindness is that sole, concentrated, direct, centralized attention to one task — the ideal of twentieth-century productivity — is efficient for the task on which you are concentrating but it shuts out other important things we also need to be seeing". She proposes a critical, though not negative, view of partial attention, arguing that "in our global, diverse, interactive world, where everything seems to have another side, continuous partial attention may not only be a condition of this life but a useful tool for navigating a complex world. Especially if we can compensate for our own partial attention by teaming with others who see what we miss, we have a chance to succeed and the possibility of seeing the other side — and then the other side of that other side" (Davidson, 2011: 289).

When looking at reading specifically, Katherine Hayles suggests that we should differentiate between close reading (which is required for formal literary analysis), hyper reading (namely in terms of Web reading) and machine reading (a kind of automatic textual analysis). According to Hayles, hyper reading introduces a number of cognitive and neurological changes that encourage neural plasticity. "Young people are at the leading edge of these changes, but pedagogical strategies have not to date generally been fashioned to take advantage of these changes" (Hayles, 2012: 11).

Thus, free-floating or partial attention consists in eliminating the traditional constraints of reason and allowing oneself to be carrying along by what Baudelaire called *correspondances,* or free association. The emancipatory dimension of distraction can also lead to a certain detachment which, by stripping individuals of specific goals, can allow them to perceive and receive information in a different manner. Evenly-suspended attention also lets individuals transcend their specific situation or setting, parameters that are inherent to any kind of expectation (Houzel, 1998: 34). "Isn't a certain *distraction* just a condition that is just as necessary for an *active* listening as total, structural and functional listening is?" Peter Szendy has wondered (2009: 128). Floating attention is therefore not only useful, but profoundly necessary — as long as it is educated.

4.3   Hyper Attention: An Autopsy

Hyper attention is thus not a sign of deficit or excess, but simply a different kind of attention. The shape, structure and temporality of this free-floating kind of focus do not fit neatly into the framework of traditional education.

The question remains whether we will be able to configure our environment so that we can protect deep experiences, without yielding to the general trend of shallowness (Carr, 2010), a shallowness that is produced by the distracting machines constantly buzzing around us in the digital world. Deep experiences are more highly represented among aesthetic experiences, as part of experiments (often collective) which correspond perfectly to the imaginary of the laboratory of attention: a time and space temporarily cut off from the everyday world, a place to test out limits, transcend borders, change perceptions, adopt new ways of thinking, or face intellectual challenges such as cognitive dissonance.

Ultimately, it is our aesthetic experiences that educate our attention, given that they help us to reconfigure "the distribution of the sensible," immersing us in aesthetic experiences that privilege unsuspected feelings and sensations, and/or encourage us to modify the values we had hitherto ascribed to the latter. Jean-Marie Schaeffer has moreover pointed out that aesthetic experiences are experiences that maximize one's attentional investment, in particular by promoting an attentional style that is characterized by a reluctance to categorize (in other words, a suspension of judgment). He adds: "the reluctance to categorize is always experienced as a sort of dissonance, since it contradicts the economizing principle of cognitive consonance. An individual's ability to pay sustained attention to the sound quality of a text is thus proportional to their ability to tolerate situations of delayed categorization" (Schaeffer, 2011: 114).

These aesthetic experiences can just as easily be associated with mainstream media products as they can be with "legitimate," high-brow culture. For example, over the last 20 years, popular television shows have taxed viewers with increasingly complex storylines, even when the themes of such shows may have remained relatively banal. By looking a bit further than the supposed or real quality of contents, we can observe the intellectual legwork required from their audiences; in fact, mass media is more a purveyor of mental gymnastics exercises than it is of life lessons. The skills associated with amateurism are therefore on the rise, as Steven Johnson analyzed in his provocative title, *Everything bad is good for you: How popular culture is making us smarter*. Johnson argues that even "the most debased forms of mass diversion — video games and violent television dramas and juvenile sitcoms — turn out to be nutritional after all" (Johnson, 2005: 9). Could it be that all the vitriol directed at video games — which are accused of detrimentally monopolizing youth attention — is unfounded? This is the stance adopted by Cathy Davidson when she highlights that the most in-depth study on the issue, conducted by the Pew Research Center, had observed that "absorption in games doesn't contradict social life, civic engagement, focus, attention, connection with other kids, or collaboration. On the contrary, it seems to promote all of the above" (Davidson, 2011: 154).

As aesthetic experiences percolate into the unlikeliest of mass cultural products, the cognitive skills used by young people only become more complex. These experiences of consuming, listening and watching are nonetheless still more individuating than individual, thanks to the reflexive attention they require, situated somewhere between immersion and criticism. These two perspectives go hand-in-hand, given that it is by diving into the details and nuances of a given object that individuals strive to preemptively address the criticisms that will be directed at their subjectivity. To be convinced of this, we can compare cultural products that are commonly consumed by young people today to the products enjoyed by their parents at the same age: if we compared *Bewitched* to *Desperate Housewives,* or *Dallas* to *Black Mirror,* it is evident that plot, character development, and storytelling techniques have all become wildly more complex, just as attempts at historic realism have become much more credible. 1960s America, deep in depression and mass consumption as portrayed in *Mad Men*; 1890s England caught in the throes of profound social transformation as encapsulated by *Downton Abbey*; contemporary Norway facing its Russian fears in *Occupied*; the diverse Spanish gang running the show in *Money Heist;* the Korean salvo to plastic surgery in *My ID is Gangnam Beauty*: all these shows help to create effects of reality based on the painstaking verisimilitude of their details. Young people are rarely duped: they expertly identify continuity errors and glitches as if playing a game. This confirms that in fact, "for decades, we've worked under the assumption that mass culture follows a steadily declining path towards lowest-common-denominator standards, presumably because the 'masses' want dumb, simple pleasures and big media companies want to give the masses what they want. But in fact, the exact opposite is happening: the culture is getting more intellectually demanding, not less" (Johnson, 2005: 9).

This gives us ammunition to respond to the two predominant criticisms of youth culture. We often hear the accusation that young people today are devoid of critical thinking skills, that they gullibly believe everything on the internet. But in reality, young people manifest a different form of critical thinking, one that disturbs their elders specifically because they become its target, due to their inability to challenge the traditional frameworks of criticism and evaluation. As Marshall McLuhan presciently explained: judging emerging cultural forms using the criteria associated with older forms will lead at best to incomprehension and at worst to blindness. Of course, critical thinking is not inherently a product of the internet or of generational renewal; it is necessary to learn how to best develop the ability of young people to interpret culture and think for themselves. But we cannot dismiss offhand the interpretive skills and forms of knowledge that stem from the experiences, lessons and processes of youth technoculture.

∴

Amateurs in the digital era are therefore characterized by the adoption of a certain cultural curriculum which combines shared references and strategies for organizing one's time, an idea of what it means to be a cultural actor in the digital world and a transformation of the aesthetics of seeing, reading, listening, and writing. This curriculum is marked on the one hand by the growing popularity of certain activities (predominantly associated with *doing*) and the accelerated consumption of contents produced by technocultural industries, which play into the various hierarchies between cultural genres. On the other, it is marked by the emergence of specific new skills largely obtained through informal training. Not all young people become professional amateurs: only those with the most cultural resources and sufficient motivation do: technoculture does not erase all former social stratification and boundaries, but merely reproduces many of them. Nevertheless, the rise of the pro-am has durably altered the cultural representation of young people, both in their eyes and in those of society at large.

CHAPTER 3

The Impact of Youth Technoculture on Cultural Myths

Technoculture can be analyzed by looking at its sociological components in two different ways: on the one hand, through the lens of the norms that it establishes in various youth subcultures and how the latter transform our conception of youth; and on the other hand, through the social myths that it helps to engender and which establish expectations, provide representations to emulate (or disdain) and govern cultural dynamics.

This chapter examines the finer traits of these myths: the high value placed on expressiveness, emotions, and mobility, as well as the importance of additive comprehension. These four elements are poised to redefine what the word "cultural" means, in terms of both inherent quality and the types of linkages produced.

1 Expressiveness

Contemporary individualism has found fertile ground in the world of technoculture. Youth culture today emphasizes and develops the need for expressiveness, encouraging the ideal of self-creation (a kind of self-birth) as an audience looks on (Delaunay-Teterel and Cardon, 2006). It places great value on individual choice, hyperdeveloped self-narratives, and the quest for uniqueness within the constraints of the group, thus redefining contemporary individualism in relation to self-expression (Bréchon, 2013; Galland and Roudet, 2012).

1.1 Expressive Individualism

Technoculture is a favorable terrain for those who lean towards expressive individualism (Allard and Vandenberghe, 2003). Contemporary emphasis on expressive individualism is also linked to experimentation, exchange, and the continual search for entertainment. Young people today idolize internet celebrities, be they alternative rock groups, makeup experts, cooking stars or amateur comedy bloggers. Most of these "stars" are practically unknown to adults, but their videos, tutorials and blogs are seen and read millions of times per month by young people. Traditional media outlets, which had long ignored such celebrities, are now suddenly fawning for their attention: the doors of the television and film industries have been cast wide open. Some internet sensations do go on to find fame and fortune (or at least steady professional income) after developing a one-man show or another offline endeavor — but this generally only becomes possible following significant online recognition.

Most productions posted online are not, however, attempts at fame and success, but rather forays into self-expression: the desire for expressing one's feelings and ideas has driven new forms of identity-building that are reliant on digital networked socialization. On social networks, the most important thing is sharing who you are or want to be: cultural contents, which are increasingly tools for individualization, are in fact used to elaborate self-representations. Here we find the distinction established by Erving Goffman between, on the one hand, the "actor, tirelessly working to shape the public's impressions and engaged in the daily task of staging performances," and on the other, the "character, typically portrayed in a positive light that highlights his strength, spirit and other sterling qualities" (Goffman, 1973: 238).

The twofold interactivity of computers, used both individually by users and collectively by networks, allows for grey zones on the internet where individuals can play with privacy and public exposure (Cardon, 2010b). Computers and the internet are in turn particularly seductive to young people because a) they provide access to personalized forms of consumption and b) they are tools that combine creativity with sociability, the latter ranging from contact and collaboration to exchange (visiting sites, posting cultural content, participating in forums and chats on various exchange sites). But there is a paradox here, given that what young people share on these networks is extremely labile: profiles are continuously updated and identities can seemingly be changed on a whim. (On the contrary, however, the right to be forgotten or to have regrets is not equally ensured). In reality, most of what is shared is selected to present a flattering portrait of ourselves, as virtuous, ethical and most importantly, *consistent* individuals — with this last attribute giving rise to the greatest degree of endogenous control. Cognitive dissonance has no place in the performance of the self, nor does inconsistency over time. One has only to look at the example of Mennel Ibtissen, a young female competitor on *The Voice France*, who was eliminated following harsh treatment by the press when old Facebook posts of hers came to light, in which she trivialized the Nice terrorists attempts (14 July 2016) and claimed to support French comedian and activist Dieudonné as well as Muslim academic Tariq Ramandan, both media figures with controversial political opinions. Even though these Facebook posts were markedly different from the message of tolerance and openness Mennel Ibtissen claimed to bring to the singing competition — in part by singing a popular Arabic song in French — the inconsistencies that they highlighted in her image ultimately led to her elimination. Nothing is forgotten on social networks; as a result, it is very difficult for individuals to make amends with regard to their past.

As a form of expression-based consumption, listening to music plays a key role in the world of youth (self-)expression. This is true at ever younger ages: the competition show *The Voice* has its own kids version, while pre-teen "bubble pop[1]" has invaded the airwaves, and some audio devices are designed using the characteristic shapes and colors of early childhood. With the rise of the digital era, music has infiltrated numerous aspects of everyday life, in part by playing with hybrid forms. Since the invention of the video clip, sound and image have gone hand-in-hand and music has become increasingly networked, ultimately leading to the dominance of the visual realm and all its secondary characteristics (visibility, looks, buzz, etc.). Today, we *watch* music just as much as we listen to it. Thanks to the countless different genres and subgenres of contemporary music, it is now possible for individuals to position and define themselves in a complex and constantly changing — but always global — manner. When young people buy their first album, put their first band posters on the wall, make their first playlists,[2] purchase their first smartphone or mp3/4 players or attend their first concerts, they are engaging in important micro-events that they can use to define themselves as individuals and cultural consumers as they become older. Through music, young people learn, albeit in a sometimes caricatural fashion, about gender roles, love relations and sexual experiences while testing out a host of different identities (whether they are fans of punk, K-pop, rasta, or techno, etc.). The hyper-segmentation of the music market allows for the dominance of amateur expertise, with all its attendant practical and symbolic benefits. Being an expert in a given musical genre or subgenre can be a way of staking out a valuable spot in a peer group, from a very young age to adulthood (Monnot, 2009).

1.2 *The Rise of Experimentation*

In a society that places great value on creation (of content, but also of identity), expressing oneself presupposes a certain degree of uniqueness, which pushes young people to multiply and experiment with cultural experiences. Jean-Marie Schaeffer defines experiences as "the set of cognitive, emotive and volitive interactional processes that constitute our relationship to the world and to ourselves, as well as the assortment of skills acquired through the repetition of these processes" (Schaeffer, 1995: 6). Individual and/or collective

---

1 "Bubble pop" is a term, used in French, to describe certain twee teen and pre-teen musical genres (See Octobre and al, 2010).
2 A list of music files that can be played in a set order, or randomly on shuffle.

experimentation plays a key role in youth technoculture, underpinning the high value placed on engagement and continuous learning. Below we shall discuss the different forms that this dimension of experience can take.

Most of this experimentation takes place in the domain of play, which is characteristic of adolescence and provides the tools that young people need to distance themselves critically from the adult world. Young people are also behind the massive societal shift from culture towards entertainment, be it comedy films or internet gags. *Jackass* is a prime example of this: this American television show produces 20-minute segments where young adults engage in dangerous pranks for (on- and off-stage) laughs. The show originally aired on MTV from 1999 to 2002, and then gave rise to a number of big screen productions thanks to a collaboration between MTV and Paramount. In 2008, *Entertainment Weekly* ranked *Jackass* as the 68th best television show over the past quarter-century. In addition, what could have remained just another juvenile prank show was propelled to a whole other level when many young people around the world attempted to reproduce the pranks and dares presented on the show (often at their own risk!) and shared their results on the internet.

Video games have similarly become emblematic of youth culture: the dexterity required to play many games has led young people to engage in new kinds of knowledge transmission and training that occur devoid of any parental involvement (Dajez and Roucous, 2010). More broadly, the emphasis placed on fun and play has influenced narrative scripts across the gamut of media productions, fostering the development of new offerings that combine culture and entertainment. Young people are massively fans of talk shows that combine news segments with comedy, as well as reality shows, which became very popular in the 2000s. On these kinds of shows, the host usually follows a series of structured sequences to create excitement rather than incite real discussion. An increasing number of politicians, both male and female, now go on talk shows in a large number of countries, from *The Tonight Show* in the US, to *Le Petit journal* or *On n'est pas couché* in France, to *Tagesschau* in Germany; these shows are rapidly replacing the more traditional cultural and political debates networks may have once aired.

Television shows also allow for viewers to vicariously experience fictional lives and emotions. As a generational marker, TV aficionados have now replaced film buffs. The former engage with current events, often mentioned with a view to establishing reference points within a shared context. Television shows also deal with transnational issues such as terrorism, climate change, public health, conspiracies, and class warfare. Thanks to their universality, these topics are used as fictional constructs that permit a kind of emotional realism which encourages viewers to identify with the show or character at hand, as studies on early soap operas observed (Ang, 1985). Finally, TV shows also grant viewers access to a wide variety of feelings and mental states, thanks to increasingly psychologized narratives. Speaking about television, the writer Martin Winckler explains: "Fiction has the twofold advantage of giving us access to experiences that we have not lived ourselves, and of shedding light on the experiences we have had. Fiction warns, informs and teaches us. Sometimes, it even comforts us" (Winckler, 2012: 98). The world of TV shows so greatly appreciated by young people is moreover closely linked to other forms of media: shows can contain references to other shows, to cartoons from one's childhood, or even to famous bloggers. Media specialist François Jost states: "This way of engaging with reality largely describes 'the children of the TV age' for whom the world exists first and foremost through mediatization and more concretely, the computer screen" (Jost, 2011: 11). In addition, this world is strongly tied to networks and the digital sphere through the establishment of dynamic fan groups: for example, amateur subtitling efforts help to disseminate content faster, just as P2P platforms facilitate information sharing. Some fan communities even go so far as to pitch ideas to the screenwriters or directors of shows they love, or create exegesis-type narratives that flesh out plot lines or give characters more backstory.

2 Emotions First and Foremost

A second trait is associated with youth culture and stems from the emphasis placed on (self-)expression: the great value attributed to emotions both at the individual and collective levels (privileging peak experiences, and the ad hoc creation of communities around high-intensity circumstances and emotions rather than longevity, respectively).

2.1 *Peak Experiences*

Since the publication of *Your Child is a Person* and the decree that individuals have the educational responsibility of creating themselves, or at least of contributing to their self-creation, the leisure sphere has increasingly functioned as a space for self-construction through the experience of myriad emotions (excitement, joy, anger, love, desire, hatred, rivalry, etc.). Leisure has thus become imbued with the ideology of empowerment through emotions, with the role played by these emotions becoming ever more important as hobbies, whether cultural or not in nature, help individuals to develop their relationship to the world (Macé and Maigret, 2005). Being a young person means flirting with intense emotions, as part of the growing-up experiences, be it by watching horror films, riding roller coasters, participating in roleplaying games, or creating online personas, etc.

In reality, the media is tirelessly creating new possibilities for young people to interact with emotion-dependent cultural content or the production frameworks of the former. A spectrum can be traced from online and television-based voting to creative participation. Moreover, the media model par excellence has become the video game, which alternates quest-based sequences with moments of gratification in a rapid cadence that sustains players' attention by repeatedly preying on their emotions. Similarly, the transition from debate shows to talk shows, the meteoric rise of reality television and the process of hybridization that has led to "infotainment" more broadly, all attest to the success of eliciting audience emotions thanks to laugh tracks, tight screenwriting, and meticulous casting.

Show formats and sequencing are increasingly based around the concept of "attraction" (as is largely the case for reality TV), leading to short clips that build suspense and which can often be watched independently and out of context. Such video editing plays on a wide variety of emotional registers and can be easily recycled on the internet, thus boosting a show's popularity and the trend towards serialization as a whole (Glévarec, 2012). Via the process of emotional attraction, audience members grow to love how a work is personalized and how an artist or author's life is showcased in it. The phenomenon of stardom, even when it occurs in a meteoric or volatile fashion, has become the norm: stardom is how affective communities show recognition for what they love, while the exchange of content by amateurs is seen as the sharing of authentic emotions. This affective functioning leads to the reconfiguration of both public and private spaces, following in the wake of the changes wrought by radio and TV talk shows, just as the register of conversation used on social media networks (which resembles reader commentary) has become the discourse of exteriorized intimacy.

The digital realm is also that of emotional publics, communities of feeling, and experience that span from the 1980s, with fans of TV shows, to online communities at the end of the 2000s. These communities are often divided along stereotypical lines in terms of how emotions are used: for women, sentimentality is encouraged (Pasquier, 1999), while sports and humor are the preferred modes for men (Détrez and Octobre, 2011). These digital audiences form communities based on the experiences they engage in and the opinions they share about these experiences. Their uniqueness lies in the fact that they center on the *individual* experience of consumption (even if the products in question are themselves industrially produced for the masses).

It should be noted that emotions have always driven taste in terms of leisure activities, but today, they are increasingly disconnected from various kinds of knowledge and know-how. For younger generations, taste and understanding do not necessarily go hand-in-hand: hating things that one knows well is much more acceptable than previously, as is stating affinity for things with which one is only passingly familiar (Octobre, 2014a). This shift is an important one: the new information economy, whose decision-making processes are based more on emotions than analysis and comprehension, differs starkly from the knowledge economy, which emphasizes the cognitive dimensions of lived experience.

Recognizing and appreciating quality (which is socially constructed) has thus increasingly been decoupled from matters of taste (which are based on individual emotions). Individual taste is now just as valid as critical judgment when assessing quality. Conversely, however, quality does not imply taste: traditional art forms that are recognized by the entities in charge of legitimizing and transmitting cultural heritage (schools and cultural institutions in particular) are no longer quite as highly prized for their quality. In the elective emotional regime offered by the rise of technoculture, institutional norms — both universal and general — are considered to be independent of taste preferences. In fact, particular and local taste preferences are viewed as the very root of selfhood: in other words, "I like things and I share that I like them, therefore I am". The logic behind Facebook *likes* and social media *friends* is that which constitutes affinity networks and circuits of expression (Lévy, 1997), where each participant intervenes to support the activity of others, and where content becomes a source of cultural attraction for diverse communities. The same can be said of the various audiovisual means by which viewers are asked to engage in value judgment processes with regard to cultural contents (Donnat, 2013).

2.2 *Presentification*

The economy of emotions operates in the present. In the technocultural world, young people consume and share music, videos, images and text in a very rapid fashion, at times even instantaneously, during all kinds of social situations: in transit, at recess, during time that should ostensibly be devoted to school or work, etc. Moreover, the new emotion economy is primarily a visual one: with *YouTube* at the helm, video steaming websites are massively used by young people to listen to music, reflecting the spectacularization of recorded music heralded in the 1980s by the progressive dominance of music clips as a form of musical appropriation and the growing importance placed on the style and visual aesthetics of musical artists (including hair styles, clothing and plastic surgery, as well as album design). This twofold shift has encouraged what Carmen Leccardi (Leccardi, 2012) has termed "presentification," a transformation of young people's relationship to space and time. Digital audio and video content is omnipresent, accompanied by an increased tolerance for blurred distinctions, temporal fluidity and interstitial space, all of which help shape today's youth and its experience of the world. Zigmunt Bauman has spoken of "liquid modernity" (Bauman, 2005), while Anthony Giddens has termed it "hypermodernity" (Giddens, 1984): both of these terms describe a young generation that has been raised on the illusion of endless possibilities. In fact, today's youth is bolstered by the imaginary of reversibility, which is strongly communicated by digital networks, where the demand to be authentically oneself can lead to the precarity of existence (Ehrenberg, 2010).

Emotional functioning thus relies on the network aspect of youth culture, this time in a metaphorical sense: what matters is visibility, and being seen immediately, inciting emotions on the spot by using visual media — whether producing or consuming said media. Visual representations of the world conceal their assumptions behind the apparent neutrality of "factual accounts," while stereotypes circulate freely to enable broader and broader channels of communication (which are perhaps based on a narrower common denominator, which such stereotypes might help to reinforce). This move towards the staging of visibility (Cardon, 2008) is highly linked to the transmedia phenomenon of digital convergence: it is possible to listen to music on Deezer while commenting about it on Facebook, snap a selfie at a concert and send it to a friend via Snapchat. In this manner, young people can share not only what they like and dislike, but also their various skills, which are in turn confirmed by their network of "friends". Since everything is always in flux, the emotion economy means that feelings become ever more volatile and prone to caricature in order to stand out. Whenever catastrophes strike around the world, for instance, buzz-worthy outbursts of malice and spite can be found alongside more sincere forms of emotion.

3   Mobility as Value

A third characteristic of youth culture is its emphasis on mobility as a value, regardless of whether the former is real or virtual, and the corresponding psychological capacity for openness and adaptation. The concept of mobility has become a sort of dogma, what Pierre-André Taguieff has defined as "the latest metamorphosis of progressivism," a phenomenon closely linked to "the economic and financial impact of globalization, […] an ideology that extols individuals who are free of associations with social class, geography or history" (Taguieff, 2006: 34–5). This dogma operates in three different ways.

3.1 The Call to Mobility

Thanks to a plethora of screens, technoculture promotes widespread access to images, texts and music from around the world. As a result, a new representation of globalized culture has been forged, creating with it a new symbolic ecosystem wherein the exotic can become familiar, and the familiar strange. By creating new points of contact, technoculture also makes it possible — perhaps even necessary — for individuals to be exposed to alterity and stray from their normal frames of reference. Living with difference has become a global imperative, as cultural pluralism has slowly morphed into the implicit condition underpinning the universalist ambitions of cultural democracy. At the same time, young generations now have the expectation that the world and all its interdependencies will be virtually unified thanks to cyberspace. These are all consequences of a new social norm, albeit one that is variously appropriated by different groups. Contact with cultural otherness, including in its indigenized forms, is a necessary component of the universalist and democratic imperative of tolerance for diversity, which has increasingly become socially desirable (Harrel, 2010), despite certain negative attitudes towards immigration and diversity that may nonetheless exist among young people (Segatti, Gavalli, Biorcio, and Lescure, 1998; Muxel, 2008).

Synchronous but multi-territorialized media experiences are often underestimated: they are not recognized as having any positive impact. Far from it: various media forms are accused of playing to the lowest common denominator, of dumbing down the population by stealing away valuable brain space. And yet social networks, mass media and widely distributed cultural goods such as music, TV shows and blockbuster movies do in fact have a major impact: in terms of the emotions they provoke, the individual and shared imaginaries they help create and ultimately, in shaping how individuals relate to the world.

This media ideal finds its parallel in how physical mobility has become a norm for young people today. The experiences made possible by travel and mobility are increasingly valued in youth education, especially since the Bologna Process, which helped to ensure Europe-wide compatibility in higher education degrees and introduced new educational credits at the European level, thus encouraging greater student mobility. The Schengen agreements and the creation of the European economic space have likewise promoted mobility for students, who can now study or work abroad more easily. Given that young people are also familiar with digital networks, which they use to communicate or simply to play games (MMORPGs[3] for instance), they are also engaged in all

---

[3] Massively multiplayer online role-playing game.

different forms of virtual mobility. Both physical and mental mobility are thus an inherent part of youth *Bildung* today (Cicchelli, 2012).

3.2 Aesthetico-cultural Cosmopolitanism

Globalization is therefore a cultural phenomenon, one with a highly tangible impact on the reconfiguration of cultural agendas and references as well as youth imaginaries. In all countries that have access to the internet, and even in those where powerful protectionism still reigns, the percentage of cultural products of foreign origin and/or consumed in a foreign language has continuously increased for young people, leading to a hybridization of the modes of reception and the cultural references that we have termed aesthetico-cultural cosmopolitanism (Cicchelli and Octobre, 2018c). More and more, TV series from Brazil and Northern Europe, as well as cinema produced in Bollywood, Nigeria (Nollywood), South Korea and Japan are exported all over the world, emphasizing the proliferation (and ease) of forms of appropriation, already foreshadowed by the popularity of the American series *Dallas* (Liebes and Kratz, 1990). Books also help to create a world of free-flowing and transnational exchanges. As Arjun Appadurai has pointed out, the various technocultural means at our disposal are playing an increasingly important role in defining the contemporary world and how we live in it (Appadurai, 1996).

Today's youth are also the one of the first generations to inhabit a truly multi-polar cultural world: they can access cultural productions from geographical regions that are not merely the result of colonialization or the flexing of soft power after World War Two. The recent fervor for Asian cultural products (manga, cinema, and music alike), television shows from Northern Europe, or African movies and music can all be better understood in this context. Aesthetico-cultural cosmopolitanism stems simultaneously from an average increase in youth levels of education and mobility, and the growing percentage of young people who are the product of immigration. These young people can now turn to television, film and music to find products from their country of origin and thus a kind of (real or imagined) cultural solace, even if this phenomenon is rarer in France than elsewhere thanks to the emphasis placed on assimilation and integration: in general, French youth are more interesting in consuming hybrid or exotic cultural products than in returning to their roots (Cicchelli and Octobre, 2018c). The trend has grown steadily since raï[4] became popular in France at the end of the 1990s (thanks to Khaled and his single *Didi*

---

4 Raï is a form of Algerian folk music that dates back to the 1920s, and which was transmitted to France by migrant flows from its former colony (Algeria). The musical genre has gained political meaning when sung in France insofar as decolonization was a very bloody process: the

in 1992 and Faudel, "the little prince of raï" and his album *Baïda* in 1997). This form of cosmopolitanism benefits from the full power of digital cultural industries, which have become masters at the art of hybridizing cultural references to conquer the global market (McCram, 2012).

This flavor of cosmopolitanism does not escape unscathed from the power struggles at play in global markets, of course: in particular, English-language (and especially American) hegemony. But we cannot, however, conclude that the cultural landscape has been "flattened" (Friedman, 2005), homogenized and largely impoverished. First of all, because globalization contains an inherent and irreducible tension at its heart: while on the one hand, it creates a new social space that individuals can assimilate into through shared practices and representations, at the same time globalization marks a return to the local (even localism at times) and encourages worldwide diversification, including through hybrid and reinvented forms of culture. As Kwame Anthony Appiah has observed, globalization can produce homogeneity, but it is also a threat to homogeneity (Appiah, 2006). In addition, the current state of power relations highlighted by cultural globalization is an impermanent one and is subject to significant local adaptation: a situation evidenced by the huge popularity of Japanese manga and anime in France, especially when compared to other Western or even European countries. Since the 2000s, when manga first appeared on the French market, this art form has radically changed the relationship of young people to the rich Franco-Belgian tradition of the *bande dessinée*, a crucial element of many European childhoods. It has prompted readers to return to the *bandes dessinées* of their youth, but it has also helped to codify a number of aesthetic, cultural, and industrial elements (reading direction, illustration, relationship between text and image; highly emphasized gender stereotypes, Shinto values of heroism; extremely defined marketing segmentation, with manga being divided into *shojo, shonen, seinen,* and *josei* types).[5] The same popularity has accompanied the discovery of anime: the work of Japanese director Hayao Miyazaki have led to newfound appreciation for feature-length animation, which is especially appealing to young people today, whose childhoods were steeped in (large Japanese) animated series. Takashi Murakami, a contemporary Japanese visual artist who has enjoyed international success while challenging the boundaries between high and low art, even claims that he chose to focus on painting because he was unable

---

Algerian War of Independence (1954–1962) was characterized by guerilla warfare, *maquis* fighting and the use of torture.

5 *Shojo*: manga for girls; *shonen*: manga for boys; *seinen:* manga for young adult men; *josei*: manga for young adult women. (Détrez and Vanhée, 2012).

to become an anime creator.[6] The Asian wave has continued with the popularity of K-pop (see the ubiquity of Psy's *Gangnam Style*) and Korean films. Cosmopolitanism has reframed the thirst for the exotic, in particular for the middle-class all over the world, including among French youth (Cicchelli and Octobre, 2018b).

The global success of Asian products is in part due to spreadable and cross-media techniques (Jenkins, Ford and Green, 2013) based on user-generated content that is disseminated through both formal and informal networks. One descriptive example would be the popularity of the Norwegian teen drama *Skam*. The web series presents a number of archetypes that allow teenagers from various countries and backgrounds to identify with them, while still highlighting a number of specific traits about Norwegian society (including its multiculturalism, thanks to a fleshed-out female character who is Muslim), and depicting teenage life without sugarcoating it (the word *skam* means "shame" in Norwegian). The series focuses on a group of young people living in a liberal and yet neo-Protestant environment, depicting their classes at school, their relationship troubles, their debaucherous evenings out, and their often chaotic experiments with sexuality.[7] The show also employed a highly successful strategy with regard to circulation on social networks, which in turn influenced its mode of production. *Skam* was first and foremost conceived of as a program to be watched online, with each episode structured as several minute-long sequences that span a week of narrative time. Characters interact with viewers outside of these episodes, blurring the lines between reality and fiction, while daily clips are posted online in a Snapchat-like model to entice new viewers. This method of production and broadcasting has reached audiences well outside the geographical limits of Norway. French viewers of the series (which is offered in Norwegian with English subtitles) received it so positively that a national version has been proposed, with even more ambitious goals for its presence on social networks. The twofold movement towards global consumption and the localization of globalized products is thus clearly illustrated by the success of shows like *Skam*.

This example also highlights the fact that cosmopolitanism is progressively expanding as the use of foreign languages becomes more standard in cultural consumption. Original language versions of cultural products are increasingly popular (whether in English or another language), especially as French

---

6 Takashi Murakami exhibit, "The 500 Arhats," organized by the Mori Art Museum in Tokyo from 31 October 2015 to 6 March 2016.

7 The purported authenticity of this series has led some to draw parallels with the English show *Skins*.

young people develop a new standard of "good taste" that is strictly aesthetic (tied to ambiance, sonority, etc.) and relies on "overall" understanding rather than expert knowledge. This new standard of good taste has made the younger generations more demanding in terms of reality effects and the appearance of authenticity with regard to both contexts and emotions (Cicchelli and Octobre, 2018a and b). The significant presence of English in youth leisure activities is thus not always a proportional reflection of their linguistic competencies, but is linked to their use of this language in more simplified forms and contexts (Héran, 2013). Far from being devoid of interest, foreign cultural products are now attractive, even to audiences that do not possess significant language skills (Iwabuchi, 2002); moreover, the forms of appropriation that they lead to are not necessarily weak (Lee, 2008).

3.3 *A New Criterion for Ranking*

Cultural mobility — whether real or imagined — has thus become an essential criterion for ranking the new haves and have-nots: the haves being those individuals who have the resources necessary to manipulate different social codes, references, and registers, manifested in a number of concrete skills ethically underpinned by the values of openness and tolerance.[8] This ideology is intimately linked to urbanity, of which it is one of the constitutive dimensions (Orfeuil, 2008, 2012, and 2013), creating both real and virtual "hyperspaces" (Lussault, 2017). These hyperspaces are characterized by the concentration of spatial, material and temporal realities as well as data, content, cultural works, and all different forms of wealth and added value. As they are simultaneously hyperspatial and hyperscalar, these hyperspaces are as dense and intense as the experiences they contain.

Global cities which concentrate countless different cultural flows in one location are examples of these hyperspaces, endowed with the capacity to transform mere exposure to globalization and diversity into veritable openness to alterity. Given their size, social and racial diversity and their high level of connection, global cities are sites of mobility between diverse cultural spaces acting as "canopies" (Anderson, 2011), where, for a limited time and under certain conditions, the rules of social, cultural and/or spatial segregation can be suspended and contact (both real and virtual) can be made between different groups. But nothing guarantees that this socialization to otherness will be successful — that remains a matter of individual responsibility.

---

8   The link between these two concepts is, in general, more presumed than manifest.

This double emphasis placed on mobility has led to the transformation of the relationship between the economic and cultural spheres for younger generations: the new elites amass greater and greater economic and cultural capital, and the latter has significantly changed in nature (Lindell and Danielsson, 2017). Cultural capital is now increasingly international, which means that it also depends less on national systems and traditional forms of education and culture. As a result, it has also become more economically divisive, as it is strongly tied to family legacy (i.e. economic, social, and cultural capital) and the ability to travel, including the opportunity to engage in international education and training as needed to acquire and maintain language skills and familiarity with different social contexts.

Interestingly enough, the value attributed to chosen mobility often comes at the expense of tolerance towards forced mobility — e.g., migrants fleeing war or collapsing economies — which leads to a paradox of physical mobility that is echoed in virtual mobility: mobility is only viewed as an asset if an individual is in control of it. In this perspective, the absence of mobility fuels the imaginaries of identitarian closure, with sedentary individuals appearing to be reactionary, and nativeness (Retière, 2003) — that is, a particular attachment to one's country, region, city or neighborhood — can look like a fear-based reaction to multicultural society. Purely national or local forms of excellence are no longer at the top of this hierarchy of values; in fact, the top positions are created by combining forms of mobility and local presence. Ultimately, the so-called "French touch" only exists because it sought to conquer the *global* market of techno music.

Only certain kinds of mobility can therefore be converted into capital, in particular when the former is combined with local roots and the accumulation of autochthonous resources, as well as reflexivity regarding cultural "distance" and authenticity (in contrast to mass tourism). However, the depreciation of national forms of capital (which are seen as corny, conservative, or kitsch) does not systematically occur. For example, the mobility of young refugees or people in exile devalues their economic, social and cultural capital, in particular because their mobility is accompanied by a transition towards anonymity, which ill accords with successful reentry into social and cultural networks. On the other hand, the young international elite are often keen to highlight their geographical "origins" (Wagner, 2010). This privileged relationship to nativeness is based on the promotion of authenticity and loyalty to one's roots, heritage, and values, in turn multiplying the effects of acquiring familiarity with international codes. The accumulation of such codes, as well as language skills and an understanding of cross-cultural differences, becomes an advantage when such experience acts as a counterpart to localized knowledge; it can thus protect against the risk of social and cultural rootlessness and also allow for an educated and reflexive reinvestment in mobility resources that may depend on national context (Cicchelli, Octobre, Riegel, Katz-Gerro, and Handy, 2018).

It is notable that this phenomenon encourages the development of a labile, affinity-based cultural mythos that touts freedom while calling into question traditional social frameworks (the nation-State and social class, in particular); this mythos likewise advocates for a new kind of youth cultural citizenship that abolishes "ancient" borders. A note here, however: the impact of social, ethnic or national stratification on individual taste repertoires and on technocultural participation — both in terms of access and modalities of engagement — remains highly pronounced, even if this impact has been transformed by mass education and the emergence of gender- and race-based cleavages (or more likely, the increased visibility of the latter), in particular because ease and fluency with language (both written and spoken) are still a crucial prerequisite for expressing curiosity about foreign cultural products. This prerequisite, once acquired, allows individuals to surmount the distance created by translation (in either written or dubbing form) with regard to the act of appropriation (Cicchelli and Octobre, 2018c) and promotes the subsequent shift towards creation and self-expression.

The space created by these new and highly valued forms of mobility ultimately becomes homogenous, either because of economics (the circulation of elite youth), or due to a (cosmopolitan) cultural attitude that reconfigures the repercussions of downward mobility and uprooting by contextualizing them within the broader scope of international socialization, which helps to produce selective, practical and yet ethical forms of behavior that are based on the strength of weak ties. A number of studies have demonstrated the effectiveness of increasing networks, in the realm of academic success (Di Maggio, 1982), the labor market (Granovetter, 1983), and career trajectories (Lin, 2000) alike.

This is also a space that requires numerous and diverse forms of capital: the ability to travel (whether physically, mentally or symbolically), to encounter diversity and the complexity of different cultures, and to understand and even master different codes (especially given the fact that with the advent of mass-scale mobility, it has become harder and hard to discover contents that are radically foreign, while some groups that are geographically close may be considered socially and culturally exotic), with a view to developing one's "cosmopolitan sensibility" (Bronner, 2004). Consequently, this is a space of variable geometry within which openness to diversity does not occur in a uniform fashion, but depends on specific attitudes concerning socialization. Bethany Bryson (Bryson, 1996) has thus shown how the music genres that are rejected by the most "tolerant" of music listeners (i.e., country, rap, folk, heavy metal and gospel) are systematically those preferred by the least educated classes. This space therefore maintains strong social hierarchies.

The value attributed to mobility, both real and virtual, engenders what Pierre Veltz (Veltz, 2005) has called a "generalized unbundling": namely, a proliferation of paths and trajectories that link together production, mediation (including intermediation) and reception or consumption, in which those who possess data and provide recommendations play a key role. The mobility imperative creates tension between, on the one hand, the requirement of ubiquity (bolstered by information technologies) and, on the other, the demand for co-presence (which information technologies likewise fulfill thanks to networks and virtual communities).

4   Additive Comprehension

The mobility imperative has gradually been linked to a transformation in modes of learning and comprehension, which now unfold through the addition of scattered elements rather than by following a pre-established, unidimensional, and linear path. This has led to a new form of comprehension (in the literal sense of the word: *to bring with oneself*) of the world around us.

4.1   *Putting Together the Collaborative Transmedia Puzzle*

Additive comprehension is characteristic of youth culture and is closely linked to the hegemony of visual media (which even dictates how individuals engage with text), as well as the emphasis placed on the social capital granted by information and communication technologies. It is necessary to jump from one media platform to another to understand the narrative world created and operated by the addition of images and scraps of information, a world that can be configured and reconfigured like a moving transmedia jigsaw puzzle — a reality that is greedily exploited by marketing strategies. While this was already the case for, say, cartoons in the 1970s (the animated series *Candy*,[9] for instance, produced stickers and paper goods associated with its intellectual property), this phenomenon became especially pronounced with the growing cross-media marketing of major franchises like *The Lord of the Rings* and *The*

---

[9] *Candy* was originally a manga created by Yumiko Igarasi and Kyoko Mizuki, published between 1975 and 1979 over nine volumes. But this intellectual property became well known in France after it was adapted into an animated series (115 episodes, each 26 minutes long) broadcast starting in 1978 on *Antenne 2* as part of children's programming (*Récré A2*); it was subsequently rebroadcast many times.

Matrix. The principle of additive comprehension also governs access to knowledge through search engines and hyperlinks. More broadly speaking, these frameworks, used to understand and appropriate cultural contents, can be transposed from one form of media to another: young people now read novels based on the narrative formats of the television shows and movies that they prefer. This is doubtless a reason why youth taste in literature has changed so much, shifting to a marked preference for post-apocalyptic and dystopian stories, in large part following the success of such genres on the small screen.

The systems involved in transmedia circulation also teach young people how to play with information and content and, as a result, to value cultural products that are created by mixing and combining different elements. These changes are layered on top of those brought about by the previous generation, which witnessed the massive cultural shift to screen culture and its subsequent reconfiguration of the cultural landscape around the all-powerful image, its decoding and its (secondary) transposition into words. The internet generation has reintroduced textuality (from the perspective of both reading and writing) into a landscape that had become primarily audiovisual. How individuals engage with the written word still remains largely visual and global, however: textuality is a branching structure that must be deciphered by adding and subtracting different language skills and registers. One metaphor for today's youth might be, as Michel Serres (Serres, 2012) suggests, the contemporary fairytale *Petite Poucette*.[10] The eponymous Petite Poucette holds the world in the palm of her hand, thanks to a digital device that is the new equivalent of an individual (and perhaps even intimate) cultural library. More than ever, it is advantageous to have, as Michel de Montaigne bemoaned centuries ago, "a head that is well-made rather than well-filled". Amidst the constant flux of cultural content swirling around her from many different networks, Petite Poucette is forced to travel a winding path, making difficult and sometimes contradictory choices and constructing cultural trajectories of experience that are diverse and sometimes in conflict with each other.

Additive comprehension also works thanks to participation, where individuals can, in accordance with their skills, contribute to developing knowledge, even when such collaboration is not required of everyone. David Buckingham and Julian Sefton-Green have argued that *Pokémon* not just something that can be watched, or read, or consumed — it is also (and perhaps even primarily) a physical and mental engagement that can take

---

10 Petite Poucette is a character roughly equivalent to Thumbelina in English-language fairytales. It is also notable that Michel Serres chose a girl's character for his metaphor, since statistically in France, girls tend to be bigger readers than boys.

place individually or collectively in a wide variety of spaces, ranging from the classroom and the playground to the home (Buckingham and Sefton-Green, 2004a and b). Consequently, what matters here is not really how much knowledge is retained, but rather the process by which the latter is acquired, a process composed of tests and linkages (which are often voluntary, tactical, and fleeting). In order for young people to participate, they must believe that what they are contributing enriches both the primary content and the experience of others.

4.2   *The Reputation Filter*

In such an additive regime, the abundance of information is simultaneously a resource and an obstacle; young people struggle to orient themselves and to separate the wheat from the chaff. The veritable explosion of cultural offerings as well as networks, where everyone can distribute their own information or creative works and acquire their own admirers and "followers" has created such a glut of content that making an "informed" choice has become a difficult if crucial requirement. As a result, indices and rankings have become more popular than ever. Although different ranking systems operate according to different criteria, they all help to erect reputation as a key element of critical judgment. In and of itself, reputation is a source of information, one which compensates for a lack of direct experience; those in charging of creating reputations play a major role in the youth cultural landscape.

What is the value of a reputation? Transactional theory suggests that reputation first helps to reduce uncertainty when faced with numerous choices: when making an online purchase, for instance, we are reassured by signs of credibility, such as buyer reviews and user comments. The condensed experiences of others mean that we do not have to personally try out all possible products; we are pointed towards the best products for us thanks to algorithms which scour our past purchases to identify relevant criteria (Cardon, 2015). This first, narrow definition is primarily economic in nature. But other spheres are affected by matters of reputation, among them the need for recognition and the quest for social capital. Reputations are not forged solely by individuals, but also by their environment (friends, fan communities, information distributors). In fact, this principle governs citation in amateur circles, where those who are mentioned the most often are by default the most well-known. Being seen is another aspect of reputation: this is what we generally call celebrity (Heinich, 2012). In the reputation game, people can be noticed thanks to their talents, but also due to their *lack* of talent (at times self-professed): Rémy Gaillard, a famous French web comedian that is very popular amongst young people, has thus proclaimed that "c'est en faisant n'importe quoi qu'on devient n'importe qui".[11][12]

When building reputations and getting recommendations, friends always play an important role: young people consult their friends to find out which "good" movies to go see, which "good" concerts to attend, and which "good" books to read. But digital networks also massively participate in reputation-building and recommendation-giving: young people consult specialized websites to read reviews of movies, exhibits, and activities and make an informed choice. The internet has thus become a vast reputation-making machine, where users use a repository of quantitative and qualitative tools to measure the impact of information on reputations and how, when used in lieu of critical judgment, reputation can impact choice (Beuscart and Crepel, 2014). The lexicon of reputation echoes that of capitalism: reputation management, astroturfing,[13] personal branding, etc.[14] Building one's reputation and monitoring it has become one of the key features of the Web: from mere rumors to critical rankings, the erection of online reputations affects any kind of shared judgment, whether formal or not, based on experience or hearsay. This separation of reputation from direct experience has produced a culture of "buzz," where media noise can itself become a kind of information. Knowing what everyone is talking about has become an important skill. However, the impact of media buzz on behavior is not always so powerful, as evidenced by a recent study on

---

11   *Translator's note:* this statement is particularly interesting in French, given that it can have two somewhat contradictory meanings. "N'importe quoi" is an indefinite (relative) pronoun that can be translated as "whatever" or "anything" in English, depending on the context. By extension, it also has a secondary meaning in French of "nonsense" — as in, "any old thing that isn't particular good or valuable; whatever". Much like in English when a frustrated individual responds "whatever!" to their interlocutor, the French "n'importe quoi" can be used to indicate that the previous statement or action is, in fact, rubbish. Similarly, "n'importe qui" can be an indefinite pronoun meaning "anyone", but it can also connote a certain degree of randomness; if "n'importe qui" can do something, just about anybody can (implying a pejorative assessment of the task's difficulty). When taken in its negative form "pas n'importe qui" (literally, "not anyone"), however, the expression can be flipped to stress that this is in fact a person of importance and selection: it's not *just* anyone, but a specific person. Taken as a whole, then, the statement "c'est en faisant n'importe quoi qu'on devient n'importe qui" can mean 1) that it is only by accomplishing things that you can become someone of note; but also 2) that (in today's age), if you do any odd thing, you can become famous.

12   This is moreover the title of his website: http://www.nimportequi.com/fr/.

13   The practice of falsifying positive reviews to improve a company, person or product's score on the internet.

14   The development of a personal brand, including by creating a visual (a gimmick, a gesture, a piece of clothing) or audio (music, accent, voice) signature.

recommendations in the film world: in fact, our close friends and family (i.e., people we know and trust) are still our most reliable (and frequent) sources of recommendations (Pasquier, Beaudoin, and Legon, 2014).

The logic behind reputation presents a certain number of inherent difficulties for culture. First of all, it is reductive: it is based on the predominance of a single strong element (an image, phrase, story, character trait, or physical attribute) to the exclusion of others. There is no room for contradictions: the strength of criticism comes from its bias, and this strength is also consequently a weakness, since the reductionism that it presupposes can lead to a lack of accuracy or reliability, at times even to a certain futility. To explain the role played by reputation-based variables, some scholars have targeted the fragility of interpersonal communications in a world of over-communication, while others have, on the contrary, argued that if gossip is on the rise, this is precisely because young people are increasingly searching for relationships, which are ultimately valued more than the information that serves to prop up such interpersonal exchanges (Dunbar, 1997; Gambetta, 1994; Origgi, 2013).

Secondly, reputation acts as a substitute for direct experience, with the discrepancy between endorsement and the quality of lived (or imagined) experience being potentially vast. In the regime of additive comprehension, two attributes become increasingly significant: expertise, which bases its judgment on competence and direct experience with contents (and is generally linked to institutions), and reputation, which is cultivated by media coverage and indirect experience (and is generally associated with youth culture more broadly). In this double game, cultural middlemen (parents, webmasters, socio-cultural ambassadors, librarians, teachers, curators, etc.) play a central role but their (growing) number and their (sometimes divergent) reasons for acting mean that it can be hard to decipher their words of advice and recommendation. Moreover, the power of youth judgment, amplified many-fold by digital networks, has led to a certain contagion of reputational properties, much like other modalities of knowledge-building, including expertise: this encourages niche specialization rather than the development of a broad base of generalized knowledge. The matter of how to interpret a shared world thus becomes crucial.

Finally, the mechanisms that help to build reputations are based on the blurring of the division between public and private: it is necessary to reveal personal things (leisure activities, taste preferences, friendships, etc.) to build one's reputation, and reputations are also bolstered (or tarnished) by what is said about an individual. While this exposure to the public can help to build one's self-esteem, it also creates the risk of oversimplification, conformism, and repetition. The rabid quest for "likes" is also a quest for visibility rather than real exchanges, even if exchanges are the pillars of this visibility: it thus runs the risk of self-caricature (emphasizing certain traits to attract attention, shock, or produce laughter) and even, for some young people whose socialization has not sufficiently protected them, exhibitionist excesses.

In order to understand the extent of the changes wrought to reputation-based logic, let us look at a concrete example. François Jost (2018) reminds us that in 2015, a "reputation application" called Peeple was designed, where everyone could provide recommendations and be endorsed by their acquaintances, in the personal, professional and even romantic spheres, with each individual graded according to a 5-star scale, like in Uber. This application was ultimately forced to change, following an outcry by its own users, and now only provides recommendations, much like LinkedIn or Facebook. This example highlights how, at the turn of the 2000s, feelings begin to be expressed less by critical arguments than by numbers, the result of what was initially often a binary equation (yes/no, for example in TV singing contests) which only later became more nuanced (see, for instance, ratings on TripAdvisor or Uber). This phenomenon also illustrates the close association between social and ethical issues and the inflation of reputation-based variables in our daily existence.

Ultimately, these observations all support the argument put forth by Guy Debord in *The Society of Spectacle* (1967): the lived experience has been transformed into representation, thus marking the victory of the visible; the spectacle is no longer just a collection of images but a social relation among people, who are reduced to their mere images, thus completing the philosophical endeavor to interpret all human activity in terms of "seeing".

• •
•

While the rise of technoculture did not invent the values of expressiveness, emotions and mobility, it has granted them a hitherto unprecedented importance. In this regard, the internet is not a mirror of our reality, but a version of reality that is amplified in every way. We do not present ourselves "as we are" online, but rather as we wish we were, depending on the circumstances — at times completely disregarding continuity and consistency (elements which are otherwise required in face-to-face interactions), even if online memories can sometimes resurface with a vengeance. This is precisely why psychoanalyst Serge Tisseron (Tisseron, 2016) suggests that we should consider the internet as a third reality (the first being the physical world and the second being the imaginary landscape of our dreams). The internet borrows from the physical and the imaginary worlds and combines them in a variety of different ways. Our desires are not truly our own — they are also a reflection of desires that are shaped in conjunction with others, which thus introduces a supplementary level of complexity in identity formation, lest we become blank spaces governed by the desires of others despite our best efforts.

The technocultural transition (from the technological revolution ushered in by the advent of the digital realm and the increasingly key role played by cultural consumption in the formation of youth identities) has thus cultivated a system of values that is based — in shockingly new way — not on the world of work or education, but on the production of cultural, digital, and media-based industries.

CHAPTER 4

How Technoculture Shapes Youth Norms

Every value system comes with a set of norms, which reflect an ideal that is sometimes quite different from actual behaviors. Nonetheless, such norms shape representation, governing individual strategies, and behavioral choices among young people to such an extent that they merit further investigation. Technocultural norms play an important role in the development of youth behavior, in part by establishing expectations — expectations that are sometimes deceptive, given that in reality, practices cannot escape the constraints imposed by frameworks of socialization, including the socio-technical mechanisms at the heart of technoculture.

1   Autonomy, an Ambiguous Standard

The first of these norms is that of cultural autonomy. Simply put, autonomy is the ability to act independently and in accordance with one's own rules and decisions. Autonomy is synonymous with freedom, characterized by the ability to choose one's direction without allowing oneself to be dominated by certain natural or collective "impulses," nor be governed by an external authority. Autonomy can sometimes be taught, via the gradual incorporation of social rules which in turn allows individuals to adopt a certain distance with regard to those same rules without fear of social alienation. But autonomy can also emerge in counterpoint to numerous systems of institutional support that accompany and assist young people in their trajectories: in this context, autonomy represents an individual's capacity for social insertion thanks to the resources they possess, in contrast to a situation of dependency on third parties and public assistance.

1.1   *Cultural Consumption: The First Steps towards Autonomy*
Cultural autonomy is a message strongly transmitted by youth culture today, which is familiar with different spaces and their respective behavioral norms. Olivier Galland explains that cultural autonomy "leads individuals to want to choose their references, their lifestyles, their modalities of participation and engagement and thus to display great reticence when faced with abstract and durable forms of categorization. Young people refused to be pigeonholed in the name of the historical permanence of values and institutions that remain

foreign to them" (Galland and Roudet, 2005: 123). Autonomy and independence are thus two distinct but intertwined driving forces for young people. Consequently, the process of empowerment is not the automatic result of increased offerings in leisure activities as well as more time to devote to them: it is the concerted implementation of reflexivity and individualization. The autonomy of young people is thus both an objective and a subjective process (Cicchelli, 2013).

Autonomy requires experience, self-responsibility (the main model of which remains parenthood, with its non-reciprocity and foregrounding of others' needs) and authenticity (that is, coinciding with oneself) (Taylor, 1989). In this perspective, the difference between an adult and a child is one of degree, not of kind; in fact, neither is truly ever done growing up (Lapalissade, 1963), given that autonomy is developed over the course of a lengthy process rather than obtained following a one-time rite of passage. We can therefore look at different life stages within the context of individual narrative identities (Ricœur, 1980), wherein the cultural dimension (practices, taste preferences) becomes increasingly important. Olivier Galland (Galland, 2001: 630) reminds us that "young people today draw on a vast adolescent culture that depicts youth itself as a value, as well as its main cultural references". Childhood and youth consequently take on a variety of different forms (Bonnet, Rollet, and de Suremain, 2012), especially given that the precise segments envisioned by different cultural industries do not necessarily overlap (Delalande, 2014). In France, for example, books and magazines are generally marketed to small, two-year age brackets, while museums and other venues usually differentiate ticket prices for those under 18, and age ratings vary wildly from movie to movie; similarly, the age limits required on many social media platforms are rarely respected in reality.

Cultural leisure activities are one of the main areas where individuals make their first forays into autonomy: choosing what music to listen to, what movies and TV shows to watch, determining and then expressing one's likes and dislikes to others, organizing one's free time. These leisure activities are where individuals can first begin to experiment with self-creation and personal trajectories by declaring what they love and what they hate — since dislikes are as important as likes when aligning oneself with a shared interest group, as Bethany Bryson has illustrated (Bryson, 1996) — and by highlighting their skills as consumers or fans. The development of autonomy can have its own internal constraints, however: being alone but with others, being unique and yet similar, taking advantage of gaps, and mediating between different social scenes. The time devoted to self-empowerment, which varies objectively from one young person to the next, is nonetheless subjectively unified around a single demand: the freedom to choose one's leisure activities.

How then should we think about technoculture? The dominant paradigm of youth in our society is tied to the democratic "passion for equality": it translates to greater equality in conditions between children and adults (de Singly, 2004), thanks to the adoption of new rights (i.e., the rights of the child).[1] But this consensus is merely apparent and does not in fact address the place of young people and their ties — cultural, in particular — to other generations. Though they may be equal in dignity to adults, young people are different in maturity and require the protection of adults, given that they have not fully entered into the triple dimension of experience, responsibility and authenticity; the cultural sphere and digital media are precisely one of the areas where young people can develop these traits. Following Olivier Galland (Galland, 1999), we suggest that youth should be seen as the age where experimentation precedes true experience.

Information and communication technologies shine a light on the question of age. The coinage of the term "serious game," for instance, illustrates how different ages in life have been reconfigured. Serious games, which have become popular amongst young adults since 2002, have invaded sectors as varied as healthcare (healthcare games), the environment (green games), commerce (advergames), education and professional development (learning games), activism (causeplay or antiwar games), and culture (especially in the realm of cultural mediation). Gaming is everywhere: it represents a global market on the rise (+47% between 2010 and 2015, or almost 10 billion euros in 2015). By encouraging players to solve problems with a view to provoking behavioral, as well as socio-cognitive and socio-affective changes (changes in attitude or metacognition, for example), serious games are a prime example of using the principle of play (which has traditionally been limited to use with children and youth) in order to stimulate the three main functions of play in adults. These three main functions are: learning (which can be compounded by the motivation and engagement of players, even if they are unaware of being engaged in a learning activity); immersion (play operates outside the bounds of regular time and allows individuals to be transported elsewhere, albeit temporarily);

---

[1] On 20 November 1989, the United Nations ratified the International Convention on the Rights of the Child, which marked the culmination of a long process seeking to emancipate children (led in many developing nations by children themselves) and consequently the recognition of the child as a citizen on par with all adults. The Convention declared that children had the right to be protected but also to be themselves, express their own opinions, and determine the course of their own lives (Hanson and Nieuwensberg, 2013).

and transfer (what individuals learn inside a game can be used outside of it, with regard to ethics, social and behavioral mores, strategy, mathematics or even literature). The adjective "serious" merely designates that a game's target demographic is adults. But the rise of serious games has spread game culture ever further, including the concept of learning through play, and has ultimately helped to redefine the different stages of life and their associated characteristics. As a result, culture and media now do what the labor market and educational system cannot: define age brackets and organize generational succession.

1.2 *Private and Public Autonomy*

The standard of autonomy requires a new relationship between public and private space, with the latter representing the realm where individuals can experiment with the autonomy that is required in the former, ranging from the possession of one's first media devices to the development of personal taste preferences and cultural repertoires (Octobre, Détrez, Mercklé, and Berthomier, 2010). The increased importance of autonomy also stems from a societal shift away from independence and the systems of responsibility associated with it (e.g., professional, spousal, and parental responsibilities). The transition from the principle of responsibility to the principle of autonomy is moreover linked to a demographic swing that has challenged existing intergenerational linkages, from both a more institutional perspective (how to organize intergenerational financial solidarity via pension reform), to a largely symbolic one: how does each generation position itself with regard to generational order? How can younger generations gain access to the wealth of attributes granted by (cultural) citizenship? And more broadly speaking, what role does cultural citizenship play compared to all the other forms of citizenship?

Autonomy is therefore a claim that can be staked by both individuals — which explains why it goes hand-in-hand with demands for authenticity, originality and freedom of expression — and by society at large. It is the product of a representation of youth but simultaneously produces a representation of youth. This representational process relies on the products of cultural industries adapted to a youth market. Some of the values frequently associated with youth, and depicted in all forms of media from advertisements to blog posts and blockbuster films, include being oneself (authenticity and uniqueness), transcending established frameworks (freedom, counterculture, progressive ideas, the ability to operate outside of time constraints), and hedonism (instant versus delayed gratification).

Generally speaking, in this model of autonomy, cultural consumption is no longer just a way to escape the alienation of labor, but in fact a way to establish one's identity (to perform selfhood in a quasi-artistic manner); it offers the youth minority a space for self-ownership and visibility. This push towards identity-building remains consistent with the social pressures and codes specific to each sub-group, as evidenced by the rampant pressure to conform observed by many sociologists among adolescent (Pasquier, 2005).

This evolution is highly visible in the behavior of young people on the internet, especially since the latter has given rise to a twofold change: everyone in society can now take a turn speaking, while many private conversations can now take place in the public sphere (as can be seen on Twitter, for instance). These two transformations are the result of ever-more entrenched contemporary individualism: the staging of one's identity, assets, skills, traits, hopes and dreams is accompanied by a quest for increased visibility to validate one's attempts at uniqueness. The invention of the telephone and the rise of the press appear to have encouraged the expansion of personal and trade networks as well the creation of imagined publics albeit in a context of strict separation between public and private space, including dichotomies such as conversation/information, individuals/citizens, public/private, community/society, etc. With the internet, this separation has largely been erased: the division between the public and private has been reformulated and individuals now increasingly mix personal life and public engagement and perform their everyday lives on a public stage.

In older forms of media, the information published was public in nature and the space in which it was presented was likewise public, given that everything had to be pre-selected by professionals adhering to ethical and/or professional standards according to which the ability to legitimately speak in the public space was highly codified (this even applies to reality TV, which is in fact largely scripted). With the rise of the internet, what is visible has become dissociated from what is public: the two no longer go hand-in-hand, for a couple of different reasons. Filtering is secondary to publishing: even if in reality not all posts are equally visible (most internet publications belong to a vast grey area, as discussed by Cardon, 2010b), legally speaking they all are. On the web, young people thus expose their private lives — what Serge Tisseron calls "extimacy" (Tisseron, 2003) — by organizing their self-presentation, pushing the exposition of intimacy heralded by the arrival of television to its logical endpoint (Mehl, 1996). The internet additionally ascribes a whole new geography to the knowledge economy, offering citizens new sources of "truth" alongside the emergence of counter-powers. We thus end up in a public space that is created "from the bottom up," founded on the supposed equality of all individuals, and which claims to evaluate the latter solely on the basis of their productions, rather than their inherent traits, in turn bolstering the imperative of individual responsibility.

1.3   The Framework of Cultural Autonomy and Its Inner Tensions

Being autonomous is not at odds with the existence of frameworks: in fact, autonomy develops in large part *thanks* to frameworks which manage everyday life (family, school) and allow young people the freedom to operate and express themselves without needing to worry about a certain number of extraneous contingencies (Descombes, 2004). In addition, autonomy is not the absence of abiding by rules, nor is it exempt from group conformity. Rules exist and are generally elaborated by young people amongst themselves; as a result, tensions emerge around the search for authenticity and individuality (or uniqueness), ideals which have become new collective norms. In particular, we can think about the relationship to time, linearity and the cumulative nature of knowledge; about the reversibility of choices, the different forms of identity-building based around labile likes and dislikes; about the growing role played by aesthetico-cultural capital with regard to the construction of social capital.

Technocultural autonomy also poses a challenge to the traditional modes of cultural transmission. For example, studies show that an appreciation for reading is generally handed down from one generation to the next. Studies show that children who grow up around books, see their parents read, have book read to them by their parents and discuss their readings (usually with their mother) ultimately become readers themselves (Wollscheid, 2014). Parents can therefore transmit implicit norms through demonstration and imitation (Bandura, 1986), but they can also model these norms through iteration (Mullan, 2010). This transmission applies to both taste preferences and the value attributed to reading culture; the effects of this transmission can span early childhood to adulthood (Nagel, 2010). Other studies have shown that what applies to reading and high-brow activities (theater and museum attendance, for instance) also applies to the consumption of digital media (Notten and Kraaykamp, 2009). The transmission involved here is not, in general, end-to-end — if only because technological shifts take place — but applies to the interest evinced in various forms of cultural engagement and participation which may jump across different modalities, devices and platforms (Octobre and Jauneau, 2008). At the same time, inverse transmission occurs from children up towards their parents, especially in technological areas where younger people are more well-versed, without nonetheless excluding more traditional spheres: the immense success of the *Harry Potter* series can be explained by the fact that many adults also read the (ostensibly young adult) books and watched the movies (the same was true for the *Twilight* franchise).

In each of these situations of transmission, adults and children define their respective positions along an age continuum, depending on their rights, responsibilities, and legitimacy as a source of cultural recommendations. This development has altered intergenerational relationships. Today's parents, often on the sidelines of their children's biographical events though the latter rarely make a complete break from older modes of consumption, can nevertheless still be cultural actors (even at an advanced age), in particular when their children become interested in older elements of youth culture. The rapid induction of 60s pop music into the realm of legitimate cultural heritage (The Beatles, The Rolling Stones), followed by a number of rock and disco stars from the 1970s and 1980s is part of this process of cultural transmission — as is, for example, the continued affection expressed for the main character of the *Mario Brothers* franchise, originally created in the 1980s.

Autonomy is also linked to the culturalization of the occupations of childhood and youth, such as when, for example, parental rules are negotiated against the right to consume certain products or to use certain gadgets — but also when the first income young people acquire through part-time jobs is used to finance their hobbies and leisure activities. It is also in the realm of cultural leisure activities that we can observe the shift from a certain logic of (frustrated) independence to a logic of (supported) autonomy. The invention of the term "pre-teen" attests to this, given that it describes a category of children who are both precocious (in terms of their taste preferences) and lagging behind (because they cannot enjoy the rights and responsibilities of teenagers). As early as 11 or 12, usually when they enter French middle school, some pre-teens can enjoy a great degree of autonomy with regard to their movement and tastes. This is a time when parents lose some amount of control over their schedules, and pre-teens see an increase in free time without supervision, the ability to move around urban and semi-urban spaces, and a more unfettered use of digital social networks. The wealth of cultural and digital devices that pre-teens can access (and which quickly replace the toys and playgrounds of childhood) is a strong indicator of the autonomy that they develop as cultural consumers, ranging from computers and tablets to game consoles and smartphones. The technocultural field offers a wide variety of spaces in which young people can develop, experiment with and validate their (potentially transferable) skills and knowledge; these skills are often associated with age markers and rites of passage.

Being autonomous is not exempt from a certain number of inherent tensions or paradoxes, however. For instance, the internet was originally developed in line with a libertarian ideology, which fed into a certain social critique of capitalism (including artistic capitalism, see Boltanski and Chiapello, 1999).

The early internet sought to emancipate individuals by letting them be more creative and "authentic" — goals which have become the basis for the new cognitive capitalism of which Google and Facebook are emblematic (Moulier-Boutang, 2007).[2] While the ideology of the internet has remained libertarian, centered around individualism, autonomy, and the rejection of collective constraints and the imposition of structures from above, this has engendered a certain number of tensions between a strong vision of autonomy — which argues for the development and intensive training of children and young people — and a vision that is more focused on protecting children and young people from any kind of infringement upon their freedom.

The tensions inherent to autonomy are also due to the proliferation of competing modes of transmission: like other forms of transmission,[3] cultural transmission tends to function more through implicit permeation[4] than through explicit interactions or attempts at inculcation (Muxel, 1984; Percheron, 2001, Berthomier and Octobre, 2019b). Generally, surreptitious persuasion is more successful than pedagogy (de Singly, 1995). Different registers comingle in various states of interdependency — be they forms of incentive, support or co-consumption — where socialization actors act as role models (both positive and negative) and resources. Moreover, these cultural transmissions operate on the symbolic level of the representation of culture, as well as on the more tangible level of practices and objects: in reality, the two registers are largely dissimilar and operate independently. Ultimately, these cultural transmissions are interwoven across the many different and sometimes competing spaces where autonomy is possible, with the cultural choices of children often being informed by multiple areas of socialization: family, as we have already mentioned, but also peer groups,[5] school (Coulangeon, 2003 and 2007; Schön, 1993),[6] and the diverse forms of

---

2　Cognitive capitalism refers to a form of capitalism wherein the production of knowledge plays the key role (as opposed to Fordism, where mass and material production is the most important element, through the specialization of tasks, material investments and the quest for economies of scale).

3　For example, political transmissions, as analyzed by Annick Percheron (Percheron, 1991).

4　This is what Bernard Lahire (Lahire, 2000) calls "silent socialization" and what social learning theory refers to as "the observation process" (Bandura, 1980): transmission occurs through the observation and imitation of the behaviors, attitudes and values of others.

5　See, for example "Gender, networks and cultural capital". *Poetics* No. 32: 2004.

6　The linkages between school and cultural consumption/practices can be explained in different ways, depending on whether one looks towards educational sociologists (who examine the impact of extracurricular cultural activities on academic performance) or cultural sociologists (who highlight the repercussions of education levels on access to certain activities and modalities of consumption).

media[7] themselves (Berthomier and Octobre, 2019a). The interdependent roles of the child, the student and the cultural consumer have thus become increasingly complex in today's world.

As a result, we can trace the gradual development of autonomy using a number of cultural markers, which operate as rites of passage into adulthood (Le Breton, 2005): acquiring one's first smartphone, creating one's first playlist on Deezer,[8] etc. Increasing one's autonomy means reshuffling one's cultural agenda as well as one's tastes, with the goal of having the right "symbolic size," in terms of both attraction and rejection. The seemingly simple concept of "taste" in reality combines a variety of levels of influence and interest, where it is necessary to "be oneself" under the scrutinizing gaze — and pressure — of others. Such rites, divided in categories by age, gender and social class, ultimately confer various cultural forms of "miniscule knowledge" to young people (Pasquier, 2002). Knowing how to use a tablet, how to surf the web and find information about one's favorite celebrity, knowing how to create and manage content online are all skills that are highly segmented by age and which can (and must) be recognized and validated by one's young peers rather than by adults.

2 Norms of Engagement, Relation and Selection

Autonomy is developed at the crossroads between three intricately linked principles: the elective principle, the relational principle, and the principle of engagement. These three principles operate objectively: it is not a question of being emancipated from any and all social and institutional constraints, but rather of moving from contexts that are pre-determined (family, school, etc.) to contexts that are (supposedly) freely chosen (in particular around the notion of taste or preference). These three traits, characteristic of autonomy in general, are particularly key with regard to how technoculture operates, given that it is based on choice, affiliation and participation.

2.1 *The Importance of Choice*
Autonomy implies the importance of individual choice. The modern and almost hyperbolic emphasis placed on choice is not just a marketing strategy, linked to customized targeting in internet advertisements. It is also a key trait

---

7 On this subject, there are fewer studies, most of which look at the alienating effects of mass consumption.
8 A French online music streaming service.

of contemporary individualism, wherein individuals are tasked with their own (re)invention.

One's relationship to autonomy is intimately linked to one's educational framework: the latter tends to be more flexible and open to negotiation at the higher end of the educational spectrum, and more authoritarian in nature at the lower end. For the past twenty years, however, the social relationship to autonomy has generally been built upon a shared ideology of the "family-as-agora" and the rejection of imposed norms of authority and obedience (Le Pape, 2005). From a young age, children learn to choose. Society places immense value on learning how to choose, freely and with informed consent thanks to education. While there may not be any traces of a crisis of authority, parents nonetheless now report that they are less confident in their role as educators: "the crisis of authority, if it exists, is more of a vague feeling or social unease than something that explodes in tense family conflicts" (Galland, 2011: 223).

We are therefore witnessing the decline of the authoritarian model, increasingly replaced by a democratic family model (Fize, 1990) and the principle of consent (Gauchet, 2010). Choices are therefore made not solely by emancipating oneself from parental authority, but also by exhibiting "proof" of one's cultural experiences as one grows up. The development of individual choice justifies both the existence of various spheres of socialization to support the individual, such as the family, and their decreasing presence and more limited role as children grow up: formal education thus plays more of a complementary role than traditional pedagogy might have.

In terms of technocultural engagement and participation, the family is largely a discursive context: today's parents were the children of the first veritable youth cultures and thanks to their own experience, they have internalized the idea that each generation creates its own cultural universe. The right to cultural tastes and styles (and by extension, the quality of the products consumed, in a sort of aesthetic reinterpretation of these moral and social rights) is no longer up for debate. What *is* a point of contention, however, is how to ensure appropriate trade-offs between school and leisure activities so that the two imperatives of academic performance and personal growth can both be satisfied. Families negotiate these murky waters differently, depending on the academic trajectory of the child in question as well as parents' expectations in the matter (both being socially determined in many ways).

The family sphere consequently becomes the first area where this freedom and its constantly renegotiated limits are tested: the labels pre-teen, tween, adolescent, pre- and post-adolescent, and young adult all refer to different stages in the elaboration of one's autonomy with regard to the family unit, often expressed through relational empowerment and in particular the use of information and communication technologies. The importance attributed to choice is likewise implicated in the use of various digital forms of recommendation. Allociné (or international equivalents like Rotten Tomatoes and Metacritic), Deezer, iTunes: all of these sites "promise a new world order of criticism, one that is less beholden to the cultural elites and closer to the movie-watching experience of ordinary people" (Pasquier, Beaudoin, and Legon, 2014).

2.2 From Relationships to the Proximity Effect

Thanks to digital connections, it is now possible to never be alone: young people today are over-equipped with devices and constantly communicating and sharing their thoughts, actions, and reactions, as well as those of others. They relentlessly position and reposition themselves — sometimes quite abruptly, given that tweets are limited to 140 characters[9] — in relationship to others, creating chains of ideas. This form of digital sociability does not replace physical sociability, of which young people are still huge fans; in fact, the two are often combined: the vast majority of teenagers' Facebook friends are also their real-life middle- and high school friends (Casilli, 2010), just as when young people joined fan clubs to find individuals with shared interests in the pre-digital world (Héran, 1988) — only sometimes with broader networks. Online tutorials are directed towards friends but also larger audiences, helping to build functional and elective forms of sociability. As a result, the time young people spend with their friends is distributed across different forms of physical and virtual sociability: some of their time is spent going out (to the movies, to nightclubs and restaurants) and some of it is spent online, in almost-constant digital exchanges (Metton-Gayon, 2009).

The importance of relationships in youth culture is not a new observation: since the 1960s, youth has been described as centered around friendship, group outings, strong ties, and the start of romantic relationships, all areas in which interpersonal dynamics are key.

It is undeniable that friendships play a crucial role as children grow up: they are central to the concept of adolescence as they help to define the latter's various cultural universes, regardless of whether one looks at sociability as a cultural practice or the discursive and practical modalities of most forms of consumption (talking about an activity or engaging in it with friends, e.g.). During adolescence in particular, friends are a kind of relational capital that individuals use to establish their identity through recognition (and even notoriety).

---

9 Faced with a number of financial difficulties, Twitter has considered increasing the limit to 280 characters.

Friendships also serve to expand the field of potential cultural models to which individuals are exposed. At the same time, cultural contents, practices and behaviors are areas where individuals can accumulate this social and relational capital, in particular by communicating their cultural choices. Increasingly, cultural consumption becomes secondary to the relationships that it creates or cultivates, especially among teenagers (Octobre, Détrez, Mercklé, and Berthomier, 2010; Pasquier, 2005). These close ties foster the relational principle, an essential trait of youth culture.

But behind the image of a group of friends lies a reality that is much more varied than might first appear: friends do not present a monolithic counterweight to the parental model. Very few young people only have a single group of friends — sometimes referred to as "a chosen family". It is much more common, apparently, for young people to belong to a number of different friend groups variously linked to their activities, interests, and circumstances, especially given the proliferation of digital networks. The diverse cultural tastes of young people allow them to engage in a wide variety of relational configurations (Bergé and Granjon, 2005).

With the advent of digital technologies, relationships have taken on new shapes and significations, becoming more porous and diverse thanks to their expansion across different platforms and networks. The strong ties of intimate friendships are now supplemented by the weaker ties of digital acquaintances — ties which can nonetheless be strong enough to break into the concentric circles of interpersonal relationships. The internet has become a vast space for conversation: rather than a door towards remote and objective documents, it has become a window onto the everyday, whose banality is its very exceptionality; it is not only a space for cultural distinction but also the creation of cultural communities (Hargittai and Hinnant, 2008).

Digital technologies therefore intensify the relational principle. It is notable that the earliest uses of the internet concerned communication: instant messaging and social media, which owe their incredible popularity among young people to the illusion of permanent contact that they create, and which was in turn amplified by the rise of handheld digital devices. Social networks also feed into this ideology of the global village and go to great lengths to improve their interfaces on phones and other mobile devices. With a connected smartphone or tablet, individuals can be plugged in at all times, always able to write to and communicate with their friends. Consequently, digital technologies have transformed social ties into a "proximity effect".

Such issues were the focus of work conducted by Tomas Legon (Legon, 2011), who first looked at the effects of greater or lesser proximity between individuals on their cultural practices and taste preferences, drawing inspiration from

Mark Granovetter's theory of strong and weak ties. What Tomas Legon discovered, was that when weak ties are diversified, they provide a significant range of exposure to diverse cultural repertoires. On the flipside, however, they fragment the different forms of self-(re)presentation, given the wildly diverse contexts to which individuals must adjust and adapt. While the strength of weak ties lies in their ability to provide exposure to cultural diversity, the strength of strong ties stems from a feeling of being able to talk about anything with one's friends: "Not necessarily because individuals share a taste preference or relationship to culture, but because they feel permitted to talk about it, permitted to represent themselves (and, as a result, to see themselves) under the guise of different cultural appearances" (Legon, 2011: 55). The uniqueness of these ties is precisely the fact that they are not bolstered by existing institutions: their centrifugal force is strictly linked to individual autonomy and is solely maintained by regular renewal in terms of centers of interest, thanks to the motivation of amateurs and the work of relevant gatekeepers.

Youth sociability has its own rules and limits, of course: the "tyranny of the majority" analyzed by Dominique Pasquier (Pasquier, 2005) replicates, in the media realm, what the 1962 film *The War of the Buttons*[10] had already intimated: friends are an essential resource when developing one's identity and social persona, but they also create a social landscape that imposes demands and requirements. These demands can be linked to the limits of the institutions that frame youth experience: friendships are developed thanks to the imposed schedules of middle and high school, as well as college, while the professional world gives rise to new relationships and hobbies offer the possibility of creating yet different affective ties. As these networks can give rise to varying structures of friendship, they often require a certain degree of negotiation to co-exist. Most of the time, however, these demands exist independently of the various institutional demands made on young people and do not call upon the same skills. Sharing, for instance, is highly valued on the internet, while it would be considered copying (i.e., cheating) in school, which tends to overlook collective work in favor of independent efforts. Similarly, remixing would often be criticized as theft in an institutional setting, given that the original author is "forgotten" in favor of an original reconfiguration.

---

10   *La Guerre des boutons* or *War of the Buttons* is a French film directed by Yves Robert. *War of the Buttons* is about two rival kid gangs whose playful combats escalate into violence. The title derives from the buttons that are cut off from the rival team's clothes as combat trophies. The film is based on *La Guerre des boutons*, a novel by Louis Pergaud (1882–1915), who was killed in action in WWI and whose works portray a fervent antimilitarism.

These interlinkages have a fourfold effect. Firstly, they produce a certain endogenization of expertise, approval and punishment: each youth community has its own rules and its own micro-culture. It is not necessary for members of the community to share the same ideal: the community of professional amateurs is *itself* an ideal (Ward, 1999). The case of the late John Perry Barlow illustrates this: a poet, rancher, and lyricist, Perry Barlow helped to establish the Electronic Frontier Foundation and the Freedom of the Press Foundation. He became particularly famous for publishing a "Declaration of the Independence of Cyberspace," a seminal document that, while often waxing rhapsodically, helped to create the pro-am community. In it, Barlow addressed world governments and Bill Clinton in particular (at the time of the declaration, the American president wished to pass the Communications Decency Act), stating: "I come from Cyberspace, the new home of Mind. On behalf of the future, I ask you of the past to leave us alone. You are not welcome among us. You have no sovereignty where we gather" (Barlow, 1996) Secondly, a certain metanarrative has developed on the subject of networks and linkages, a metanarrative to which young people have largely contributed. The most extreme of these metanarratives are political in nature: Edward Snowden and his leaks, Anonymous and their spectacular actions … (more on this in chapter 6). Thirdly, the generalized growth of connectivity had led to a certain loss of prominence for the art world in favor of cultural industries. Paul Di Maggio (Di Maggio, 1987) has shown that amateur youth communities have cultivated recognition for cultural industries and challenged the superiority of high-brow, "legitimate" art since the 1990s. Similarly, Janssen *et al.* (Janssen *et al.,* 2011) demonstrated, by analyzing the various themes addressed in the media, that attention paid to popular culture tended to increase as youth amateur cultures grew in visibility. This phenomenon has obviously been amplified by the rise of the internet, which multiples many-fold the impact of selection and visibility. Finally, interconnectivity has led to renewed creativity: new aesthetic genres have emerged from the internet, like so many exquisite corpses penned during recess. Online writing has been a particularly fruitful terrain for new forms and authors on networked platforms, allowing for the layering of narrative and metanarrative over created content and encouraging the transmedia hybridization of genres, likewise also facilitated by the various tools at hand. It has become increasingly easy to combine images and sound, to create films, to record and to compose music.

2.3   *What Engagement Signifies*

This relational principle goes hand-in-hand with a principle of engagement that can be understood from two perspectives: through the lens of participation in new cultural genres (which young people are particularly fond of), and through participatory engagement in cultural and artistic associations or certain digital platforms. We saw this in terms of devices: more and more young people are technophiles. But this also applies to tastes and choices with regard to content: young people are increasingly open to new genres and participate more readily in innovative artistic and cultural practices, in particular when these practices are technologically advanced in nature (Octobre, 2014a). Moreover, the digital revolution has pushed young people towards new forms of network engagement that they do not necessarily classify as "hobbies" or amateur practices (ranging from crafts to computer-based songwriting). As illustrated by the example of *booktubers*,[11] these new forms of engagement are attracting ever-greater numbers of young people (Donnat, 2009a and b).

However, participation does not always entail loyalty: forms of engagement can be circumstantial and ad hoc, without nevertheless losing any degree of intensity when they occur and are accompanied by different types of experimentation. In this regard, cultural engagement resembles what Jacques Ion has called "distanced engagement" in the political sphere: it is reversible, circumstantial and wary of institutional mechanisms, preferring horizontal and interpersonal linkages and putting an emphasis on the individual and his or her "identity" (Ion, 1997; Franguiadakis, 2005). It is still important to specify what kind of engagement is involved, however. In this context, there are no references to external principles (the supernatural, nature, society), as is often the case in the more commonly studied forms of participation (religion, metaphysics, anti-globalization, ecological movements, ideologies, politics, and humanitarian efforts). On the contrary, new forms of cultural engagement are founded around an internal principle — the self — that individuals must cultivate and develop. New forms of participation are presented as a way to enhance a source of internal meaning: the conscience, a combination of intelligence and intuition, with the former prompting reflexivity and the latter expressivity, which has become an imperative for self-realization.

These principles underpinning relationships and engagement also play out against the ideology of youth, which favors a vision of youth-as-resource rather than youth-as-obstacle. This vision is based on twofold principle of regulation and self-control, arising from the personal appropriation of contents, emotions and experiences and the collective negotiation of personal identities and cultural values with one's family, peers or institutions. The various forms of subversion that young people are fans of — fake commercials, doctored clips,

---

11   See the special issue of *Lecture Jeune* on the topic of "*Booktubers* et communautés de lecteurs" [Booktubers and Reader Communities], summer 2016, no. 158.

mashups[12] — as well the types of peer-to-peer learning they consume — tutorials,[13] memes,[14] gameplays and playthroughs[15] — express just how youth cultures are balanced against sociocultural frameworks, a delicate process of negotiation that simultaneously affirms the specificity of youth culture for certain age groups and gradually integrates a number of skills that will be transferable to future social roles. These three dimensions, with regard to relations, engagement and endogenous control, define cultural autonomy as a process, a socially situated form of learning that is inherent to youth identity, which combines difference and belonging and presumes a certain reflexive capacity on both the conscious and subconscious levels (with regard to discourse as well as practices, behaviors, and habits).

3   The Vices and Virtues of Eclecticism

Eclecticism is what happens when the transition to cultural and digital industries, characterized by a vast increase in offerings and the expanded circulation of content, is paired with a change in the concept of self-construction, which has now become active, expressive, demonstrative, collective, and at the same time highly individual. In short, eclecticism is what happens when the autonomy imperative plays out against the backdrop of technocultural abundance.

3.1   *Revisiting Youth Omnivorism*

The question of how youth cultural repertoires are composed in this context of abundance — as the traditional divide between high-brow and low-brow culture is being challenged (Coulangeon, 2011) — has been a subject for cultural sociologists for many years, from early works by Olivier Donnat (Donnat, 1994) on eclecticism and Richard A. Peterson's (Peterson, 1991) on omnivorism.[16]

---

12   Mashups combine several different media elements into a single creation (songs, videos, sounds, information sources, images, etc.).

13   Tutorials are short online videos where individuals film themselves doing something they are an expert at; these videos are often posted on blogs or on YouTube and are used as tools by their relevant communities.

14   According to Wikipedia, memes are "image macros paired with a concept or catchphrase," though they recently evolved in complexity.

15   Short videos posted online where young people film themselves playing video games and showing how to beat challenges or levels.

16   This approach gave rise to a significant number of international studies on the different spheres of cultural consumption, even if the practice of listening to recorded music has remained the most popular realm of study.

Both approaches shed new light on cultural consumption, with a view to reconfiguring the linkages between cultural and social hierarchies: social hierarchy is no longer seen as a counterpart to singular practices (e.g., attending the theater), but rather to the plurality and diversity of consumption patterns in general, ranging from traditional high-brow tastes associated with the elite to the supposedly "popular" tastes of the lower classes. Bernard Lahire (Lahire, 2006), on the other hand, drew attention to the non-homogenous nature of cultural legitimacy, including the likes and dislikes of the younger generations. Today, the same individual can read literary masterpieces, Harlequin novels and manga; can listen to classical music and electronica; can enjoy arthouse films and horror movies. Hervé Glévarec encourages us to radically challenge the hierarchies that govern "distinction," located at the crossroads of newly legitimized amateurism (which shapes the experience of consumption) and the emergence of eclecticism in a context of increased cultural diversity (Glévarec and Pinet, 2009). According to the latter, differences are wrought within genres and subgenres, creating myriad constellations of micro-localized dispositions and plural forms of legitimacy.

However, most studies fail to account for the transition from media culture to technoculture, sometimes even concealing to what extent technological evolution and the proliferation of devices have automatically prompted eclectic taste preferences for many individuals, who combine mainstream consumption habits with niche amateur practices, as well as the artificial narrowing of the cultural offer (faced with overabundance, most people follow the recommendations of their friends and acquaintances) and the multiplication of microlocalized micro-markets for cultural amateurs of all stripes. It is not surprising, therefore, that although the French movie business has never produced so many movies, the vast majority of its financial success comes from a limited number of blockbusters, whereas the number of films reaching audiences of fewer than 10,000 has increased in tandem.

When we look at music listening habits, this also becomes evident: the dominance of certain musical genres for certain age groups (pop being associated with late childhood, rap/R&B with tweens and early teens, metal/rock/hard rock with adolescence) nevertheless does not negate the fact that getting older is broadly associated with an increased number of musical tastes (Octobre, Détrez, Mercklé, and Berthomier, 2010: 135–51). Adolescence and young adulthood are indeed a period of experimentation in terms of musical likes and dislikes, especially given that such preferences are often indexed to interest communities with strong cues for behavior and dress which produce important opportunities for group identification. In short, most consumption remains concentrated on a small number of products, platforms or contents — even if these can gradually shift over time — while a plethora of products, platforms and contents manage to attract a minority of consumers in relatively niche markets.

3.2   *The Challenge of Eclecticism*

Young people today have grown up with interactive media and a broad spectrum of cultural options, leading to the assumption that they can consume what they want, when they want. Simultaneously, media platforms have become increasingly collective *and* individualized in terms of the wide variety of consumption options.

This eclecticism, which is characteristic of young people's relationship to technoculture, is also its own challenge, given that it requires numerous resources to be implemented and generate rewards, both individually and collectively. First of all, because in order to be eclectic, individuals must be able to handle an excessive amount of information and a plethora of options, and exhibit mastery over a vast number of genres and subgenres that form the basis of judgments on quality, taste and (self-)positioning in a stratified social, cultural and technological sphere. And secondly, because individuals must be able to take advantage of cultural abundance without being overwhelmed by it: risks include addiction, idleness, conformism, withdrawal from the world and loss of creativity, all different reactions when faced with the individual and/or collective inability to find guiding threads (again, either personal or collective) amidst the abundance of contents and modalities of consumption. Finally, eclecticism is also a daunting challenge because, as a generational form of relationship to culture, it constitutes an inclusive but simultaneously exclusive norm: not being able to join in on a conversation because one doesn't know the latest Pink song, or hasn't heard of *Breaking Bad,* or because one isn't familiar with Musical.ly[17] or Dubsmash[18] automatically means being excluded from certain peer groups. Keeping up with technoculture is a constant effort, one that becomes especially demanding as innovations emerge and social usage changes at an ever-accelerating clip. The feeling of cultural shame that transpires when individuals feel like they are out of the loop with regard to youth cultural flows is especially strong given that nowadays, this no longer concerns behaviors that are relatively notable — going to a museum,

---

17   A smartphone app that allowed individuals to create short videos based on musical clips that can be slowed down or sped up as desired. Released first in 2014, it reached over 90 millions users in 2016 and was acquired by ByteDance Ltd in 2017, then merged in Tik Tok in 2018.

18   A smartphone app that allows individuals to create short videos based off of existing songs or film dialogue.

attending the theater, seeing a concert, even accessing a library — but rather elements that constitute the everyday life of most young people. In addition, the results of a recent international survey on adolescents has indicated that the latter experience worry and significant pressure to be "in the know,"[19] in particular due to the role played by screens and the messages they convey.

∴

All of the youth norms discussed so far are all largely implicit: nowhere it is written or otherwise stipulated that young people must be culturally engaged and have diverse tastes. The relationship to the world that is governed by these implicit standards is consequently a source of important cleavages. There are in fact two youth populations: one which enters society with a good understanding of its codes and cultural expectations, and one which enters society without these assets.

It is rarer today to find a young person who does not invest any energy in culture, who experiences scant cultural autonomy, or who expresses highly homogenous taste preferences. Such individuals will experience significant and successive exclusion from various peer groups, which will be increasingly hard to disentangle from the complex web of factors determining inclusion. Accepting this means perhaps reconsidering the objectives of cultural democratization, in order to reformulate them in a plural fashion so as to account for all technocultural values and standards. It also entails investigating the factors behind the development of inequalities, while taking into account the general context of cultural diversity with regard to contents, publics and expectations. This will be the focus of the following chapter.

---

19   There are numerous local studies. One of the most recent important studies is *Health Behavior in School-Age Children,* 2016.

CHAPTER 5

Technoculture, Education and Self-Education

There is nothing "natural" about the digital and cultural education that we receive. The fact is that not all young people end up developing the same skills, acquiring the same knowledge or learning how to adequately present themselves on the digital stage. Not all young people are able to pivot to lucrative or otherwise valuable fields and obtain social recognition. Ultimately, technocultural citizenship is not equally accessible to all. In this chapter, we shall examine what forms of knowledge are developed through cultural contents, and in particular via digital literacy.[1] How is education transformed by the digital ecosystem that now surrounds it? How can new forms of knowledge associated with digital literacy be incorporated into a broader educational program? What skills should be encouraged to promote digital literacy? And finally, how can education best support young people on their journey to become technocultural citizens?

1 Is Technoculture an Alternative Form of Education?

"The king is dead, long live the king." While there is no broad institutional consensus on the matter, can technoculture, perhaps even better than its predecessor media culture (Maigret and Macé, 2005), provide an alternative form of education? One may very reasonably express some doubt on the matter. Google, for instance, is not an educational institution, but a private corporation that is funded through advertisements. Google is not in charge of verifying the quality of content, but of creating algorithms that help to sort and rank data depending on the latter's pertinence to given search criteria, this pertinence in turn being influenced by the search engine optimization techniques deployed by many companies to improve their performance online. Economic actors are nevertheless forced to take a stand on various ethical dilemmas, be it out of veritable conviction or simply marketing strategy. For example, Unilever threatened to pull its advertisements from all digital platforms if the latter did

---

[1] The American Library Association's digital-literacy task force offers this definition: "Digital literacy is the ability to use information and communication technologies to find, evaluate, create, and communicate information, requiring both cognitive and technical skills." Cited in: http://edweek.org/ew/articles/2016/11/09/what-is-digital-literacy.html.

not work harder to combat fake news and other toxic content. The company's chief marketing officer made the following statement: "Unilever, as a trusted advertiser, do not want to advertise on platforms which do not make a positive contribution to society".[2] The potentially massive financial impact of such a boycott pushed social media companies to emerge from the fog of neutrality: Facebook now regularly tweaks its algorithm in an attempt to fight against the vast number of conspiracy theories that crop up on the network. Users have also begun demanding increased content regulation on digital platforms, in order to obtain a granular understanding of the violations being flagged. For instance, posts including thumbnails of Courbet's painting *L'origine du monde* or photos of breasts in the fight against breast cancer were originally taken down, based on the sole fact that they contained nudity. Such examples demonstrate that media culture is educating us all through an accumulation of rules and experiences.

1.1 A "real-world" Education

Anne Barrère (Barrère, 2011) was the first to use the French expression *education buissonnière* to describe what teenagers learn from media culture outside of school. A play on the standard phrase *école buissonnière*, meaning truancy, this new expression roughly translates to a "real-world" education where individuals can become "street smart" rather than "book smart". The forms of "miniscule knowledge" derived from narrative and fictional works (music, TV shows, movies, etc.) are, in our technocultural world, also accompanied by newer forms of knowledge regarding how to be ideal consumers, contributors and distributors of content, including self-promotion. As the birth of cultural studies highlighted, all undertakings linked to the cultural industries, including reception, are now viewed as full-fledged activities. Numerous studies have in fact observed the richness of miniscule knowledge, especially as conveyed by media culture, with TV shows at the fore (Chaillan, 2015 and 2016; Milner, 2014).

These traits are further accentuated in the technocultural regime, given that it is now possible for all individuals to create their own cultural agendas and act upon cultural content directly. As the media landscape increasingly calls upon individuals to decipher, (re)interpret, contrast and combine content, nothing about reception is entirely predetermined, automatic, or linear. Differences in genre and age segmentation mean that these are high socialized and

---

2 See http://unilever.com/news/press-releases/2018/unilever-will-not-invest-in-online-platforms-that-create-division.html.

socializing activities. Participating in technoculture means developing specific skills linked to the manipulation of information and a variety of typical media platforms; these constitute an informal education associated with the use of technology and the "technologies of the self" that the latter entails. This informal education may or may not work in tandem with formal schooling but can also function independently (Brougère and Ulmann, 2009). The ability to interpret moving images, to manipulate interactive content, to process multiple sources of information simultaneously and to react rapidly to all of the above are examples of important technocultural skills. And these competencies have their own internal systems of assessment and regulation: for example, Facebook "likes". Let us not forget that for all technocultural curricula, the principles of choice and taste are essential and further support the value placed on individual expression. While the technocultural universe has not eliminated our relationship to the collective, it has significantly reshaped it. Social capital in today's youth culture sometimes takes the highly specific form of a media competition that outweighs the meritocratic world of school and work. Finally, digital media culture allows young people to discover who they are as individuals and as such, provides a certain number of trials and challenges to overcome and initiation rites to undergo.

Moreover, the highly prized uses of cultural contents, with reappropriation at the fore, tend to exhibit a dual logic. On the one hand, this logic runs on reputation (or celebrity), which implies a certain uniqueness or creativity (being the leader of a fan group, launching a new trend, having lots of friends, etc.) that is usually evaluated by one's peer group. On the other hand, this logic also demands a certain degree of conformity, given that individuals must ideally consume the same products and adopt the same tastes as their peer group (in terms of age, gender, social situation, etc.) in order to fit in and be accepted. Individuals must thus be familiar with what everyone else knows, even if this knowledge is sometimes superficial and/or devoid of any personal interest; they must also develop their own areas of cultural curiosity — even if these are not shared by their peers — in order to be unique. This twofold obligation is in many ways paradoxical: "it requires effort and consistency, but also initiative and ease with informal education" (Barrère, 2011: 11). This double requirement may require skills that are similar to those rewarded in school (looking for information, interpreting it, developing one's knowledge through accumulation of data), but enjoys no formal recognition within the educational system. It moreover presumes that individuals have a certain capacity for autonomy concerning their choice of cultural contents, the search for information and the development of knowledge — a degree of autonomy that schools often require of their pupils without granting them equivalent leeway with regard to cultural education.

Another major transformation wrought by youth technoculture concerns its relationship to popular culture. The skills that young people acquire through their consumption of popular culture (including passive reception, play, and manipulation) have a significant impact on how they learn, how they work and how they participate in pedagogical, political, civic and social processes more broadly. The skills that are derived from previously "low-brow" cultural products have now become powerfully inclusive. Such skills largely center around the communication-based assets of cultural contents and their use by individuals as resources for self-construction, helping the former to interpret the world around them and elaborate repositories of potentially shared references which heavily favor cultural industrial productions, with television in the lead. The stakes of this inclusion are quite high given that it involves a new kind of cultural citizenship.

But is cultural citizenship something that is widely shared? Pierre Lévy writes: "the knowledge possessed by a community of thought is no longer shared knowledge, as it has become impossible for any one person — or even group — to gain mastery over all the skills and data required. These new forms of knowledge are fundamentally collective and cannot exist within a single individual" (Lévy, 1997: 27). The things that everyone knows in a given group are limited, pertaining to what sets the group apart as a community of shared interests. But what is the scale of this shared knowledge: is it national (as desired by national education programs) or local, based either on discipline-specific skills or cross-cutting managerial and interpersonal ones?

Amidst this "democratization" of knowledge, systems to refocus and reconstruct hierarchies have nonetheless emerged: brain trusts and experts work to establish an elite that has access to information that is not otherwise widely available. These thought leaders are entrusted with the responsibility of choosing what should or should not be shared collectively.

As the masses have gained access to the internet, the latter has undergone a transformation similar to that experienced by the school system at the end of the 20th century, as increasingly diverse populations were gradually granted admission. These new populations are geographically, socially, and culturally different; some are even embedded within the commercial sphere. The dissemination of information and subsequent knowledge-building are only made possible by a certain separation between contents and their authors — and yet this separation is unequally distributed. While early adopters of the internet knew how to manipulate their identities, these newer populations possess less cultural capital and are less familiar with information and communication technologies more broadly; as a result, they tend to have a more identitarian usage of these tools. Mass access to the internet has thus led to the creation of enclaves, niches and micro-communities of individuals coalescing around a handful of shared traits (which are not necessarily, or solely, sociodemographic in nature) (Cardon, 2010a).

1.2 *The Return of Aesthetics*

The rise of technoculture has also heralded the return of aesthetics: never before have so many images, words and sounds been shared, viewed and modified. But this new form of aesthetics is likely multidimensional. Aesthetics does not refer to a category of objects, but a specific type of attention which can be brought to contents, both cultural and others: the aestheticization of individuals' relationship to the world can take a variety of paths. Jean-Marie Schaeffer (Schaeffer, 2016) has defined aestheticization as the implementation of a form of cognitive attention that constantly evaluates the pleasure we derive from a certain activity and which in turn reinforces this investment. The exact nature of aesthetic behavior will depend on the various properties of the object(s) of focus and the attention-based and cognitive competencies of individuals, as well as their previous experiences, expectations, contexts, preferences, and prejudices. As a result, automobile tuning, knitting, tattoos, manga and video games can all become aesthetic practices. A similar divide occurs between aesthetics as a category (one in which we would normally place reading, going to visual arts exhibits) and aesthetics as an experience: young people who read books because they are forced to or visit a museum as part of a class trip do not always have an aesthetic experience, far from it!

New aesthetics have surfaced thanks to TV series (Colonna, 2010; Esquenazi, 2011; de Saint-Maurice, 2009; Trudy, 2010), which have had knock-on effects with regard to "major" art forms such as cinema and literature (for instance, when popular novels are adapted into TV shows or movies, the latter eventually start to account for audience reactions in a way the books never could). The growing legitimacy of TV shows is a relatively recent phenomenon (Jost, 2011), dating from the turn of the millennium and owing to the aesthetics of media specialists, including in the academic realm, as well as increased sociological attention to television publics (Glévarec, 2012).

On the one hand, TV shows have given risen to important innovations in cinematography, evidenced by the fact that they are increasingly welcomed into international festivals, from Toronto to Paris and Berlin. The serial nature of television allows it to engage in significant character development and multi-faceted plots with professional, social and personal components. In 1999, *The Sopranos* marked the tipping point: for the first time, the season and not the episode was the unit against which the narrative arc was plotted. The show also illustrated the aesthetic evolution towards storylines that were focused on private lives (or at least where the private lives of individuals occupied a significant portion of the air time). The growth of intimate spaces in television, which requires a certain number of easily recognizable tropes to allow for viewers to identify with a show, translated in particular into the use of voiceovers to bring storytelling closer. This does not entail moving away from realism, as some have suggested (Pourtier-Tilian, 2011), but on the contrary it involves making reality seem more intimate: general statements drive verisimilitude and the narrative obeys its own internal logic, rather than relying on abstract deductions. In TV series, there is also a shift toward intimacy, as relationships have become the focus of so many of them in recent years. Thanks to digital technology, watching television contents has also become increasingly intimate in nature: individuals can watch what they want, when they want, from the comfort of their smartphone or their smart TV, including sometimes with unofficial subtitles drafted by amateurs.[3]

On the other hand, the cognitive scope of television shows has exploded, now drawing on a quasi-encyclopedic knowledge of the various sciences, social and professional skills as well as practical know-how. Television also allows young people to learn interpersonal and behavioral skills — this can take the form of what Dominique Pasquier has termed "the grammar of love" (Pasquier, 1999), or the modelling of maternal and female behavioral roles, as identified by Tania Modlelski (Modleski, 1982).

The internet has also prompted some young people to return to the written word, where it had often been neglected during the media era. But the written word takes on a very different guise today, with blogs replacing journals and diaries. The internet also values the act of reading, but not so much of literature, even if some studies have highlighted the role of digital platforms in disseminating the work of authors old and new (Beaudoin, 2012). Reading on the internet does not follow a linear, pre-determined path: it wanders amongst hyperlinks, drifting to and fro as individual curiosity and interest dictate.

The return of aesthetics thus takes place according to new modalities. First of all, the sped-up circulation of images and contents has created a repertoire of shared references, which is transmitted in an increasingly porous fashion across different types of media and cultural genres, as well as national borders (even if localized forms of reception continue to exist). The principle of transmedia storytelling likewise encourages highly diverse forms of participation, exchange, and even confrontation among young people, who thus shape a generational sociability in playgrounds, rec rooms, and public spaces alike.

---

3   These are called "fansubs" (Dagiral and Teissier, 2008).

This is what Henry Jenkins considers to be the uniqueness of our current culture, which has prompted a shift away from contents that are designed for a specific medium or platform, to contents that can circulate freely across various forms of media. This phenomenon has also led to the interdependence of communication systems, in a context where there are multiple different ways to access any given media content. This transmedia ecosystem fosters the development of intricate relationships between cultural industries and the media, leading to the reversal of a traditionally top-down system into one that is highly participatory and relatively bottom-up (Jenkins, 2006). And finally, the concept of multitasking has brought about a sea change in youth culture, which is illustrated quite clearly in the case of video games. The technocultural aesthetics of the latter force individuals to establish priorities, make choices, and quickly evaluate situations; they also reward trial and error as a method for learning. The rules of a video game are usually broad enough to allow for various different types of game play between which players must constantly negotiate. Multitasking consists precisely in this ability to handle numerous audiovisual inputs at the same time in an environment that contains sometimes contradictory goals nevertheless loosely tied together by a shared aesthetic. In other words, young people today are far from being overwhelmed by video games: this in fact invites us to consider a more nuanced form of attention that is continuously partial and well-suited to this kind of aesthetic experience.

The preferred reading experiences of young people today — be they heroic sagas, dystopian novels, or Japanese manga — are selected because they elicit strong emotions (even sometimes to a saturation point) and allow for self-identification. These works draw on complex imagery and narrative universes which create an aesthetic that is very different from the learning model associated with traditional literature and the great works. Reading for emotional pleasure has long existed, of course, but it has been looked down upon: Emma Bovary does not die because of her adultery, but because she placed too much faith in the romantic novels she voraciously consumed. Just as certain kinds of literature have long been (wrongly) disparaged, the powerful attraction of fictional universes, especially for young people, has likewise been underestimated, even despite the recent growth of youth literature.

Thanks to technoculture, what has accompanied the return of aesthetics across the board is the rise of fictional competency, a skill that young people develop very early on and which technoculture ceaselessly stimulates (regardless of the quality of this stimulation). This skill concerns the ability to dive into any one of a number of counterfactual or virtual universes (the principle underpinning video games as a whole) and to create a sort of patchwork from transmedia contents. Even though individuals know these media contents are not real, this patchwork accumulation allows them to engage emotionally and cognitively and develop many new skills.

Youth culture thus prompts a reconfiguration of aesthetics, moving away from erudite models towards a combinatory, partial, and emotional one. In this context, some activities are less privileged than before. For instance, we can observe that reading rates are down while education levels are up, even despite the strong link that exists between academic achievement and a penchant for reading. It is not certain that reading is still part of a shared cultural capital for all the different youth subcultures (depending on age, gender and social demographics), even if some young people massively enjoy reading. Correlation with social class does not equate to usefulness within that social class: reading can serve as an external mark of distinction without serving any corresponding purpose *within* one's social group. While the children from upper classes continue to read more than their peers, and children who grow up reading remain attached to this practice, this activity does not necessarily create a shared universe (Octobre et al., 2010); in fact, it even struggles to establish intergenerational linkages, given that adult expectations in terms of youth reading practices remain overly influenced by academic traditions.

This aesthetic is associate and deliberative. It may give rise to aesthetic publics, as evidenced by the work of Laurence Allard on young videographers (Allard, 2002): the members of a given community experience the same stakes, without necessarily needing to have those stakes explicitly stated. They share a mode of access to and interaction with the world; similar challenges and goals make up the fabric of collective experience through discussion and exchange. But mostly importantly perhaps, this aesthetic reminds us of what Bernard Manin has called "the democracy of the public" (Manin, 1995), with its cult of personality and in particular, its infatuation with images. Young people have thus developed modes of aesthetic consumption that can critique *Hélène et les garçons*[4] and then parody *Loft Story* in the same breath. These new forms of aesthetic consumption have also emphasized the shift to the first-person. The rise of aesthetic discourse in relation to the emotions and reactions it provokes has also meant the proliferation of first-person narratives. The media is overrun with eyewitness accounts, talk shows, audience discussion programs (Livingstone and Lunt, 1994), and reality TV (Jost, 2001), not to mention the plethora of personal pages and blogs on the internet (Beaudoin and Velvoska, 1999). As emotions and anecdotes come to substitute debate and opinions, a

---

4 One of the first French sitcoms targeting teenagers, which depicted the adventures of a group of young students in their romantic and personal lives outside of college (first broadcasted between 1992 and 1994).

subtle value shift has also occurred from "truth" to "authenticity": sweeping generalizations and abstract classifications are no longer as valuable as specific taste preferences and critical responses, which have become legitimate precisely on account of their specificity. This leads to a double paradox: on the one hand, the overexposure of emotional intimacy in the public sphere is accompanied by the banishment of expert opinions to the private sphere; on the other hand, expert rankings and categorizations are challenged in the name of individual and immediate experiences, whereas the recognition and appreciation of subjective micro-differences governs the normal regime of public speaking. In other words, whereas the aesthetics of cultural legitimacy — somewhat arbitrary but largely collective in nature — used to institute strong standards against which individuals could choose to rebel (in the name of creative, social or individual freedom), now the aesthetics of individual emotion, sensation and perception is struggling to produce a shared discourse that can be the subject of dialogue, debate and negotiation: in short, to establish social ties.

1.3 *Modes of Learning and Affinity Spaces*

All of these reflections invite us to investigate the various modes of learning that have developed within this new landscape dominated by cultural industries. The opposition between technophiles and technophobes has become a radical cleavage in this regard. Optimists are likely to agree with Michel Serres and see new forms of learning as a major cognitive leap for humanity, opportunities to stimulate creativity and open up new avenues for knowledge (Serres, 2012). Pessimists, on the other hand, will tend to agree with Nicholas Carr and argue that technoculture makes us stupid, in large part because it encourages us to abandon reading and critical analysis for mere data consumption, in the process fostering new forms of addiction and creating higher risks of scattered attention (Carr, 2010). We should therefore discuss the prospect of a shared cultural agenda, which would become possible with the help of cultural (re)mediation.

Let us start by examining the new modes of learning. James Paul Gee describes these as "affinity spaces" (Gee, 2004) which operate thanks to amateurs harnessing the amateurism of others. These autodidactic mechanisms are especially robust given that the level of training increases with each generation. However, skills are developed in a fragmentary fashion, depending on the sometimes fleeting, sometimes long-lasting desires and interests of individuals (Cardon and Levrel, 2009). This is the case for fansubbing communities, for instance, which play a crucial role in disseminating television shows by creating almost immediate subtitle tracks, thus embodying the values of free sharing and solidarity — values which are entirely contradictory with the utilitarian and sometimes harmful aspects usually mentioned when discussing internet piracy. The same applies to a wide variety of fan art in the literary, visual, and audiovisual realm which circulates on dedicated sites like fanfiction.net.

These affinity spaces largely operate according to an elective principle rather than a selective one (unlike in the academic sphere, where selection by educational achievement, and thus ostensibly by knowledge, is overwhelmingly used) and erect internal rules that govern the use of individual expertise within an amateur community as well as the circulation of information. Affinity spaces can cut across all ages, genders, and social groups. The concept of learning within the technoculture landscape can thus be envisioned as a spectrum: it goes from information (collecting information thanks to familiarity with contents and uses, contact with technologies and practices which encourage learning a certain limited, but practical know-how through repeated exposure) to knowledge (use and manipulation of information), meta-knowledge (about the practices and information that make up an individual trajectory), and likes and dislikes, with the linkages between these points being neither linear nor causal.

Looking at affinity spaces allows us to both revisit the supposed decrease in intelligence among young people and to consider the role played by technological shifts in how knowledge and culture have changed for younger generations. Do the brains of young people today work differently, having been irremediably altered by playing video games and surfing the web? In general, two new forms of learning stand out. The first involves sequential intelligence: this applies to coding and the logical sequencing of thoughts in language. The second form of learning draws on fluid, simultaneous intelligence. It allows individuals to handle information from different realms of perception (watching a film or contemplating a painting, for instance) in parallel and without establishing any logical order or hierarchy. These two forms of intelligence are inseparable: the use of language amplifies perceptions by making them objective realities that can be communicated, while perception allows individuals to grasp extra-linguistic nuances. Video games tend to favor the second type of intelligence, whereas social networks call on a variable combination of the two. In addition, we must clearly distinguish between interactivity, a characteristic of many modern technological products that is determined by the creator of a given content, and participation, which depends on the aptitude of individuals to exploit this potential (with said aptitude being largely governed by socially constructed norms).

2 The Challenge of Transliteracy

The various skills and modes of learning that are exploited by technoculture in turn foster new forms of literacy, leading to new possibilities for education.

2.1 *Literacy, Media Literacy and Digital Literacy*

Literacy has traditionally been defined as a set of skills related to listening, verbal eloquence, reading, writing, and critical thinking, skills ideal for molding active learners and thinkers that can engage in socially effective and meaningful ways. Historically, proponents of the Beaux Arts similarly developed criteria for learning how to contemplate a painting. To this day, such skills remain indispensable for any citizen wishing to fully participate in social life, especially given that technoculture has caused the convergence of hitherto separate sensorial dimensions and forms of appropriation: sound, imagery, video, text, and hypertext. In addition, some key elements of literacy — the idea that cultural contents and works are constructs; that the public deciphers or interprets their meaning; that works have social and political implications; that each art form has its own distinct aesthetics — are still applicable. Through its power of convergence, however, technoculture mobilizes pre-digital skills while also requiring new competencies in relation to new technological configurations and sociotechnical uses. As cultural practices are evolving and media and communications platforms gradually converge, we are no longer mere spectators or consumers of information and entertainment, but rather participants in an immersive media culture (Hobbs, 2010). This shift requires us to expand the notion of literacy. We must now speak of transliteracy, which can be defined as "a set of interaction-based skills implemented by users when using a wide variety of information and communication platforms, incorporating voice, text, icons, and other digital forms, primarily in digital contexts and environments" (Delamotte, Liquette, and Frau-Meigs, 2014: 145).

Video games have traditionally unfolded in a linear fashion; in both early video games like *Pac Man* and newer games such as *Final Fantasy,* narrative predetermination is the rule rather than the exception. However, a newer generation of online games like *Warcraft III, The Sims* and *Second Life* operates differently, since players interact with the game and with each other, modifying storylines and outcomes in the process. In this environment, players develop new skills — how to collaborate and exchange information with other players — while still needing the traditional competencies of media literacy (analyzing game content, determining prerequisites and expectations). Today, digital literacy includes the ability to produce and consume multimedia content and to grasp the sociocultural implications of the contemporary changes

(Poyntz and Hoechsmann, 2008). Digital literacy requires critical thinking, communications management and information processing skills (i.e., intellectual, technological, and psychological skills), as well as an arsenal of practical know-how (responsiveness, handiness). As a result, digital literacy is composed of multiple skills, most of which are crosscutting, including reflexive thought on digital uses and the consequences of these uses, political and civic action and artistic creation (Combes, 2010). These skills can be grouped into three broad categories: using, understanding, and creating.[5] Using refers to the knowledge needed to manipulate computer programs of various kinds (word processors, web browsers, e-mail and other communications tools, cloud computing, etc.). Understanding refers to the ability to assess and evaluate within a given context, and thus make informed decisions with regard to digital uses (though such decisions can be made without a conscious reflection on actions and the consequences of those actions in terms of how they will be perceived and whether they are appropriate, fair, or likely to hurt anyone's feelings). This kind of understanding is positioned at the center of the knowledge economy required for the 21st century. And finally, creating refers to the ability to produce cultural contents by using digital tools, combining image, sound, video, text and hypertext; as well as the capacity to share these productions using various features of Web 2.0 (social games, blogs, tweets, wikis, file sharing sites, etc.). From this perspective, creation is also a form of participation in cultural citizenship.

2.2   *The Components of Transliteracy*

It can thus be argued that transliteracy mobilizes a number of successive elements. Literary, visual, and auditory literacies correspond to the linguistic and perceptive functions that are most frequently called upon in acts of communication and exchange (note the absence of smell and touch, which are less commonly enlisted). In all three cases an individual receives and handles a message (text, image or animation, sound), extracts information that might influence their behavior, emotions, or worldview, and engages in a reflection on how the message was produced and its desired impact. These different forms of literacy combine to form media literacy. Technological literacy, on the other hand, adds another level of reflection concerning the ergonomic

---

5   The International Society for Technology in Education (ISTE) has a more nuanced definition of digital literacy, divided into six dimensions: creativity and innovation; communication and collaboration; ease with research and information; critical thinking, problem solving, and decision making; digital citizenship; technological concepts and operations. See https://www.iste.org/standards.

and technological structures that shape the production and usage of multimedia messages (shooting a movie, writing an algorithm to generate cultural recommendations). It is inseparable from information literacy, which allows individuals to examine critically the information produced and evaluate what is pertinent to their needs; individuals with information literacy can conduct online research to find the data they need, analyze it thoroughly, and put it to good use. The concept of information literacy was first elaborated to support the work done by library scientists, but it can easily be applied to the digital sphere. In the vast ocean of unfiltered information that is the internet, critical thinking is essential to evaluate sources and contents and determine their value. This information literacy is also deployed in the context of communication literacy, which brings together skills involved in reflecting, organizing, or interacting with others. Not only are young people today expected to incorporate information plucked from multiple sources like music, video, online databases, and other media forms, but they are moreover required to use a vast panoply of resources to share and distribute this information.

Communication literacy in turn fosters social literacy: in order to fully participate in society, young people must be able to express themselves through a "participatory culture" that develops thanks to collaboration and networks. This social literacy consequently demands a kind of ethical literacy, given that the numerous different dimensions require skills and attitudes that allow individuals to identify best practices through reflection, critical thinking and sense of responsibility. These skills can also prevent harassment and conspiracy theories from prospering, on the contrary encouraging forms of technocultural citizenship that variously creative, participatory, individual, and collective.

2.3   A Weapon against Bullshit

Transliteracy can also be used as a weapon against the tidal wave of bullshit (Dieguez, 2018) wrought by the advent of the technocultural age, as it can produce structured and crosscutting skills in a variety of social fields. The concept of bullshit — which is not a form of lying so much as it is indifferent to truth — has become a subject of interest for philosophers, linguists, psychologists, sociologists, information and communications experts and political scientists alike. If post-truth can easily be mistaken for post-fiction, and if it is the product of mimetic, but uneducated technocultural skills, this is precisely because we are so used to interpretive activities, often encountering "alternative truths" that say more about individual worldviews than reality itself. Hence the importance of delegating authority to individuals, institutions and other voices that we deem — sometimes mistakenly — capable of helping us to co-produce meaning. But without an established process for creating meaning — we are not all semiologists, sociologists, or political scientists — our trust can be misplaced in gurus (of pseudoreligious or pseudoscientific ilk). As a result, intuitive beliefs and half-truths proliferate (Speber, 2010): the validity of an argument is often determined ahead of time, depending on the reputation of the person making the argument and the context in which it is uttered. Why? Because it is impossible for us to cognitive process all the information that surrounds us (and too costly even if it were possible, as we are not adequately equipped all spheres of knowledge). Amidst this context of informational opulence, we all suffer from confirmation bias, which leads us to trust information that reinforces our pre-existing ideas rather than information that carries a risk of cognitive dissonance. This phenomenon is not new of course — our brains have not been completely altered by technoculture alone — but it has become more pronounced as reputation has become a major asset in the technocultural regime (it is crucial for recognition on social networks as well as in real life, thus explaining the constant efforts at image management made by young people today). The risk of making a mistake, of contradicting oneself or changing one's mind (which according to scientific reasoning is an indispensable skill) is now seen as unbearable. We can therefore observe a vicious circle wherein projecting oneself as an authority figure inspires confidence, and confidence bolsters authority, without this authority ever having been established as legitimate in any of the realms where it reigns supreme. The specialization principle is thus undermined, with many "experts" pontificating on a wide variety of subjects on which they do not have specialized knowledge, arguing that they have "some authority" on the matter. The reign of thought leaders is now upon us, especially in the realm of technoculture: YouTubers, bands and music groups with online fan communities, etc. The trait shared by all these thought leaders is that they develop a particular aesthetic or style, whose success ends up being more important than the actual message or substance. In fact, the message *is* aesthetic rather than epistemic, whether we are talking about text, images, or video.

This subterfuge stems from a certain confusion between style and intelligence, between brio and talent, between grandiloquence and creativity. According to Cohen, this confusion has become particularly prevalent in France, a country known for its creation of "the intellectual," a figure at the crossroads between the thinker, the artist and the journalist (Cohen, 2013). These elements are mutually reinforcing in the case of technoculture, whose operating mode in fact borrows from the economics of attention, visibility and aesthetics. What is at play is therefore equally tied to psychological mechanisms as it is to sociocultural and institutional settings. For example, a French unemployed young man named Cem Cem became famous after posting videos on

YouTube that depicted him performing a variety of banal activities for 10 hours straight (listening to the Netflix jingle on repeat for 10 hours, or staring at a taco, or handcuffing himself to the radiator).[6] Paradoxically, the lack of quality of these videos becomes interesting in itself, and the creator of the videos is seen a conveying an important message. A national radio station even devoted a whole program to analyzing this phenomenon.[7] As curiosity and buzz grows surrounding such a phenomenon, viewers engage in cognitive processes to try to extract meaning. In fact, the value of a given content is measured against the mental activity it prompts. A vicious cycle begins, despite a lack of interest in the original content. This system rewards anything that incites debate and controversy, rather than real interest or value; it fosters emotions and opinions rather than reason and logic.

Knowledge is by its very nature analytic: it is the result of progressive stages of reasoning, including contradictions and confirmations, and the iteration of empirical truths. Accumulated over time, knowledge is ultimately provisional and hypothetical, local and circumstantial (as evidenced by the common saying that "the more you learn, the less you know"). It is possible, however, that inhabitants of the technocultural world view knowledge in a more holistic fashion: knowledge (or ignorance) is a statutory quality that is almost universally valued. It is equally possible that knowledge is propagated in the rush of constant technocultural flows. This holistic vision positions itself against (specialized) experts and substitutes opinion for knowledge, with an important emphasis on the identity of the people expressing these opinions (unlike knowledge, which exists largely independently of whoever imparts it). Impartiality is less important than engagement, circumspection is less valued than a rapid response rate: what founds the legitimacy of discourse is rooted in every individual's democratic right to think for him or herself.

Given that performative technoculture (in terms of both contents and self-representations) rewards the virtues of spontaneous inspiration and creativity, even creation that is seemingly "from nothing" (Pennycook, Cheyne, Koehler, and Fugelsang, 2015), it does not require a specific method. In this context, it is cognitively comforting to have seemingly omniscient authority figures. The important thing is not so much expressing the "correct" opinion (especially since statements are usually accompanied by a number of analytical hedges that limit their scope of application) as it is merely expressing *any* opinion at all. And what drives such cognitive shortcuts is not really credulity (if that were

---

6 https://www.google.com/search?client=safari&rls=en&q=cem+cem&ie=UTF-8&oe=UTF-8#.
7 "Cem Cem ou l'art de ne rien faire" ["Cem Cem or the art of doing nothing"]. *France Inter*, 1 May 2019.

the case, it could be targeted with education in critical thinking skills) but rather the increased value placed on intuition and the belief that the latter is a true path towards the acquisition and production of knowledge — which is sort of what happens when we learn how to use digital tools through trial and error. Similarly, greater value is awarded to sincere intentions than to the quality of results obtained: sincerity has come to replace accuracy. The technocultural system now tempts us to sin through epistemic omission (Kimbrough, 2006).

3 Mediation and Remediation

If we look at these new aesthetics, multiple forms of literacy and the fact that sincerity is the new standard against which statements are measured, it is evident that our relationship to culture has changed dramatically. This poses the question of which forms of mediation are desirable. How can we build knowledge on the basis of often scattered and fragmentary competencies, disseminated equally through banal acts of everyday consumption and rare or exceptional practices? Below, we shall examine how we can connect the different forms of literacy in a single educational model that ensures individual empowerment.

3.1 *A New Organizing Principle for Knowledge?*
Since every choice is dependent on the individual preferences of the person making it, the privatization of cultural acts has entailed the loss of a general organizing principle, especially given the almost total lack of discourse on a hierarchy of shared cultural values that is not immediately countered by arguments for cultural diversity. This is particularly true since the contemporary cultural offering asks each producer to offer their own programs and frameworks of reference and reception, without any kind of dialogue other than potential competition for overlapping publics. But these frameworks are not organized in a convergent manner. As a result, cultural programs have multiplied. One can look at, for instance, the model espoused by music schools and the model of self-production that is widespread on the internet. Both models correspond to the logic of different private or public bidders: institutions versus cultural industries, as well as certain industries versus others (see, for example, the long debate contrasting cinema and video games (Aufray and Georges, 2012)). It is therefore outside of any unified cultural institutional program that young people evolve, craft their identifies, develop their likes and dislikes, affiliations and distances, have fun, discover new people and things and ultimately, grow up. The French Senate thus titled a 2008 report *Les nouveaux médias : des jeunes*

libérés ou abandonnés ? [New media: Have young people been liberated or abandoned?] (Assouline, 2008).

Youth eclecticism, accompanied by the fragmentation of standards in terms of cultural, aesthetic and artistic value in micro-communities (which sometimes remain impermeable bubbles), has also led to the heterogenization of cultural combinations. Moreover, it expresses the ideology of individualized cultural repertoires, which takes its concrete form in television and radio shows that encourage audience participation and voting, as well as in social networks, amateur artistry and self-production. In this context, what is shared across generations, or even just within a single generation? It is necessary to look at how different amateur communities that are highly cohesive internally can communicate with each other in order to constitute, at the very least, a shared cultural foundation for a generation — or perhaps a geographical region, or even a nation. "Thanks to all its possibilities, is the internet the form of media that will abolish mediation?" Benjamin Loveluck wonders (Loveluck, 2008: 165). Or, on the contrary, do various forms of amateur micro-expertise offer so many new types of (inter)mediation, allowing for the relative and fluctuating transversality of knowledge?

3.2   *Self-Organization and Remediation*

There are many examples nowadays of self-organized mediation. Since it was launched in London by the artist Ahmet Öğüt, The Silent University has cropped up in Stockholm, Hamburg, Amman, and Athens. Led by displaced persons and refugees, the group brings together almost as many individuals as it does languages, and establishes a chain of translation that allows for the circulation of ideas and knowledge. Founded as a knowledge-exchange platform for migrants, this university allows those who know something and those who want to learn it to connect, independently of academic validation or the institutional recognition of titles and diplomas. The platform offers many courses in spoken and written languages as well as music, dance, and history and civilization. In short, The Silent University is a utopian endeavor that seeks to promote global cultural citizenship.

The example above prompts us to distinguish between mediation and remediation. Mediation refers to what is exchanged within the enclaves of expertise that are amateur communities: amateurs discuss, criticize each other and produce metanarratives. These enclaves of expertise are especially prevalent among young people, as we have already seen, especially since the general education level has risen, as well as the level of technophilia and the amount of time young people can devote to their hobbies and leisure activities (where cultural investment is significant). Remediation, on the other hand is the mediation of mediations: it refers to what must be implemented to create shared, crosscutting lines across these amateur communities or enclaves of expertise. We should not therefore speak of the elimination of mediation, but rather of its transformation. As it has become increasingly fragmented, mediation has come to rely equally on technology and the users of technology. This transformation is evident with regard to the institutional mediation of culture, as it occurs in museums in France for instance (Serain, Vaysse, Chazottes, and Caillet 2016). This remediation incurs a number of very real stakes: while young people massively derive access to culture and information through electronic media, the latter does not allow most children and adolescents to spontaneously develop an understanding of how media works; it may in turn exacerbate existing social inequalities. On this basis, it is possible to outline the three main responsibilities of remediation: 1) To take into account the digital culture of children and adolescents, even if this is largely popular and standardized in nature; 2) to develop a critical understanding various media uses, including production and self-production; 3) to establish reference points in media practices by elaborating technocultural pedagogies but also by transmitting legal norms and information with regard to the risks posed by digital media (Jehel, 2011). Beyond pithy phrases referencing "digital natives," "millennium learners," and "generation Y," what do the institutions in charge of mediating and remediating youth culture know?

∴

Faced with the impasse of relativism and commodification, we are thus well poised to build a new model of cultural education in the broader sense, one which helps to strengthen the social fabric and is also capable of establishing linkages with the emancipatory function of culture for human development. Transliteracy is at stake: namely, connecting all the different forms of literacy. Even though the diverse forms of literacy outlined above all rely on the exercise of critical thinking, they are used differently for educational purposes: traditional literacy informs school-based learning, while media literacy is primarily concerned with teaching young people how to become savvy media consumers who are capable of critically assessing products. Digital literacy seeks specifically to equip young people with the tools they need to participate in digital media in a safe, informed, and ethical fashion. But it is important to remember that the skills mobilized by these different literacies do not exist in separate worlds: in fact, they tend to be complementary and mutually enriching. As they constantly evolve, these skills overlap and combine in new intersections that continue to astonish us with their emotional impact (Jenkins,

2007). They generate forms of mediation that lead to requests for remediation, and which challenge (again) the relationship between educational institutions and young people. We must strive to avoid the pitfalls of excessive navel-gazing (Barrot, 2000) and the siren call of infinite information flows, in order to fully assert the need for a cultural vision of the world and describe the role that it should play.

CHAPTER 6

Technological and Cultural Fault Lines

The norms, figures, operating modes and mythologies that govern representation in the technocultural regime have perpetuated and even fueled a number of significant inequalities with regard to how young people approach culture. These inequalities mean that we must examine the educational, political and ethical dimensions of youth culture and integrate them into the broader social debate.

On the whole, the media depicts young people from all walks of life as experts when it comes to using digital tools, as evidenced by designations such as "digital natives" and the various generational markers (X, Y, C and alpha) that are frequently used without defining any exact limits. But such media narratives gloss over the difference between using and understanding, between engaging in a practice and having mastery over the same. Most importantly, this globalizing image of young people does not account for the diversity of uses, the different intersecting dimensions of inequality (civic, aesthetic, psychological, pedagogical, or related to leisure activities and entertainment) and the policies the latter require: cultural (and educational) policies, in addition to the promotion of e-inclusion.

Consequently, the power of the representations analyzed above concerning youth relationships to technoculture often conceals the existence of deep cultural inequalities provoked by the digital divide. Often referred to as digital natives, young people have largely been depicted by the media as intuitively capable of using and mastering a wide variety of technological devices. While the majority of studies today concur that young people are familiar with an increasingly digital landscape, many scientific publications have also challenged the concept of digital "natives," instead choosing to refer to these individuals as digital "naïfs" (for France see Boubée, 2011; for English-speaking countries, see Daniels, Gregory, and McGillian Cottom, 2017; Ostashewski, Howell, and Cleveland-Innes, 2016). Some young people are in fact not so "native" to technology but remain quite naïve about it. This is partly true because, on the one hand, young people do not have homogenous digital uses and capabilities, and on the other because the digital skills and know-how acquired during leisure time are not always, and not entirely, transferrable to other realms (school, professional life). By taking this into consideration, we can avoid reproducing the age-old quarrel of "ancients" against "moderns" — that is, the old against the young — and instead focus on describing how young people use their technocultural resources as they inhabit the world.

1 Technocultural Fault Lines

The issue of the digital divide has long been addressed in a straightforward fashion devoid of nuance, putting those who have access to the internet on one side of the divide and those who do not on the other. The "technologization" of the issue has often overshadowed its inherently cultural dimension. It is more accurate to speak of digital fault lines, as there are a plurality of divides within young generations that affect inequalities in technological use and access. These fault lines are quite varied, ranging from the technological and socioeconomic (with regard to access conditions) to the psychological and sociological (relating to cultural uses). They intersect, creating a variable geometry of technocultural inequalities with regard to the primary dimensions of use, access, re-investment, and reflexive capacity.

1.1 *The Access Divide*

Inequalities in terms of broadband access and the necessary equipment represent the first technocultural fault line. Studies have shown that young people are better equipped than their elders, and that the presence of a child in a household correlates with the purchase of a computer and internet access. Children and young people today are moreover becoming increasingly well equipped with digital devices.

Only a little more than half of the world's population has access to the internet (with penetration rates ranging from more than 80% in Europe and more than 70% in the United States and Canada to 34% in Africa); the same proportion of people belong to social networks. Even if 15 to 24-year-olds are the most technologically plugged-in cohort (for example, 96% of them are connected in Europe), worldwide, 29% of them do not have access to the internet. According to UNICEF, important inequalities persist, given that more than 60% of young people in Africa do not have access.

In France, inequalities also begin with equipment (Bigot, Croutte, and Daudey, 2013; Brice, Croutte, Jauneau-Cottet, and Lautié, 2015). Despite increases in the size of smartphone screens, tablets are still massively present in French households with children; equipment rates have only risen, from 22% in 2013 to 46% in 2014, 62% in 2015 and approximately 70% in 2016. Most the time, tablets belong to the parents, but about one-sixth of children ages 1 to 6 and one-third of those 7 to 12 and 13 to 19 have their own devices. 13 to 19-year-olds are especially well equipped compared to their younger peers with regard to smartphones (68% compared to 12%), televisions (41% compared to 17%) and computers (73% compared to 20%). As a result, they are increasingly present on social networks as well: Facebook (78% of teenagers are on it), Twitter

(25%) and Instagram (14%), even if the percentage of young people on Facebook has continually dropped since 2013 (85% down to 79% and then 78%), whereas rates of account creation on Twitter and Instagram have gone up (8%, 22%, and 25% for Twitter; 7% and 14% for Instagram). Forty-six per cent of young people in France regularly check Facebook Messenger, 26% use Skype, 23% Snapchat and 6% WhatsApp. As the hyperconnectivity of young people increases — as observed by the majority of studies on the subject — individuals who are poorly connected or not connected at all are prone to exclusion. Given that high-speed broadband coverage is not universal (and is necessary to stream video in optimal conditions, among other things), certain geographically stratified segments of the population cannot develop the same practices and relationships to technology. When speaking of access to culture, the digital divide is therefore a complex problem with multiple dimensions.

Differences in access are the most commonly discussed facet of the digital divide, leading in many countries to the implementation of public policies with a view to ensuring that all citizens can enjoy a high-quality internet connection, and that access to the internet (and thus cultural contents), as well as necessary equipment, remains affordable. *The* Alliance for Affordable Internet's stated goal of reducing the cost of internet access everywhere is thus a commendable one. The inventor of the World Wide Web, Tim Berners-Lee, has carried this message far and wide with his World Wide Web Foundation, which collaborates with some 30-odd corporations (including Google, Alcatel-Lucent, Cisco, Ericsson, Facebook, Intel, Yahoo and Microsoft), as well as institutions, public foundations, associations and governmental agencies. This alliance supports several objectives, including the adoption of best practices designed to reduce the cost of internet access at the international level and an annual publication on the subject of the cost of internet access throughout the world as well as the official positions on access costs held by various States.

1.2   *The Usage Divide*

As has been widely observed, digital uses are subject to an important generational divide. According to a 2016 report by the *Centre de recherche pour l'étude et l'observation des conditions de vie* [Center for Research on the Study and Observation of Living Conditions, CREDOC[1]] in France, 84% of young people ages 18 to 24 use digital technologies while on the go, thanks in particular to smartphones (compared to 52% of those aged 40 to 59). Young people also massively download and stream music (83% of them, compared to 36% for the older

---

1   https://www.credoc.fr.

cohort) and also use applications (80% of young people, compared to 30% of those aged 40–59). Many members of the younger generations likewise have social media profiles on one or more platforms (88% versus 40%), and they are more likely to contribute content in various media (36% versus 22%). Overall, young people spend twice as much time online: 27 hours per week, compared to the 13 hours spent by those aged 40–59. Early exposure to the internet can create generational differences in how individuals use it, including their dexterity and problem-solving ability, and levels of intuitive understanding developed through trial and error, etc. However, these differences will fade over time as digital natives grow older (Croutte, Lautié, and Hoibian, 2016).

This generational cleavage should nonetheless not completely overshadow an intra-generational one that is perhaps even more striking in its inequities. According to the ECDL Foundation,[2] the world's leading authority in computer skills certification, a non-negligible percentage of young children and students exhibit only rudimentary competencies with regard to information and communications technologies. An even larger percentage display a lack of critical thinking with regard to online search tools and the cultural content they consume. And yet, in a service- and knowledge-based economy, the lack of these skills mean that many individuals are at risk of being "left behind," unable to derive any benefit from their use of ICTs as students and citizens, employees and entrepreneurs.

In fact, many of the "skills" that are highlighted when describing young people as a digital generation are first and foremost *lifestyle* behaviors: for example, sending texts, playing video games, posting clips online. While most young people know how to bookmark web pages they want to remember, only about one-fifth of them know how to select different fonts in a word processor application; even fewer of them feel comfortable identifying false content online, as evidenced by the proliferation of fake news, alterative facts and the rest. Marc Prensky, the inventor of the "digital natives" concept, has written that the concept originally implied a kind of technological wisdom and the ability to critically assess the tools being used — an ability that has nonetheless not always been present in young people today (Prensky, 2001).

This second digital divide does not separate those who have access to the internet from those who do not: it marks the difference between the entertainment realm (lifestyle interests) and a broader realm of reflexive, critical, and creative engagement with cultural contents and uses. In other words, there is a deep, intra-generational cleavage in the digital world with regard to how tools and resources are appropriated. This appropriation itself depends on the variable aptitudes of young people, as well as the contexts and situations they

---

2   http://www.ecdl.com/.

encounter. This is especially crucial given that most digital uses occur in the intimate seclusion of "bedroom culture" as described by Sonia Livingstone in the United Kingdom (Livingstone, 2007) and by Hervé Glévarec in France (Glévarec, 2009); most uses are never subject to corrective actions, institutionally speaking or otherwise. Young people are confronted with strong social requirements that are often unspoken and sometimes contradictory. Their varying abilities to meet these requirements thus determines their future in subtle ways that can nonetheless be highly decisive.

1.3   *The Transferability Divide*

The third technocultural divide concerns the re-investment of digital skills, transferring them from the realm of hobbies and entertainment to other spheres. Most young people use the internet in their leisure time; many fewer of them use it in other aspects of their lives. While many young people know how to download an episode of their favorite show, they do not necessarily know how to efficiently and effectively search for information online. Some young people are incapable of filling out a web-based registration form, despite spending more than 10 hours a day listening to music or talking to their friends online. In other words, individuals can only transition from an everyday "leisure" use of digital technologies (for play, entertainment or otherwise elective activities) to the more complex demands of social life when they can make sense of the vast amounts of information that swirl around them, when they can decipher the conflicting hierarchies presented online. As a result, lack of access or cultural variations in use are no longer the sole sources of inequality. Social conditions can also influence the transferability of skills from one sphere to another. Certain young people are faced with situations that do not allow them to transfer the skills they acquire during their leisure activities to other domains, on account of the unequal development and distribution of social capabilities across different backgrounds.

Until the end of the 2000s, public policy primarily focused on the relationship of young people to the internet from the perspective of the risks to mitigate: data privacy, web security and how to incorporate digital training into school curricula (Brotcorne, Mertens, and Valenduc, 2009). As a result, this third cleavage took longer to be identified, with important prospective studies such as *France numérique 2012* [Digital France 2012] (published in 2008, and followed by its successor *France numérique 2012–2020 Bilan et perspectives,* published in 2011) and *La société et l'économie à l'aune de la révolution numérique,* published in 2009 [Society and the Economy in Light of the Digital Revolution] neglecting to address digital inclusion for young people having recently graduated or looking for their first job.

In France, actors in both formal and informal education settings use digital tools to fight against illiteracy and increasing school dropout rates. They tend to emphasize certain uses over others, given that studies have shown that skills are more likely to be added than subtracted: digital skills often supplement pre-existing competencies in terms of literacy and numeracy. In this fashion, educators work to avoid the "double penalty" suffered by young people facing difficulties: exclusion from the traditional objectives of schooling (reading, writing, and arithmetic), as well as digital exclusion. As even recruitment turns virtual — with one out of every three jobs posted being only accessible online (AFUTT-ANSA, 2011) — digital technologies are increasingly employed to help re-insert young people who have left school or the workforce. However, even though young people are much more familiar than their elders with the digital environment and are more likely to use ICTs in their spare time, the stakes of digital inclusion are exponentially vaster for young people. In France, more than 1.9 million young people between 15 and 29 years old are not in school, are not receiving any form of training, and are not employed, thus accounting for about 17% of the age cohort (*Conseil d'analyse économique*, 2013); 900,000 of them are not even in the process of looking for a job. Among these individuals (often designated as NEETs: "not in education, employment or training"), 85% did not continue their studies after high school; 42% did not get further than middle school. Moreover, 23% of young people are unemployed, compared to 10% for the active population as a whole. This is a problem further entrenched by social reproduction, given that 48% of school dropouts are the children of blue-collar workers (only 5% are the children of white-collar executives). The social stakes of technocultural inclusion are thus massive for young people, and depend on their ability to transfer the digital skills they learn (at least partially) during their leisure to time to other dimensions of their lives, school and work primarily.

1.4 *The Reflexive Capacity Divide*

Access and use are also accompanied by reflexive capacities which help to develop youth identities. In many ways, watching a TV show on the internet today is similar to reading a novel in the past, given that both experiences call on individuals to step outside of themselves and their immediate experiences to develop a kind of individual meaning that will help them to grow, including through strong and sometimes addictive emotional reactions (Cordier, 2015). The TV show enthusiasts interviewed by Hervé Glévarec (Glévarec, 2012), like the manga fans interviewed by Christine Détrez and Olivier Vanhée (Détrez and Vanhée, 2012), can clearly explain their passion and the effect that it has had on their lives.

These inequalities are thus more cognitive or psychological in nature, even if they are based on significant social constraints. They can impact the following:
- The ability to consume information and culture across a variety of modes. Cognitive psychology has long demonstrated that our brain can only process multimodal information in limited quantities (Citton, 2010 and 2017). The dynamics of hypertextuality, which is by essence multimodal, thus requires a certain level of adaptation, which has its limits. Certain multimodal contents will in fact be less well read, understood or assimilated on account of their multimodal nature. For example, our visual acuity is at its best in the foveal region of our retina; moreover, scanning eye movements — which occur on average every 40 seconds — alternate with pauses, which last 250 microseconds. As we become more comfortable with reading, we increase our skill at deciphering complex information (for instance, annotations on a music score). But the quantity of information that we can perceive visually (our realm of perception) cannot expand; in fact, different aspects of textual presentation (the degree of brightness, the addition of images or musical content) can negatively impact the quality of our reading. Studies have shown, for instance, that backlighting — a standard practice across digital devices — causes a significant degree of eye strain. Similarly, scrolling is detrimental to spatial encoding, which allows us to locate information that we already consumed at any given moment. Finally, hypertext links create an overwhelming landscape of reading possibilities, which can lead to cognitive overload and lead users to stray from their original goal.
Managing multimodality is a challenge in itself, one that presents a number of inequalities. Christopher Wickens' attentional model thus indicates that in order for multimodality to be beneficial, all the different modes must ultimately share the same purpose, so that the brain can elaborate a coherent mental representation (Moreno and Mayer, 2000). This is especially true since individuals possess specialized information-processing resources for different activities. But individuals elaborate their mental representations in highly different fashions, especially depending on their cultural capital and social background.
- Confidence. The process of validating cultural and informational contents now falls to users, in a context where overabundance poses a serious threat to the ability to establish universal standards with regard to quality. Amidst all these flows, how can we know what is "good" and what is less good? As a result, young people often develop an emotional relationship to cultural contents, without nonetheless verifying the reliability of the latter. The fact that something is available on the internet is good enough for them, an argument that is bolstered by the various pages they automatically consult

such as Wikipedia, Google and the sites of pure play companies.[3] Young people primarily obtain information through social media platforms, where genuine information (albeit often from specialized sites) may exist side-by-side with hoaxes and commentary that combines bare-bones analysis with visceral emotional reactions.

As a result, the digital world often seems like a form of counterculture for young people, picking up where television left off (Stora, 2012). The internet creates a sort of "masquerade," where identities are labile, reversible and interchangeable, fake but real within the context of the online world. It would therefore behoove us to revisit the criticisms levelled against social media. While it may be true that some young people do not realize that the information they post online about themselves is available to people outside of their close circles, we should not underestimate the number of young people who exploit the possibilities of playing with their identity. For some, this is a way of finding a space where they can act freely, a possibility which has been greatly reduced for many young people as public concerns for safety (e.g., "stranger danger") have increasingly confined children to their bedrooms and curtailed their access to public spaces (boyd, 2014).

In Europe, the focus is primarily on "protecting" young people, no doubt underestimating the degree of manipulation tinkering and dabbling that many of them engage in, and which makes monitoring them almost impossible. And yet, "fake" culture is one of the very things that attracts young people to social networks; much like Oscar Wilde once wrote, "a mask tells us more than a face" (Wilde, 1891). This culture is hard to understand and even harder to master, however: some young people have a clear-headed relationship to images, and develop the necessary distance to appropriate them; others lack this ability and are thus more easily manipulated. In reality, conspiracy theories thrive online and within certain youth circles, given the insufficient tools many have to consume information and the fact that the criteria determining trust sometimes conflict with the criteria governing information quality (Bronner, 2013). In other words, it is easier for some to trust the validity of the conspiracy theory voiced by their best friend than it is to believe an explanation provided by a specialized newspaper (Cicchelli and Octobre, 2018b). In fact, our convictions are highly resistant to facts. During the 2016 American presidential election, researchers asked American citizens of all political leanings to determine whether various statements made by then-presidential candidate

---

3   Pure play retailers are those that focus exclusively on a specific product or activity; by extension, the term can also refer to companies that operate solely online without a brick-and-mortar component.

Donald Trump were true or false. Logically enough, Trump supporters determined that his statements were true more often than Trump opponents did. More interestingly, however, when Trump supporters were shown how certain statements were patently false, they easily adapted their beliefs, recognizing that Trump had lied (regardless of the source of the correction and whether it was pro- or anti-Trump), without this having any impact whatsoever on their voting intentions (Swire, Berinsky, Lewandowsky, and Ecker, 2017).

– Belief and desire. Linked to the issue of trustworthiness, the question of noise amidst the plethora of available sources of information is also an important one. Recent political and electoral events in both France and the United States have reminded us that information and noise are two different things. Noise is in fact a kind of misinformation: hoaxes, rumors and bad faith arguments dotted campaigns on both sides of the Atlantic, with a very real effect on voting (or at least, accounts of voting). The overabundance of information and media signals likewise heralds the advent of the reign of rumors, analyzed by Gabriel Tarde in his *Lois de l'imitation* [The Laws of Imitation] originally published in 1890, well before the birth of the media society, let alone the internet. Gabriel Tarde originally proposed two concepts to explain social behavior: imitation and invention. Everyone imitates what they admire, what they believe is good and can serve as a role model, but crafts in a unique way a series of imitations selected from a variety of sources. History thus presents itself as a succession of different imitation flows, a series of models that are likely to prompt imitation by a large number of people. At the heart of life in society, then, is a hall of mirrors. Underpinning the processes of imitation and invention, Gabriel Tarde identifies "desire and belief: they are the substance and the force, they are the two psychological quantities which are found at the bottom of all the sensational qualities with which they combine; and when invention and then imitation takes possession of them in order to organize and use them, they also are the real social quantities" (1903 [1890]: 145–46). For Gabriel Tarde, "belief" refers to the trustworthiness that an individual grants a set of representations, or the person conveying them, or even a value system as a whole. Belief allows for imitation; and desire, by reinvesting different beliefs, allows for invention. A perpetual cycle ensues, with belief feeding into desire and desire feeding into belief. This twofold flow can create public opinion but can also manipulate it. This is still true today, given that contemporary youth is just as influenced by belief and desire as its 19th-century counterpart.

– Pleasure and emotions. The concept of pleasure is behind the existence of leisure activities and likewise governs much of youth identity, especially with regard to play. But there are different forms of pleasure: short-term gratification which is inherently bulimic in nature and even addictive at times, and long-term enjoyment which helps to develop both taste preferences and personality. These two forms of pleasure are more complementary than they are conflicting: instant gratification must exist for longer-term taste preferences to be developed, while emotional involvement favors informational research (Meyers, Fisher, and Marcoux, 2009). But the individual capacity for such development presupposes a number of specific skills (in particular, resistance in the face of thwarted desires and the suspension of judgment), as well as a stimulating environment with diverse cultural contents on offer — prerequisites that are, once again, unevenly distributed among young people. The challenge is therefore allowing young people to transcend their short-term perception of the internet as a mere platform for hobbies and discussions with friends, to instead fully embrace it as a means to further their education and knowledge, in a context where temporal acceleration and the illusion of instantaneity are primordial.

– The key role of the individual actor. Both the emancipatory rhetoric surrounding the birth of the internet and the figure of the professional amateur that emerged shortly thereafter were focused on the role of individual actors who were masters of their own destiny. A UNESCO report explained it thusly: "a specific Web culture is built up by a process of distribution in which all the actors have a role to play, if only through the choices and sifting they make between all the available sources of information, thus contributing to a continuous creative circulation of information and knowledge, of which no one person or institution is the originating source" (UNESCO, 2005: 53). There is a lot at stake therefore in terms of young people and their relationship to culture: the high expectations of academic and political institutions, the possibility of self-empowerment through cultural and media practices, the individualization of one's relationship to information and knowledge, the crisis of mediation ... Institutional discourse holds the individual responsible for overcoming all of these challenges. Three observations can be made here. First of all, cultural technologies favor individual inductive reasoning skills, multitasking and visual information processing. They promote doing rather than learning (or learning while doing) and instant gratification. However, the skills developed by cultural technologies do not add up to mastery of a given context or task, instead leading to a lack of respect for intellectual property and increasing confidence in popular opinion rather than in traditional authority figures (CIBER Group, 2008). Second, individuals online are first and foremost individuals that exist offline; as a result, they arrive with unequal baggage, experience and knowledge (or lack thereof) as developed in the wider social sphere. Finally, the competencies that

are prized in the digital sphere have implicitly become hegemonic. Information skills play a central role in the information society; education is no longer limited to schools in that regard, and initiative is valued as a skill in of itself. The set-up required to master vast digital environments is increasingly linked to the private sphere and individual resources (Aillerie, 2012). These resources are unevenly distributed and particularly difficult to compensate for, particularly because they are presented as private in nature. The rhetoric of the individual actor is thus used to gloss over structural inequalities.
- Mastery over the visibility of one's identity. Self-expression is characteristic of young people, especially adolescents (it is a facet of subjectivation), but it is important to distinguish what belongs to an individual in an embodied and durable way (age, gender) from what is ascribed to one's persona (from the Latin for "mask") and the representation of one's actions. In this second register, individuals can "pretend" — that is, play with the opposition between everyday, real characteristics and those that belong to a virtual representation of the self (an avatar or pseudonym, for instance). Christophe Aguiton and Dominique Cardon thus identify several different uses of digital identities by young people, which range from "masks" of concealment to exhibitionism, but whose most common configuration remains somewhere in between; namely, a partial unveiling of one's intimate life for an inner circle, but without a clear understanding of how such disclosure may travel outwards (Aguiton and Cardon, 2012). For young people, the question of visibility is very important: both recognition and safety are at stake. But young people have varying degrees of awareness when it comes to possible consequences, in particular when it is a question of discerning truth or verisimilitude.
- An understanding of technological and physical constraints, or what danah boyd calls "affordances" (2014).[4] Each technology and each venue (a theater, for example) has a set of unique constraints imbedded within its design and which dictate how it will be received and/or used. Individuals must therefore understand these design constraints to exploit what serves their own objectives best. Anyone who does not know that the audience should be silent while watching a piece at the theater will fail to properly receive the piece and feel excluded from the space, just as any individual too naïve to realize that social media is a game of masks and that professional websites are

---

4 According to danah boyd, the concept of "affordances," which was previously used by Donald Norman to describe human/machine interactions, should also take into account the role of users. It can also be applied to other kinds of interactions, for instance features pertaining to physical reception.

specifically crafted to give ideal self-presentation will experience the pain of rejection and failure.

In all of these dimensions, the presence — or absence — of reflexivity is key. Young people can have consumption practices that are creative and still remain quite gullible when it comes to the fate of their creations or the impact of their consumption. They can produce videos and post them online without understanding how to (re)present themselves, elaborate a discourse or alter their perception by others. Much like cultural products have progressively become part of transmedia storytelling, individuals, whether they like it or not, leave behind traces of their trajectories through the transmedia landscape.

Transmedia reflexivity can lead to openness: how many young people who were not previously voracious readers devoured *Harry Potter, The Hunger Games* and *The Maze Runner* sagas after watching the eponymous movies? Similarly, the lengthy discussions of "booktubers" encourage many to pick up a book. How many young people have discovered new music on YouTube just by seeing an image? Different forms of media can in fact attract new publics. The predominance of image and speech in contemporary hyper-communication society has dethroned the written word and returned us to an earlier orality, but according to different modalities that can lead to cleavages, given that knowledge still remains tied to the written word and the spoken word is more often associated with conversation. Should we view the beauty tutorials posted by EnjoyPhoenix[5] as existing primarily in the realm of conversation, given that the focus is on providing (verbal) explanations? Similarly, Snapchat operates according to a visual format, but those images are in turn commented and discussed by users. Transmedia reflexivity is therefore not just possible but frequent. But can it be taught?

2   A Universe Where Important Inequalities Persist

For a certain percentage of the young population, then, access to knowledge and leisure activities operates through a variety of platforms and cultural modalities, including heavy use of screens at home. Some of them keep an eye on "the Gutenberg Galaxy," whereas others dive headfirst into the digital world. Still others find themselves excluded from certain cultural spheres (social networks, cultural consumption practices, etc.). All of these factors lead to

---

5   https://www.youtube.com/user/EnjoyPhoenix.

cultural inequalities that are often hidden behind the issue of access to digital technologies.

2.1 An Argument against "the tribalization of youth culture"

While the digital universe has opened its doors to many different populations, it is not the great equalizer that many hoped for. In 2010, US Secretary of State Hillary Clinton gave a speech at the Newseum and proclaimed the following: "the internet can serve as a great equalizer. By providing people with access to knowledge and potential markets, networks can create opportunities where none exist ... Information networks have become a great leveler, and we should use them together to help lift people out of poverty."[6] In his work *From Counterculture to Cyberculture. Steward Brand, the Whole Earth network, and the Rise of Digital Utopianism* (2006), Fred Turner established a filial relationship between the hippie counterculture that developed in the 1960s in America and the rise of new technologies, in Silicon Valley specifically. The concept of a digital utopia — taking the guise of an ideology and a cyber culture that believes in making the world a better place through networks and technology — brings together three different elements: the hippie counterculture, the military-industrial complex (which has long been embedded in the region) and American puritanism, with "the elect" of Puritan doctrine becoming today's entrepreneurs. Revisiting the history of the internet through the figure of network pioneer Stewart Brand, Fred Turner highlights the internet's multiple political affiliations. It has been successively associated with the New Left, engaged in the fight for civil rights, the New Communalists, who turned inwards to build a new society, and the New Right, which disseminated its libertarian ideas with the publication *Wired*. In all these cases, the internet is praised for its ability to promote collaboration and to create new, alternative communities focused on individual freedom, according to a certain universalist rhetoric. The utopian promise of the internet is that of individual empowerment: everyone can freely express themselves and be creative, against a backdrop of unbridled innovation and fully embraced diversity. Adam Smith has been replaced with the invisible hand of hi-tech. The advent of the Arab Spring initially seemed to confirm all these utopian promises — until even optimists were forced to admit that technology has not rid us of tyranny and has even helped some dictators consolidate their power.

In reality, observing how technologies are appropriated differently by various youth sub-populations illustrates just how long-lived this belief is. For

---

6   https://2009–2017.state.gov/secretary/20092013clinton/rm/2010/01/135519.htm.

example, MySpace was a social network targeted at young people that was vastly more popular — and more diverse, from an ethnic and racial perspective — than Facebook, which ultimately dethroned it, while Snapchat, Instagram and their ilk swooped in to create new market segments for which they recruited increasingly younger customers.

It would thus be a mistake to think of youth cultural practices, uses, and leisure activities as homogenous in nature, just because they are all part of the technocultural landscape. Some behaviors are indeed shared across the board: for the most part, young people go out with their friends, to movie theaters, nightclubs and sporting events. Listening to music on an MP3 player, a cellphone or online is also a common practice, as is attending concerts, both of which help to create differentiated identities for teenagers as they develop affinities for rap, metal, rock, R&B or other musical subgenres. Watching TV shows in one's bedroom or while in transit and joining micro-communities that pop up around a show or a genre is also a staple of adolescent behavior today. Young people massively use social networks and more broadly speaking, have more intense cultural practices and leisure activities than the rest of population. They moreover tend to be more attracted to novelty, whether this takes the form of new technologies or new aesthetic subgenres.

Thanks to general increases in education levels and an explosion in the cultural offering worldwide, many cultural practices, uses and consumption patterns have become widespread over the course of the last twenty years, with the result that certain leisure activities are indeed enjoyed by all young people today, without important variations observed depending on gender or socioeconomic background. Nevertheless, if we look more closely, important inequalities still remain with regard to access, for both young people in particular and the rest of the population more broadly. The inequalities that young people from different social backgrounds face when trying to engage in technocultural leisure activities stem both from material elements (income, geographic location) and more intangible ones (education level, reading and writing skills, family environment). The social homogeneity initially promised by the internet was therefore an illusion: the "tribalization of youth culture" prophesized by some has not come to pass.

2.2   *Factoring in Gender*

With co-education having become vastly more common, the question of gendered differences has long been overlooked when examining leisure activities, which are ostensibly freely chosen according to natural individual preferences which may mask inequalities (Détrez, 2015). And yet, public, commercial and cultural professionals all know that men and women (and the boys and girls that they start out as) do not like the same things and do not make the same choices with regard to cultural products. In fact, a lot of work goes into establishing gender differences in this regard. Market segments are consciously created for gendered preferences, while public offerings generally fail to take this dimension into account and end up creating contents that are gendered by default (Octobre 2014b; Octobre and Patureau, 2018 and 2020). Far from eliminating gender boundaries, the technocultural revolution has in fact (re)produced existing differences. Girls are still overrepresented in traditional cultural practices and structured leisure activities (dance classes, music lessons, museum and library visits). Not only are girls seen as "spontaneously" developing a liking for legitimate cultural practices and the values they convey (a certain cultural, aesthetic, and at times even social conservatism), these practices and values neatly line up with institutional and academic expectations (discipline, diligence, dedication). In reality, of course, these are not inherently "feminine" traits, but rather the result of social constraints and gender stereotypes.

Gender expectations and stereotypes play a role at various different levels. The first level is the social classification of practices (consumption patterns, usages, behaviors) as male or female, depending on whether more men and boys like an activity or more women and girls do. Secondly, practices are subject to certain inherent gendered stereotypes. Activities and behaviors related to relationships, care, aesthetics, discipline, softness, and grace are seen as areas where women excel, while competition, inventiveness, originality, and resourcefulness (but also lack of discipline) are seen as primarily being the purview of men. The latter skills, of course, embody more closely to the spirit of technoculture. At the third level, we have the modalities by which cultural contents are used or consumed, in particular with regard to the balance between the individual/collective (things that individuals do behind the scenes for themselves, compared to the things that they share using various communication channels). The fourth level is the categorization of behavioral and verbal interactions, be they in person or at a distance. Certain topics are more likely to come up in female conversations than they are in male conversations, and vice versa; this is true both within a given generation and across generations.

The educational aspect of many childhood leisure activities means that mothers pay particularly close attention to them (and often provide support), which prompts girls to identify with their mothers and thus reinforces the "feminine" dimensions of these practices. Among siblings, when boys and girls alike are engaged in a "serious" leisure activity, the girls are often more patient and diligent than their brothers and receive encouragement to this end. These four registers, all of which are strongly influenced by gender expectations, frequently intersect. Consequently, if girls read more than boys (Clark and Foster, 2005; Octobre 2011 and 2014b), this is because cultural transmission (regardless of the medium) is largely conducted by women and is more likely to target girls directly, both in terms of the time devoted to a given activity with a given child (depending on gender) and the interest expressed for it (Guthrie and Anderson, 1999). For all its novelty, the digital era has not changed much in this regard.

The personalization of technocultural uses makes it seem like our activities are freely chosen, despite the fact that they are largely governed by social constraints (imposed by our families, our peer groups, or our socio-economic class); as a result, it has also obscured the resurgence of gender-imposing mechanisms, which are especially prevalent in the commercial sector. Some technocultural niches have witnessed a kind of silent revolution, however: the entry of young women in world of video games is a good example. Technoculture thus has a twofold impact: on the one hand, it has "technologized" the relationship that women and girls have to culture (an aspect which was highly gendered for previous generations). On the other hand, it has given men and boys a way to access intimate "bedroom culture," which had hitherto been the purview of women (Buckingham and Sefton-Green, 1994; McRobbie, 1990), owing to the traditional opposition between inside (feminine/protected) and outside (masculine/adventurous). The "digital bedroom"[7] described by Buckingham and Sefton-Green allows boys to develop skills and interests in what was long deemed "girl's bedroom culture," embodied by the traditional female use of the telephone. In fact, the internet gives boys and young men access to conversational modalities that are sometimes entirely lacking in other aspects of their lives, just as blogs may reintroduce them to writing (Kredens and Fontar, 2010). Online games, where game play is interspersed with exchanges between players, also supports real — and not just virtual — interpersonal development and digital socialization among boys, given that what is said is less important, in the grand scheme of things, than the fact that communication is occurring (Martin, 2004). Similarly, some have suggested that digital technologies have "brought boys back" to reading (Mazin, 2017), albeit a different kind of reading that may be more serial and/or cursory. But if this supposed return to reading exists among boys, it remains a minority phenomenon and does not last as long as it does for girls.

---

7   We are using the concepts of the digital bedroom and girls' bedroom culture developed by Buckingham and Sefton-Green, as well as McRobbie.

2.3 Cumulative Inequalities?

Technoculture does not, therefore, exist outside the realm of social constraints, as previously shown in the case of gender inequalities. In reality, the digital era has merely reproduced existing constraints within the four walls of "bedroom culture". We can therefore observe a twofold cumulative effect, where symbolic boundaries between social groups are redefined (Lamont and Molnar, 2002). As Michèle Lamont, Mark A. Pendergrass and Sabrina Pachucki explain, "'symbolic boundaries' are the lines that include and define some people, groups, and things while excluding others. These distinctions can be expressed through normative interdictions (taboos), cultural attitudes and practices, and patterns of likes and dislikes" (Lamont, Pendergrass, and Pachucki, 2015: 850).

The growing heterogeneity of social groups in the contemporary world is thus echoed by the increasing significance of aesthetic classifications, used as markers of boundaries to distinguish different social groups (DiMaggio, 1987). The middle classes and younger generations, which are particularly drawn to the aestheticization of everyday life (Featherstone, 1987) are the main drivers of this shift in the global context, much as they instigated the trend of omnivorism (Peterson and Kern, 1996). Urban youth have developed a taste for innovation and novelty as a way to distinguish themselves, sometimes leading to the emergence of new forms of cultural capital and distinction, especially among their peer groups (Katz-Gerro, 2017).

The first divide takes place between pre-digital inequalities and digital ones: the existing research overwhelmingly shows that the mechanisms which produce inequalities with regard to cultural practices (including reading, hobbies, and attending events) are the same ones that determine digital inequalities. Young people from families with the most cultural capital (in particular, those with the most educated mothers) have a significant comparative advantage when it comes to developing reflexivity, a skill whose importance was discussed above.

The second divide takes place within systems of exclusion themselves, as illustrated by the following French examples. An anthropological study conducted by Emmaüs Connect (Davenel, 2014) on young people dealing with social, professional or educational exclusion highlights the difficulties these individuals face in terms of digital access and use, which in turn significantly hinders their chances of reinsertion in the professional or academic spheres. Even if they belong to the generation born between the beginning of the 1980s and the beginning of the 2000s — which is assumed to have increased familiarity with digital tools on the whole — these young people have less access to a computer or a smartphone than their peers and, more significantly, are less equipped to use these devices correctly. This study emphasizes the fact that young people aged 18 to 24 years old and facing difficulties entering the socio-professional world or at the risk of dropping out of school also encounter obstacles when dealing with digital technologies. These young people first suffer from inequality when it comes to equipment: 82% of the young people interviewed by local youth support organizations (*missions locales*) reported having a computer at home, whether individual or shared, and 59% reported having a smartphone — this compared to 99% of those aged 12 to 17 years old and 94% of those aged 18 to 24 on average. More importantly, however, the study also highlights the differences in terms of digital device usage between these young outliers and the rest of their cohort: 73% of young people who interact with local support organizations connect to the internet at least once a day, compared to 91% of all 18 to 24-year-olds. Similarly, they are less likely to have an email address (or to check it regularly, which can have a negative impact on their job searches) and less skilled at performing Google searches.

Not all young people are thus "natives" when it comes to technoculture, if what we understand by this term is a certain degree of ease in all three of registers identified above. It is crucial to avoid reifying younger generations as a homogenous social group when it comes to digital and cultural practices. While lack of access does explain certain cases where young people do not use digital technologies, there are also other situations, where individuals have access they chose not to exploit, or where they are unable to transfer their existing skills to any digital uses. Finally, some young people engage in a reflexive non-use of digital technologies. It would be logical to assume that in countries with the most widespread access to the internet, the rate of digital usage among young people would be the highest. And yet, Malaysia is ranked fourth in the world (ahead of the USA, in sixth place), illustrating that this middle-income country's initiatives to promote the internet among young people have borne fruit. Once again, this proves that technoculture is not inherent to young people, that a certain level of material access is necessary but not always sufficient to give rise to durable practices — and that implementing cultural policies around digital education is more important than ever before.

In other words, the use of the word "native" may be overly facile and ultimately counterproductive if we seek to understand inequalities with regard to how young people apprehend culture, the vast majority of which is transmitted (if not produced) using digital technologies.

This observation logically leads us to challenge some of the highly prolific rhetoric on youth culture. Why continue to designate young people as "digital natives" if all indicators point to the absence of a single youth culture? We can envision several different explanations (which are not mutually exclusive). At the top of the list is marketing. To create and durably target markets, the concept of youth culture, based on a certain fascination with young people mentioned at the beginning of this volume, is used to identify products, consumption modes, and even consumption sites. The second explanation is political: youth policies likewise need a way to designate their targets, including to create hybrids. The cultural policies targeting disadvantaged youth in France are thus combined with the urban policies targeting the banlieues and semi-urban periphery. As a result, a paradoxical use of the expression "youth culture" comes to designate the intersection of public policies with dissimulated intentions — cultural policies ostensibly implemented to ensure the peace in "difficult" neighborhoods. The third explanation is social: the ability to refer to youth cultures with a single term thus allows for the reduction of their power as forms of counterculture. The apparent homogeneity conferred to youth culture conceals its internal conflict and, as a result, mitigates its subversive vitality. Similarly, it masks the need for strong, diverse and targeted public policies with regard to education. The fourth explanation is more strictly cultural in nature; it concerns the gradual recognition of cultural forms formerly viewed as "popular" — in the twofold sense of being widely disseminated and ultimately low-brow — and whose popularity has now permeated to all segments of the population, thus significantly redefining cultural legitimacy (and lack of legitimacy) among young people (Coulangeon and Duval, 2013), as well as the associated policies of recognition.

∴

The social utopia promised by technology is not a new hope: Charles Briggs and Samuel Augustus Maverick imagined that the telegraph was going to link all the nations of the Earth together, while, in his novels, Jules Verne proposed a vision of the world that was condensed thanks to travel in the air or underwater. Each time a new means of communication and exchange appears, the promise of utopia is renewed, as we hope that this new technology will alleviate existing cultural and social inequalities — not realizing that technology does not inherently possess this power, independently of those who use it and the social constraints by which they are bound. Alas, no technology can solve all of society's problems. The cultural inequalities of technologically advanced cultures are thus numerous but often concealed behind a homogenizing social discourse on the one hand, and by individualistic representations of digital autonomy on the other. Even if, in reality, only a minority of young people aged 16 to 25 are cut off from digital tools and the traditional sites of physical culture — the percentage of "excluded" youths is estimated to be about 10% in France (Octobre, 2014a) — these individuals are subject to radical forms of exclusion. And for some young people who do have a digital life, it remains very difficult from them to go beyond what is "their" digital universe (the internet, instant messaging, downloading or listening to music online, watching videos, going to nightclubs or the movies) and translate the cultural skills that society expects of them into useful behavior as employees, entrepreneurs and most importantly perhaps, as citizens. The role of educational policies and mediation thus remains essential if we want to offer forms of support, in public spaces or the media, that allow young people to grow and develop, including as auto-didacts, and to transform diverse and widespread individual digital experiences into the much rarer phenomenon of digital mastery.

CHAPTER 7

The Political and Ethical Implications of Youth Technoculture

There are also political implications to the rise of the technocultural era, given the twofold movement encompassing the culturalization of technology and the technologization of our relationship to culture, as well as the norms and mythologies this movement engenders and which help to reconfigure cultural citizenship more broadly. Not least among the implications of the technocultural regime is the fact that it has convinced many that cultural participation and consumption are inherently apolitical, even though cultural activities are by nature political and have become progressively more so as traditional forms of participation have collapsed and technocultural industries have produced new modalities of civic validation. The new forms of culture that have emerged thanks to the advent of digital technology are inherently flexible, as required by capitalist ideology, and embody the libertarian and liberal values at the heart of democracy (Cardon, 2010a). The Internet is seen by some as a realm of freedom, offering the possibility for a kind of direct and perhaps even radical democracy (Loveluck, 2008), while others view it as a form of counter-democracy (Rosanvallon, 2006).

Digital citizenship draws on civic-mindedness in the traditional sense of the word, while also emphasizing the importance of understanding and skillfully exploiting digital media with a view to actively participating in modern society. As media messaging has come to dominate political debate and platforms like Facebook and Twitter are increasingly used by activist and political movements throughout the world, critical thinking, creativity, and access to culture — in short, digital and cultural citizenship — have become major issues. We must therefore examine the political and ethical dimensions of these new forms of culture, not specifically in terms of issues like economic concentration, net neutrality or the reconfiguration of cultural markets in the digital world, but rather to identify those traits that are shared generationally and intergenerationally.

1 Technoculture Is (Inherently) Political

Technoculture possesses a political dimension, both because it proposes a vision of the ideal individual and because it creates linkages between public and private spaces in society. In the 18th century, Friedrich von Schiller argued that arts and aesthetics were political by nature: the development of imperatives regarding creativity in the technocultural world has only bolstered the validity of this centuries-old statement. Is creativity a demand, or a new standard of democratic education? And how should this political dimension be handled when young people are seen as subjects (rather than actors) in anticipation of their trajectories into adulthood? (Dupeyron, 2012; Ottavi, 2012)?

1.1 *Becoming a Political Actor in the Era of Technoculture*

One of the goals of national education is creating well-informed citizens. The fact that the concept of "culture" has gradually shifted away from the realm of knowledge (including the unique French flavor of "general culture") to the realm of expression (everyone has their own culture) only highlights the need for civic education. This lacuna both signals and challenges the transition of culture towards cultural goods and services (particularly dramatic among young people), the impact of multiculturalism and the meaning of "academic culture". The social pressure felt by young people to embrace eclecticism, norms of interpersonal relations, elective choice and engagement in the technocultural regime likewise pushes them to search for authenticity and self-actualization. As Danilo Martuccelli suggests, "in terms of singularity, what is important is not necessarily what differentiates me from others, nor what traits I might share with others, but rather what hinders me from achieving my singularity" (Martuccelli, 2010: 61). The cultural sphere can therefore help individuals self-actualize, through empowerment and the gradual shedding of dependencies. For Rousseau as well as Dewey, the advent of the subject is made possible thanks to education, which includes a primer on a democracy not in terms of preparation but action. Technocultural practices are not a form of training or knowledge to be acquired prior to exercising one's responsibilities, but rather the implementation of capacities for autonomy allegedly already present in children — autonomy also being required for all sorts of political skills. What kind of political subject comes of age in the technocultural era?

Although the political nature of technoculture is often concealed under its liberal and commercial aspects, the same cannot be said of youth, which is constituted both administratively and politically by surveilling governance bodies. As soon as national and international institutions started focusing on youth (UNICEF, *Declaration of the Rights of the Child*,[1] etc.), the latter became a political topic. There are numerous signs of greater attention being paid to youth and more specifically, childhood development. Diverse initiatives have thus been developed, seeking to grant children and young people the same rights that have long been recognized for adults, in part by introducing the concept of "the best interests of the child" as a juridical person and no longer just a subject of legal discussion. In direct reference to cultural expression and production, Article 13.1 of the Convention on the Rights of the Child states: "The child shall have the right to freedom of expression; this right shall include freedom to seek, receive and impart information and ideas of all kinds, regardless of frontiers, either orally, in writing or in print, in the form of art, or through any other media of the child's choice." Meanwhile, Article 17 addresses the relationship of children to the mass media. But Article 31 is the most explicit in defending the cultural rights of the youngest members of society:

(1) States Parties recognize the right of the child to rest and leisure, to engage in play and recreational activities appropriate to the age of the child and to participate freely in cultural life and the arts;

(2) States Parties shall respect and promote the right of the child to participate fully in cultural and artistic life and shall encourage the provision of appropriate and equal opportunities for cultural, artistic, recreational and leisure activity.

But are the development and mastery of moral and political autonomy truly equivalent processes? And how can cultural authority be wielded while ensuring the representation of the child as a legal person? There are two clashing visions of children and youth in society today. On the one hand, children and youth are encouraged to develop autonomy at earlier and earlier ages, and they are lauded for their creativity as well as their ability to rapidly adapt to new technologies and tools. On the other hand, children and youth are seen as vulnerable to the nefarious effects of these same technologies and tools, at risk of falling under the perverse spell of the machines that subjugate them. In one perspective, children are fully fledged actors; in another, they are victims, exposed to greater perils given their status as minors. This paradox permeates much of the discourse on youth culture; in many cases, referring to youth civic participation operates as a kind of mantra rather than a real tool for analysis or action.

---

1   The *Declaration of the Rights of the Child* was adopted by the General Assembly of the United Nations through resolution 1386. https://www.ohchr.org/EN/ProfessionalInterest/Pages/CRC.aspx; https://www.un.org/ga/search/view_doc.asp?symbol=A/RES/1386(XIV).

1.2   Towards a Technocultural Public and Political Space

Changes in the modes of cultural consumption and self-production have had repercussions on the political world. Some of these effects make for interesting anecdotes. For instance, it is said that Nigel Newton, the founder and chief executive of the British publishing house Bloomsbury and the editor of the *Harry Potter* series, was contacted in 2005 shortly before the release of the sixth volume (*Harry Potter and the Half-Blood Prince*) by British intelligence services. At the time, a copy of the manuscript had allegedly been stolen by a security officer; the British secret service, who Nigel referred to as his "allies," had spotted this act of online piracy and ultimately determined that the version published on the internet was a fake. Contacted by the British press, a spokesperson for the secret service — generally averse to speaking about ongoing cases — stated: "We don't comment on our defence against the dark arts," echoing one of the subjects taught at Hogwarts Academy in the Harry Potter universe, "defence against the dark arts".

Other consequences have been more serious. On 3 June 2014, the French newspaper *Le Monde* ran the following headline: "Rallying sign used by Katniss Everdeen imitated by anti-coup protestors in Thailand" [original headline: *Le signe de ralliement utilisé par Katniss Everdeen a été repris par les manifestants thaïlandais anti-coup d'État*]. The article went on to explain that "the three-fingered salute (with the thumb and pinkie finger touching) used by Katniss Everdeen, the heroine of the *Hunger Games* sci-fi trilogy, played an important role in the popular book and movie series. It has increasingly appeared in the popular protests against the coup in Thailand, where demonstrators have adopted the signal as a rallying sign".[2] Anne Muxel adds that, in response to a certain disillusionment among young people, new forms of protest have developed, accompanied by demands for new forms of democracy that incorporate digital tools and references (Muxel, 2010). As democratic expectations evolve, new forms of direct and participatory mobilization have emerged, often enabled and communicated by social media (Feixa and Nofre, 2013). In addition, social exclusion has taken new guises, prompting significant reactions in a variety of cultural contents on social networks.

The year 2020 has given us several more serious examples: it's common knowledge that the concept of "fandom" has often been used by celebrities to encourage voting or specific actions, such as to fight against climate change. But things are shifting. Fandoms now emancipate themselves from their

---

[2] See http://www.lemonde.fr/pixels/article/2014/06/03/en-thailande-le-signe-de-hunger-games-contre-le-coup-d-etat_4431166_4408996.html?xtmc=katniss&xtcr=1, 3 June 2014.

putative sources and gain power in the process. They can spontaneously and effectively mobilize for political causes that they choose independently. For example, K-pop fans — and especially the fans of the group BTS, one of the world's most popular groups — sprung into action after the death of George Floyd, a black man suffocated under the weight of a white policeman in Minneapolis, which led to many demonstrations against racist police violence. After police called for residents to post videos and photos of illegal activities taking place during these protests on a specific app, K-pop fans, who exert great mastery over certain sectors of the internet, started flooding the app with photos, videos and gifs of their favorite stars, in a well-calculated strike against racism that also rendered the app useless. The fight against racism was taken a step further when various fans decided to counter white supremacists on the internet, using the same technique: in order to hinder coordinated action by racist communities, as soon as a hashtag grew in prominence (such as #whitelivesmatter or #exposeantifa), K-pop fans appropriated it, thus preventing white supremacists from using the hashtag in question to organize. Moreover, without waiting for BTS to act, some of the band's fans collected donations for various associations supporting the Black Lives Matter movement, amounting to a total of $50,000 in four and a half days (Mayard, 2020). K-pop fans even disrupted Donald Trump's meeting in Oklahoma by reserving seats *en masse*, initially making it look like a success, while the ultimate audience was ultimately quite sparse (Brandy, 2020).

These examples shed light on the political potential of the cultural consumption and engagement patterns of young people as they cross borders, languages and nations, as well as on the new nature of fandom in the technocultural era. The picture of fandom painted today in fact contradicts prevailing notions regarding K-pop fans, who are usually seen as a community of lighthearted young people, without political commitments (Tiffany, 2020). And yet, many fans feel a kind of responsibility and use the technocultural skills that form part of the communities' DNA. K-pop aficionados are experts in the art of helping YouTube videos go viral, of creating hits, of broadcasting memes and fancams. They have proven that they are also capable of taking political action using the same methods, working to reach millions of people in a single day without waiting for the source of their fandom to take a position.

Derived from cultural participation, this political engagement occurs both across nations, linking together the members of the same generational cohort, and within nations, across different generations, groups and communities. If, regarding the latter, cultural conflicts seem to have dissolved into a kind of peaceful co-existence, does this mean that culture has become a common good? Or on the contrary, does this reveal that countless cultural archipelagos exist alongside each other, sometimes in complete ignorance of each other? More broadly speaking, is the cultural dimension re-politicized when the culturalization of clashes becomes the argument used to resolve difficulties (Appadurai, 2006) — for example, when secularism is used to resolve the issue of wearing headscarves in public spaces, or culturalism is used to explain the various terrorist attacks that took place in France since 2015 — a scenario in which the media, in particular social media and the internet, play an outsized role?

In terms of the relationship between public and private social spaces, youth internet practices have established a new political equilibrium between conversation and information, between culture and communication. While the telephone and the press initially encouraged the globalization of exchange and the expansion of personal and professional circles, ultimately leading to the creation of "imagined publics" (Sola Pool, 1990), a strict separation between public and private spaces was always maintained. Gatekeepers of various kinds (editors, journalists, webmasters, critics) helped to ensure the preservation of this separation, which structured social life around dichotomies such as conversation/information, individuals/citizens, community/society, etc. In "old" forms of media, the information made visible was inherently public in nature: there was thus an overlap between visibility and publicity. The naturalistic tendencies of terrestrial television, which are particularly expressed through the rise of reality TV, remained tightly controlled by script writers and other gatekeepers. Such spaces are public because all of the information they convey has been carefully selected by professionals obeying various ethical and/or professional standards which govern public speech and its legitimacy.

With the internet, this separation began to disappear, as the relationship between professionals and pro-ams was scrambled and a system of mutual interdependence was created. The dividing line between public and private spaces was redrawn in light of a new tendency for individuals to exhibit their lives while seamlessly combining personal and public issues. These two shifts have only deepened the force of contemporary individualism: the presentation and staging of oneself, with one's attributes, skills, hopes and dreams is accompanied by a quest for greater visibility, seen as a way to validate one's claim to uniqueness. In addition, the ideology of freedom, collaboration and permeability between designers and users that stems from the internet's genesis as a volunteer project spearheaded by researchers and computer enthusiasts continues to influence the political representation of the internet, in particular when collective intelligence — or mass intelligence (Surowiecki, 2008) — is viewed as a triumph of participatory democracy.

In 1980, Langdon Winner thus wrote an article provocatively titled "Do Artifacts Have Politics?" (Winner, 1980), to which Bernward Joerges replied in

1999 with his own pithily named "Do Politics Have Artefacts?" (Joerges, 1999). Notwithstanding the 19 years separating these two texts, and the fact that the second was written in a world where digital technologies already played a sizeable role, this opposition poses an important question: where is politics in technoculture?

For young people are also responsible for the phenomenon of "democratic deconsolidation" (Foa and Mounk, 2016; Mounk, 2018). They vote less than their elders, and more often for fringe political parties that operate outside of traditional government circles. Most importantly, only 47% of young people in France believe that voting is the best way to effect change (compared to 61% of all French people), while almost three-quarters of them support lowering the voting age to 16 (Roudet, 2014). In France, the breakdown of civic engagement has been accompanied by intense skepticism regarding traditional political parties. Political contests are increasingly democratic, as evidenced by the *Generation What* study conducted by France Télévision in 2016,[3] and the fact that 51% of young people voted for a radical party in the 2017 French presidential election.

1.3 *The Technocultural Regime Threatened by Rumors*

There are two main reasons why the rise of technoculture has reconfigured the political landscape. First, the ideology of the web promotes the strength of weak ties — *likes* from strangers, as well as short-lived commitments that may be unstable or "liquid" (Bauman, 2005). Second, the internet operates primarily on the consensus model (Urfalino, 2007), even if such consensus can be entirely fleeting: collectives are loosely defined and lack structure or leaders. One of the main forms of consensus regards the fact that values associated with leisure, in particular self-expression and autonomy, should also carry over into the professional sphere (Gershuny, 2000), which has led in one particular vein to the development of "cool capitalism" (McGuigan, 2009). The drive towards consensus poses a number of risks, however: as individuals adopt the opinions of others without factchecking them, rumors can spread like wildfire. Especially given that one of the technocultural paradoxes is that large-scale conversation can only happen if centralized and unified institutional structures are properly maintained. As a result, this libertarian ideology conceals the repetition of many socio-cultural strata and systems of power from the pre-digital era.

---

[3] http://generation-what.francetv.fr.

In the democratically-oriented technocultural regime, what is most important is not truth, but credibility. One's digital identity is not derived from an assessment of truth, but is rather "a reflexive process of self-creation that is only truly achieved when recognized by others" (Denouël and Granjon, 2010: 29); this process can only exist contextually. The first person is becoming increasingly popular even in traditional forms of media, as journalists and commentators start saying "I" and providing "emotional" reactions online, thus transforming the entire cultural ecosystem. From the invention of the printing press to that of the internet, successive waves of technological change have gradually stripped spatial and temporal limits from cognitive offerings and have allowed for "on the one hand, the right to speak in public to be extended to the whole of society; and on the other, for part of all private conversations to be integrated into the public sphere" (Cardon, 2010a: 11). Consequently, and perhaps paradoxically, democratic polyphony (what Weber called the polytheism of values) contains within its core a risk to democracy.

In turn, this amplifies confirmation bias: despite the ever-greater quantities of information available — the information produced in the last 5 years of the 20th century surpassed the volume of all printed media since Gutenberg (Autret, 2002) — there has not been a corresponding growth in informational competition. Individuals may be tempted to paint a picture of the world for themselves that is plausible rather than true, thus avoiding the cognitive cost of assimilating new information that doesn't fit into the picture. Studies have shown that in cases of information saturation, we tend to pick the option that produces the greatest cognitive effect for the least mental effort (Speber and Wilson, 1989; Fiske and Taylor, 1984). Unlike what has been argued by Nicholas Carr (Carr, 2008), the internet does not reprogram our brains, but how search engines organize information does play a major role how we structure our thoughts.

And yet, consensus is not sufficient to build commonalities (in contrast to politics). Culture depends precisely on its ability to be shared over time; it thus needs more than consensus to create hierarchies and rankings, to be shared, celebrated and remembered. We must determine what frees individuals from their particularities and transforms them into members of society, thus allowing them to find their place in a shared world, and what helps them to develop their discourse, their judgment and their emotions as adults. While the traditional model of culture has lost some of its luster and may seem old-fashioned, out of sync or downright repellant to some, in the kingdom of rumor and consensus, cultural policies remain essential — for they alone can elaborate cultural programs that can create long-lasting social ties at the local, national and even transnational level. But cultural policies are increasingly hard-pressed to define "shared" or "ideal" objectives, categories which had traditionally deferred to existing standards of truth and beauty. Praising diversity does not square with preserving hierarchies, and yet hierarchies are necessary to make well-informed policy decisions. Similarly, commending participatory democracy is hard to reconcile with conserving existing political decision-making processes, which are ultimately concentrated in the hands of experts.

1.4   Far from the Technocultural Crowd

Every day, millions of posts are made on social networks on an endless variety of topics: politics, of course, but also sports, cooking, fashion, social activities of all stripes. This plethora of opinions is produced outside of any external demands or organized forums for debate. The alleged spontaneity of tweets, blogs and comments is proof of their equally alleged authenticity. Appearing as forms of direct access to the thoughts of ordinary people, such comments thus help to create a new court of public opinion (Kotras, 2018).

As we can see, technoculture runs the risk of resurrecting old fears related to crowds. Etymologically speaking, in French, the word *foule* (the equivalent of the English "crowd") comes from the Old French *fouler,* meaning to "press" or "crush" (the Old English equivalent would be "crudan"). By the 16th century, *foule* had come to refer to the crowd itself, with an implicit if minor threat to individual freedom and integrity. The crowd (*foule*) conveys the idea of a separate and irrepressible power that goes beyond the will of its individual actors. This notion, originally theorized by Gustave Le Bon in his 1895 *Psychologie des foules* (translated in English as *The Crowd: A Study of the Popular Mind*), has many contemporary illustrations. In fact, thanks to the increasing ease with which individuals can communicate and exchange content, the contemporary era has become one of mass gatherings, be they sports-related (the Olympic Games, national and international competitions), musical (Woodstock, rave parties, stadium concerts), political rallies or religious events. Examples can also be found in the movements of technocultural crowds, including how a given piece of information, a hoax or a challenge (e.g., the Ice Bucket Challenge)[4]

---

[4] The Ice Bucket Challenge, disseminated online through short videos, consisted of dumping a bucket of ice water over a person's head (either oneself or someone else) and then challenging someone else to do the same. This activity was designed to raise awareness for ALS (amyotrophic lateral sclerosis) and encourage donations to research to fight the illness. Various celebrities participated in the challenge, including Mark Zuckerberg (the CEO of Facebook), Bill Gates (the founder of Microsoft), Larry Page (the co-founder of Google), Oprah Winfrey, Jessica Biel, Justin Timberlake, etc. The campaign went viral during the summer of 2014 and raised over 100 million dollars in donations.

is disseminated far and wide. According to Gustave Le Bon, crowds have a collective soul that is more than the sum of their individuals. The crowd is like a living organism of its own, possessing autonomous traits that cannot be boiled down to the individuals that constitute it. Within a crowd, emotions are cumulative but rationality is not. A crowd is very different from a public (*un public*), which Gabriel Tarde analyzed as "a crowd at a distance" — at a distance from itself (members of a public are generally not in direct physical contact with each other), but also from its emotions. However, examining the crowd in the 21st century also means returning to one of Tarde's initial objectives: analyzing the "science of conversation". The stakes of this analysis are enormous: the meaning of words, the meaning of politics, the meaning of shared ideals and ultimately, the meaning of democracy.

The data provided by our digital activities — our digital "traces" — are of significant interest to social scientists (Boyadjian, 2016) and to private companies. Since the 2000s, countless start-ups, software companies and consulting agencies have sought new ways to measure public opinion, with regard to both political and commercial concerns. This has revealed a wide variety of sometimes conflicting views of public opinion, including how the latter is shaped and disseminated. Among the most pervasive approaches to opinion: a focus on surveillance, based on the continuous observation of all individuals, which has somewhat come back in favor recently; a focus on truth, with heavy reliance on polling since the invention of representative sampling techniques; a focus on current opinion, which, far from considering that public opinion is the aggregation of individual preferences (as supposed by polls), views it instead as a collective and socialized phenomenon, where the unequal influence of different actors plays an essential role. Whereas the invention of representativeness was based on the moral principle that the statements of all individuals/citizens were of equal worth; whereas representativeness anchored the truth of such statements, thus concealing all the power struggles behind the scenes that may have helped to shape public opinion; whereas, ultimately, polling was a tool of political rationality that helped to generate more political rationality, the new tools used to comprehend public opinion are a different beast all together. From a sociological perspective, it is now impossible to know who is speaking (representation is not the issue in question), but information is available on how power dynamics help to produce public opinion. In reality, sociodemographic variables (operating according to a historical representation of society based on social classes with different interests) are no longer as important with regard to the development of individual opinions; instead, data concerning individual mobility, community affiliations, and media visibility play a larger role. Thus composed, not all opinions carry the same weight: mathematical logic is replaced by a properly political view of opinion, since opinions are that repeated the most frequently and give the rise to the most comments are the most valuable in the web ecosystem (Didier, 2013). Opinions are seen as authentic by some who analyze big data, given that they are not influenced by the structures and biases of surveys or polls. Shared spontaneously and directly, no longer filtered through layers of mediation, opinions are now seen as the true voice of the social body. The new public opinion is thus based on the size of three criteria: audience, popularity and authority (Cardon, 2015). Newspaper readers do not constitute a "crowd," therefore, because they remain physically distant; nor do they represent "the masses," as they can preserve highly different sociological traits as well as interests. In short, Gabriel Tarde's public is much less despotic and dogmatic than Gustave Le Bon's crowd. Opposition takes a new guise in digital democracies: cultural publics (theater, museum, newspapers) are overlaid with throngs of internet users, with individuals remaining stakeholders in both groups. In its current mode of functioning, democracy happens at the intersection of publics (composed of citizens) and crowds (which express and circulate opinions, in particular using mass forms of communication including the press, radio, television, and the internet), preserving a delicate balance between rationality and reflexivity on one hand, and emotions, sensationalism and immediacy on the other.

In the context of interactions between the public and the crowd, this balance is constantly affected by the opinions of one group on the other, and vice-versa. For example, the discrepancies observed between pre-electoral polls of public opinion and the votes cast are one indicator of the crowd's power, constituting a kind of "imagined community" (Anderson, 1983) derived from such opinion polls as well as the signals it conveys on social networks, in tweets and in forum posts. Researchers frequently wonder whether the results of opinion polls in fact alter voting intentions, especially when voting results confound all forecasts, as was the case for the American presidential election in 2016, and the left- and right-wing primaries of the French presidential election in 2017. The same has been pondered, albeit to a lesser degree, regarding the Brexit vote. The surprise unanimously expressed when discovering such discrepancies is likely due to the fact that many of us have forgotten about the permanent transaction that exists between the public and the crowd: the crowd produces representations that the media organizes (or attempts to organize) into publics that are political in nature; however, as the crowd is labile and always changing, it will forever thwart rigorous attempts at organization. It has thus been admitted that leaks — regardless of their presumptive credibility — can influence the opinion of the masses by interfering with this transaction.

In France, it is not just the less educated or less cultured that are at risk of being lured into false beliefs by the digital crowd: Jean-Bruno Renard (Renard, 2010 and 2011) has observed that middle and senior managers are statistically more drawn to fringe beliefs (such as UFOs, telepathy, spiritualism, etc.); Françoise Bouchayer illustrated the same with regard to the use of alternative medicines and the existence of the Loch Ness monster (Bouchayer, 1986). In fact, the more well-informed young people believe that they are, the more likely they are to doubt scientists and other experts, instead believing that they can uncover "hidden" information online. Such delusions are of course supported by the fact that the internet favors a plural definition of truth, placing all contributors on equal footing regardless of their skills and expertise on any given subject. The more individuals are taught the basics of critical thinking without pursuing a rigorous methodology — i.e., without an appropriately scientific mindset — the more they are likely to be gullible or engage in cognitive nihilism. This is the paradox described by Gérald Bronner (Bronner, 2013 and 2016): as knowledge increases, education becomes increasingly a mass commodity, and as a result credulity grows more rampant. There are many ways for reason to be perverted, some of which have been analyzed by Nicolas Gauvrit and Sylvain Delouvée (Gauvrit and Delouvée, 2019) and Sébastien Dieguez (Dieguez, 2018). Such failures of reason include the guru effect (where individuals adhere to powerful but vague ideas and statements), confirmation bias (the tendency to search for information that reinforces one's existing ideas and to overlook any contradictory ideas), and even interpretive charity (which presumes that every statement has logical meaning). These tendencies are all based on the human drive to find experts (especially in areas where individuals are conscious of their own intellectual limitations) and to mitigate one's ignorance (the result of our imperfect and often specialized cognitive abilities). In other words, the failures of our reason are linked to the normal functioning of our intelligence and our need for reference points. Hans Rosling, Ola Rosling and Anna Rosling Rönnlund provide countless examples that show how easily we are led astray, especially in today's world of immediate overabundance of information, as compared to the printed world of yesterday (Rosling, Rosling and Rosling Rönnlund, 2018).

It is an arduous task to identify our mistakes and thwart our own error-producing tendencies. This is precisely where scientific reasoning becomes so important, provided that theoretical reasoning and empirical verification (traces, documents, experiences, and observations) are clearly delineated. We must not, however, fall prey to the illusion that purely mathematical logic is the model to follow: mathematical truth is the product of abstract deductive reasoning (stemming from axioms and theorems) and is based on true/false dichotomies and the impossibility of a third alternative (which would be neither true nor false). In everyday life, very few situations look like a mathematical problem: both an "all or nothing" attitude and the law of noncontradiction are refuted on a daily basis by the complexity of human emotions, which make it possible to wish simultaneously for a thing and its opposite. We face similar difficulties when trying to provide proof. The utterance "the Earth is round" is considered to be true not because each and every one of us has ascertained its validity, but rather because it is stated by scientific experts; in a contradictory fashion, the statement is thus ultimately deemed to be true without requiring any form of direct observation on our part. In addition, direct observation can itself be deceiving, as optical illusions prove.

To avoid being trapped in the snares of our reasoning, we use subjective probability (our personal judgment of whether something is credible or not), and assess certain elements as representative of entire categories (which liberates us from having to analyze every case in a given category). Alas, daily life does not provide us with axioms or theorems — we are much more likely to operate via induction and deduction, using our (naturally limited) senses. Moreover, the overwhelming predominance of the visual dimension in a transmedia context (where visual proof can be cross-posted in different contents) stimulates our sensorial perception and our emotional reactions. Doesn't it look weird how the Twin Towers fell? Isn't it suspicious how, in the car belonging to the Kouachi brothers during the Charlie Hebdo terrorist attack in 2015, the color in the rearview mirror changes? The new realm of public opinion is no longer so easily shaped by the mass media; now, opinions tend to be influenced horizontally (peer-to-peer) or from the bottom up (with individual opinions online forcing change in politics and the media more generally). Current fears arise from the opposition between, on the one hand, the reality of incontestable facts and their descriptive data and, on the other hand, the world of individual perceptions, emotions, and interpretations. It is actually striking to see this reversal at play: critics of mass media used to decry the risk of conformity and adherence to the lowest common denominator, whereas critics of the digital era lament the irrationality and hyper-fragmentation of digital publics.

2 Political Activism and Technoculture

The observations made above lead us directly to the issue of democracy in the technocultural era. As they enter into civic and political life, armed with the skills they have learned throughout the course of their digital and pre-digital activities, young people are increasingly confronted with difficulties when attempting to become active members of society. Politically speaking, are they capable of changing how democracy works? Should the relatively high level of electoral abstention among young people be interpreted as a sign of their disdain for collective social functioning — an interpretation which would seem to contradict the participatory engagement required by technoculture — or should it rather be viewed as a call to rethink social and political ties as they currently exist? Is their engagement in the digital world and public space alike a reaction to the restrictions regarding access to public space with which young people grew up (youth investment in the digital sphere could then be seen as a sort of counterspace where they could achieve the freedom otherwise denied)? Or as a call to mobilize the imagined communities of the internet to political ends? Have public spaces been replaced with networked publics (Ito, 2008)?

2.1   *Political and Cultural Media Activism*

Media activism — in French, sometimes spelled as one word *médiactivisme* (Blondeau 2007) — is the most common way that cultural consumption can be politicized. It occurs through the intertextual collage of different images borrowed from archival footage, live television, cartoons, video games, songs, movies and speeches. Facilitated by new digital editing tools, the products of this creative process are called "found footage" (Habib, 2014). The video *Soral Sauve,* posted on YouTube on 28 March 2016, is a prime example of found footage. In this video, visual elements from the TV show *The Walking Dead* and audio from the song "The Time is Now" are reused to political ends. This re-aestheticization of content remixes pre-existing material to convey a political message that is external to the sources sampled, but whose effectiveness is proportional to the emotional ties the wider public has with regard to those sources (Giry, 2017).

Driving the politicization of such cultural consumption patterns is the belief that each and every individual must interpret the world for themselves; in this world, moreover, the truth is often concealed (Boltanski, 2012; Olmsted, 2011). It is often argued that, thanks to cultural productions, we have all become used to interpreting, deciphering and unmasking content (Citton, 2010), a situation that has ultimately blurred the lines between fact and fiction, truth and lies (Lavocat, 2016; Jameson, 2007; Karbovnik, 2015; Cicchelli and Octobre, 2018b). In fact, popular cultural products frequently allude to conspiracy theories: from the French graphic novels *XIII* and *Histoire secrete* to the television program *Le vrai journal,* series such as *Black Mirror, Stargate SG-1, The West Wing, X Files* and *Utopia,* or movies such *The Matrix, Rosemary's Baby,* the *Divergent* series, *The Pentagon Papers,* and even card games like *Illuminati* and video games like *Assassin's Greed and Deus ex Machina.* ... not to forget books both fiction (Dan Brown) and non-fiction (David Icke). These are not just mass consumer goods: they are also channels through which different aesthetics and ways of interpreting the world are conveyed (Kniht, 2000; Coale, 2005; Arnold, 2008).

This politicization is also fostered by the new dynamics of information in the internet era. A number of different hypotheses have been put forward to describe these dynamics: a certain hardening of attitudes towards public spaces; decreasing reliance on "vertical" channels of information dissemination; greater space awarded to alternative sources of information and a broader notion of what constitutes media (with the inclusion of social media platforms in particular); the development of horizontal use and creation, etc. All of these changes are occurring as the proliferation of data makes an exhaustive analysis of all existing information ever more impossible (Bronner, 2016).

These traits emphasize the idea that all individuals have the right to be the authors of their own narratives in the new public space constituted by the internet and social networks. In addition, freedom of expression and demands for transparency (both touted as values) and the participatory network ideal further encourage the simultaneous diffusion of information of a wildly diverse nature and quality, while the pluralism of ideas and opinions means that (almost) anything is up for debate by anyone in any forum — thus encompassing democratic principles through multiple identical channels, while supporting the idea that everyone narrating their own life is part of the democratic public space. "The very conditions of our democracy favor the diffusion of this appeal to ignorance (*argumentum ad ignorantiam*) in the public space as well as its corollary: the possibility for anyone claiming the right to doubt to bury their opponent's speech in a flurry of arguments" (Bronner, 2013: 3).

Finally, the impetus behind the phenomenon of cultural politicization can also be found in rising education levels, including the development of critical thinking skills. The latter encourages individuals to be independent thinkers, not trusting anything that they cannot verify themselves and to systematically challenge even minor details (because "everybody lies about everything"). However, it can also perversely justify the rejection of established forms of knowledge, which are seen as potentially manipulative (and manipulated), given that they are emitted by instances of power. Ultimately, this situation generates a feeling of extreme insecurity. In addition, the fleeting nature of knowledge is accompanied by the moral expectation of tolerance, which sometimes helps to re-enchant the world. The educational paradox, with regard to disseminating a culture of doubt, finds its counterpart in the cultural media paradox. In the context of cultural media, the important role played by fictionalization has lent substance to a new vision of critical thinking, seen less as the rational ability to determine whether a given statement is true or false, and more as an interpretive stance with regard to content, including acts of tinkering, dabbling and reconfiguring. As discussed above, this stance has in fact become a way to express one's individuality.

2.2   Political and Cultural Hacktivism

What forms do new democratic experiments take in the era of technoculture? One product of youth technoculture, hacktivism, represents a political extreme of cultural militancy. It fuels both institutional projects and the counterpowers of civil society. Two examples will suffice here: the open government project and the *Anonymous* collective. These two entities are governed by contrasting aims: institutional on one hand and anti-institutional on the other. The latter can, in a certain way, be seen as an institutional response to the demands for information transparency, cultural equality and democratic participation as expressed by the former. One operates underground, the other officially: both initiatives are like two faces of the same technocultural coin. In both cases, the ideal of a new democracy is fueled by the internet, bursting with content and multiple, co-constructed cultural references. While young people are of course not the sole actors of these new democratic developments, they nonetheless play an important role, both in terms of their direct participation and how these initiatives are justified: altering democracy thanks to digital tools is often a goal expressed by and for the sake of young people.

The *Anonymous* collective, a loosely organized group of internet hackers active since 2003, has grown on the fringes of the institutional world, which it deems overly opaque and insufficiently democratic. At first, *Anonymous* brought together a number of internet hacktivists who shared certain values (freedom, exchange, transparency), denounced what they viewed as violations of individual or collective freedoms, and presented themselves as the web's — and the world's — "moral and ethical conscience". The cultural codes of this collective remain faithful to the original participatory ideals of the internet: its members are anonymous and wear masks, and all their actions are performed collectively, receiving collective blame or credit as a result. Awash in the heady ideals of the internet's early days, the *Anonymous* collective was composed as a team of global avengers fighting to address gaps in State infrastructure and laws. In the wake of the *Charlie Hebdo* terrorist attacks in January 2015, *Anonymous France* launched a vast campaign called #OpCharlieHebdo through its YouTube account. The operation's goal was to track down and denounce jihadists throughout the world. But the group is just as likely to attack States for what they view as democratic failings. When the French government was debating the project to bury nuclear waste in a town called Bure, *Anonymous* was once again in the news when it deployed its IT skills to pirate certain public websites. The group has operated around the world: in 2020, *Anonymous* took action in the wake of violent protests surrounding the death of George Floyd, promising to expose "the many crimes" of police forces around the world. It conducted various cyber-attacks in reaction to the protests, taking control of the city of Minneapolis' website, then turning the website for a minor United Nation agency into a memorial for Mr. Floyd (displaying the message "Rest in Power, George Floyd," along with the *Anonymous* logo) (Molloy and Tidy, 2020).

Here again, there is a close relationship between politics and culture: the Guy Fawkes mask used by *Anonymous* members is an important cultural and historic reference. Guy Fawkes was an Englishman from the 16th century who helped to plan the Gunpowder Plot.[5] During the 1980s, this historical figure became popular thanks to the popular graphic novel *V for Vendetta* (by Alan Moore and David Lloyd), which tells the story of a kind of Robin Hood-terrorist. The authors used Guy Fawkes' face as inspiration to create the mask worn by V. Later portrayed on the screen by the eponymous film (starring Hugo Weaving as V and Nathalie Portman as Evey, a young working-class woman caught up in V's mission), this mask became famous across the world. In the movie, V lives in a futuristic England governed by fascists. He admires Guy Fawkes whom he views as a freedom fighter ready to die for a noble cause; he wears a mask of his likeness while fighting for the preservation of various art forms threatened by the tyrannical powers that be (opera, sculpture, painting, etc.).

In 2016, the *Anonymous* collective recently crossed another political threshold when it announced its intention to launch a worldwide political movement, the first of its kind. This movement was called "The Humanity Party" (also referred to by its acronym THumP); a long video was posted on YouTube to mark the movement's launch. This 30-minute documentary video was titled "The Way to World Peace 'Imagine' " — perhaps an allusion to the John Lennon song. The Humanity Party is a new kind of political party that draws heavily on technocultural references.

Despite its evident differences compared to *Anonymous*, the open government project may be viewed as a public response to the same issues regarding transparency, participatory democracy, and cultural inclusion. The concept was born in 2009 in the United States when a newly elected Barack Obama launched the Open Government Initiative, calling upon the various agencies of the US

---

5 The plot was a failed assassination attempt against King James I, his family and most members of the English aristocracy in one fell swoop by blowing up the House of Lords during the State Opening of Parliament in 1605.

government to work with citizens in a transparent, collective and participatory manner. In September 2011, 8 founding members (Brazil, Indonesia, Norway, the Philippines, Mexico, South Africa, the United Kingdom and the United States) created an international alliance, the Open Government Partnership (OGP), with a view to improving democratic functioning. This partnership now has 69 member States, as well as NGOs and civil society representatives, all working to promote open government and transparency in public action in order to fight against corruption, harness new technologies (including digital ones) to reinforce public governance, promote innovation and stimulate progress. France joined the OGP in April 2014, published its national action plan in July 2015, and hosted the 4th Global Summit of the OGP in Paris from 7 to 9 December 2016.[6]

The operating modalities and end results of these summits concern the same aspects of digital culture that are so important to young people: its collective and participatory dimensions, its horizontal and volunteer-based nature, and its heavy reliance on a transformative ideology (which brings together issues as varied as protecting the planet, ensuring political transparency, the equitable sharing of resources, sustainable human development and the co-construction of digital tools). The OGP summits thus present a toolbox that is deployed at various collaborative events. A single platform brings together the summit's digital services as developed by the administrations and civil society of the entire world; participants are allowed to list their software products on this list, thus creating a global catalogue of digital tools designed to consult, mobilize, or exert citizen control and to foster participation in public debate (open data portals, consulting platforms, tools for tracking and collaboratively developing legislation, participatory budgeting, civic tech, monitoring of national action plans, etc.). Most importantly, this experiment seeks to reinvigorate citizens, in particular young people. At the opening of the OGP Summit on 9 December 2016, the mayor of Paris, Anne Hidalgo declared: "citizen capacity is an antidote; the OGP produces this antidote, hence the importance of the relationship between governments and citizens […]. This is the way forward to ensure a better future for our children."

There is no leader in this kind of movement: just collectives of actors that favor collaboration. Nonetheless, one figure does stand out as an exemplar of the democratic renewal made possible by digital technologies: Audrey Tang. Originally from Taiwan, Tang grew up in Germany, where her father

---

[6] I would like to thank Myriam Terny, a founding member of the Grand Poitiers (France) collective governance development board and a participant at the first citizen meeting of the SGMAP (Secretary-General for Government Modernization) at the 2016 OGP summit, for the information provided on this subject.

was a doctoral student studying the Tiananmen student-led protests. Assigned male at birth, Tang later changed her name and gender identity in 2005. A self-educated genius programmer (Tang left school at 12 years old), a precocious entrepreneur (she also created her first start-up before turning 15), Tang grew up with one foot in Silicon Valley and the other in the lawless world of the early internet. In the 1990s, she operated both as a programmer and a cultural actor: she was very active in several online communities, especially open-source code communities. In addition, she has translated several programming books into Mandarin, written for Wikipedia and Freenet, and helped to encourage the free publication of out-of-print texts on the internet, all the while pushing the widespread diffusion of cultural content. Her political engagement in favor of inclusive democracy where the cultural internet plays an important role took shape in 2012: in reaction to a budgetary law passed in Taiwan, Audrey Tang then joined a group of hackers who decided to "free" the government's budget data and make them available to the public on an easily readable site using crowdsourcing.[7] The project drew in about 9,000 individuals in 24 hours and was quickly given the name g0v (pronounced gov-zero).[8]

Now 35 and already retired from the corporate world for a few years, Tang now devotes her time to public action and creating tools to change the world: she describes herself as a civic hacker. In fact, Audrey Tang embodies the values of digital culture. Her actions seek to establish a new politico-cultural ecology of society based on the individual contributions of citizen actors.

3   Democracy and Technoculture

Media activism and hacktivism both express and consequently transform the modalities of democratic participation: the values of transparency and self-expression find fertile ground in the world of technoculture. But what may initially appear to be the fulfillment of a democratic promise also contains risks to democracy, centered around the issue of both civic and technocultural education.

---

7   Crowdsourcing is a model wherein a large number of people on the internet contribute knowledge (whether for a specific project or more generally, as in an open-source project) and help to undertake tasks that would have traditionally been performed by companies.
8   Today, there are g0v versions of all the major ministries in Taiwan: the Ministries of Education, Labor, Health, etc.

3.1 Democracy and Polyphonic Regimes of Truth

The plethora of alternative realities that have proliferated thanks to the democratic belief in the value of individual opinions, emotions and informational productions poses a certain challenge to the Enlightenment legacy that undergirds our democratic models. Alternative facts,[9] fake news,[10] hoaxes, post-truth,[11] trolls[12] and conspiracy theories abound on social networks and peer-to-peer media, especially given that professional amateurs are seen as legitimate sources of information and democratic principles enshrine the right to free self-expression, regardless of the opinions being emitted. This new regime of parallel truths undoubtedly poses a challenge to the very notion of political consensus. While Enlightenment thinkers argued that reality was a philosophical criterion for truth — that is, reality is an ontological category that concerns being, whereas truth is a logical and gnosiological category that concerns language and knowledge. In other words, reality was a criterion of truth that could be rationally and objectively confirmed through the scientific process. This notion of truth-correspondence is contradicted by the digital realm in two different ways, which highlight a number of philosophical obstacles. Kant thus argued that, in order for the truth/reality relationship to exist, reality must be given, it must appear: and yet we only deal with representations of reality, a situation that has only been exacerbated by the digital era's emphasis on the diversity of expressions, cultures and opinions. The German philosopher Gottlob Frege had already pointed out the incommensurability of realities and their representations, an aspect which has likewise only been further reinforced as emotional expressiveness has become a marker of individual authenticity, increasingly valued and rewarded on digital social networks. As these two arguments have converged, a generalized subjective relativism has proliferated. This relativism is quite different from the objective relativism at the core of all scientific thought: what Gaston Bachelard refers to when he

---

9   A concept invented by Kellyanne Conway, counselor to the American president Donald Trump, during an interview on NBC (22 January 2017). An alternative fact is, in short, an untruth. This term rose to prominence in public discourse following the election of Donald Trump. On 23 June 2017, *the New York Times* attempted to make a definitive list of Trump's lies, listing at least 74 that occurred during the first 13 days of his presidency (often several lies per day).

10 Fake news can refer to any kind of false information that purports to be a valid media source. On this subject, see the study conducted by *Le Monde* on Facebook (Senecat, 2017).

11 Idea according to which emotions and beliefs are more important than objective facts.

12 A troll is an individual who makes digital posts or statements with the intention of stirring up trouble. When individuals "troll," they flaunt the rules of conversation, including sincerity, relevance and the desire to have a constructive exchange.

writes that there is no first truth, there are only first errors. This generalized relativism prevents both alternative truths from being discredited and scales of truth from being established, given that ascertaining truth has become simultaneously much more difficult and much less socially validated.

This explains why rationalist arguments are not enough, since the latter are weakened by growing mistrust of scientific discourse in general. Science scares people — just look at the types of cultural content that are popular among young people today: dystopian and post-apocalyptic films, shows and novels that are frequently based on the idea of "the end of the world" provoked by scientific experiments gone haywire, be they genetic manipulations, virus outbreaks or nuclear or natural catastrophes (nonetheless always related to human activity). The storytelling era — as well as its successor, the era of the clash (Salmon, 2019) — in no way entails assessing the truth of statements; the latter operate on the register of pleasure and identification, drawing on the growing permeability between reality and fiction but also mounting skepticism regarding "official" accounts and a tendency to search for "secret" reasons.

Mistrust with regard to science, experts and power, especially political power, go hand-in-hand (Rosanvallon, 2006). Likewise, Bernard Williams (Williams, 2002) has demonstrated the existence of two concomitant forces. On the one hand, he observes strong mistrust with regard to the values of rationality, scientific progress and objectivity, including within intellectual, educated circles, the media and society as a whole (as evidenced by recurring debates regarding vaccines). On the other hand, he also argues that the impression of being duped by the powers that be (political, scientific or other) that embody the aforementioned values has only augmented as the desire for trust has increased. Science is an object of mistrust (though it should be noted that since Popper, science has itself revised its relationship to truth and reality), but the history and narratives that a society develops about itself are particularly susceptible to vicious ideological battles whenever the question of identity is at stake. Counter- and pseudo-science play an important role in generating fake news, alternative facts and countless conspiracy theories: revelations regarding how the Pyramids were built and the prophesies of the ancient Mayan calendar are just two examples of attempts at producing scientific discourse to rebuke official expertise, as well as narratives to help explain the world — by uncovering hidden meaning, which can be ostensibly used to prevent the looming apocalypse (Karbovnik, 2017).

Tensions thus center around the issue of information and who distributes it: the media, and in particular the internet. In general, the proliferation of fake news and conspiracy theories in the technocultural era is explained in one of three ways. The "echo chamber" theory negates the power of social networks, arguing that the latter only magnify phenomena that predate the internet. A second theory, the so-called bullet or "hypodermic needle" hypothesis, counters that social networks have a massive, anesthetizing effect on users, who are subject to the most radical influences and denied free will. However, it seems appropriate to consider the relationship between networks and individuals from a third, more systematic perspective: networks have specific traits that produce communication modalities that are well-suited to persuasion leading to engagement … or persuasion leading to manipulation. In fact, social networks prey on the desire that young people have of engaging in "extimacy" (as defined by Serge Tisseron, their penchant for expressing the most intimate details of their lives to strangers). Social networks are adept at bringing together otherwise unrelated strong emotions, using these as a kind of bait to create affective ties. Philippe Breton has shown how information cannot be successfully transferred solely by using logic: such transfers also require an emotional and intersubjective buy-in (Breton, 2008). This explains why virtual communication, which manipulates questions of identity, extimacy and performativity, is so powerful. In addition, the value placed on curating unique repertoires of individual knowledge flips the relationship between the expert and the layperson, leading to a new consideration for "popular" opinion. The French movie *Le Ciel attendra* [*Heaven Will Wait*[13]] which recounts how two young women are gradually radicalized on the internet, clearly illustrates this shift: the anti-globalization and green sensibilities of the protagonists are exploited for political aims, with successive techniques combining the imagery of animal killings, human massacres, and intimate discussions ultimately used to radicalize the girls.

3.2   *Knowledge Societies and Cognitive Bubbles*

Thanks to the multiplication of images, sounds, and information, Jean Baudrillard's famous phrase — "what mass communications give us is not reality, but the *dizzying whirl of reality* [*le vertige de la réalité*]" (Baudrillard, 1998: 34) — has never been truer. Successive technological revolutions, from the invention of the printing press to that of the internet, have gradually freed the cognitive offer from spatial and temporal constraints.

In France, official filters no longer exist — see for instance, earlier State legislation on the monopoly of information distribution that performed an *a priori* selection and triage and which was abolished on 29 July 1982.[14] Editorial

---

13   Directed by Marie-Castille Mention-Schaar and released in 2016.
14   Law number 82–652 passed on 29 July 1982 put an end to the State's monopoly on radio and television broadcasting, which had been established in 1964 and amended various times, leading to the creation of the High Authority. This organization granted radio and

control now only happens after the fact in many cases (look at Wikipedia, OhmyNews or AgoraVox). This only strengthens confirmation bias: despite a vast increase in the quantity of information readily available, there has been no correlated rise in competition regarding information. It is often tempting for individuals to elaborate an acceptable vision of the world — one that matches the individual's beliefs — rather than a true representation, thus avoiding the cognitive cost of assimilation new and potentially contradictory information.

Consequently, a cognitive oligopoly reigns over most of the web. As they are always highly motivated to disseminate their ideas (in particular because this dissemination helps to create reassuring cognitive universes for them), extremists are legion on the internet, whereas scientific experts are relatively rare. Belief actors are always much more engaged in proselytizing, which leads to paradoxical cognitive oligopolies. The proliferation of cognitive bubbles can also threaten the very principles of knowledge societies, which strive for political emancipation through the acquisition of knowledge. The knowledge society's agenda thus "reveals an error of judgment concerning the non-selective processes of information diffusion that characterize the relationship between cognitive supply and demand, on the internet in particular" (Bronner, 2013: 59).

To understand this phenomenon, we must look at the nature of radical ideas: they are not irrational, but follow their own logic, values and notions of commensurability. Radical ideas are developed in direct relation to the advancement of knowledge, given that the latter increases awareness of what remains unknown (and the attendant discomfort), while also providing young people, through education, with the rudimentary skills of scientific thought. Science and belief thus share the same foundational hypothesis: reality is not immediately evident and must be "discovered" behind sometimes misleading appearances. In both cases, doubt is wielded as a tool, while skepticism and critical thinking are adopted as the modus operandi, establishing a kind of rational bedrock. In the case of science, however, there exists a burden of proof, whereas belief requires no such thing. We are thus faced with one of the paradoxical consequences of the widespread dissemination of education and the democratic value of self-expression. "Education grants individuals a certain mental capacity, broadens their intellectual horizons. The problem is that this broadening often entails weakening the authority conferred to official sources of knowledge" (Bronner, 2016: 62). As a result, by sharpening critical thinking skills, education also serves to make truth less absolute. In addition,

---

television stations the right to broadcast, selected the presidents of public channels, established contractual specifications and monitored competition rules. In short, this law liberalized the audiovisual sector.

by being inherently relative, the regime of truth governing the social sciences has helped to diffuse the idea that there are many possible interpretations (Passeron, 1991). In many works penned by individuals ascribing to "alternative truths", such as cult leaders, rationality and the trappings of scientific proof are used to convince readers (Sauvayre, 2012).

Both users and institutions have reacted strongly to the rise of conspiracy theories and other perversions of scientific thought. Debunking conspiracy theories is now its own subject, integrated into national education programs as well as specialized courses (see for example, the #FaceAuComplotisme[15] and #OnTeManipule initiatives led by the French government). Certain individuals also take it upon themselves to attack conspiracy theories (see *le Debunker des étoiles, La Tronche en biais, Hygiène mentale, Defakator, Temps mort* in France and *Captain Illusion, Myles Power,* and *The Utopia Show* abroad), with audiences ranging from 25,000 to 1 million subscribers and 200,000 to 73 million views per video (Signoret, 2018). But the binary thinking of both conspiracy theorists and anti-conspiracy theorists is not sufficient to account for the many more alternative worldviews found around the web. One video arguing that the Earth is flat obtained 1.1 million views, whereas one claiming that Emmanuel Macron is the Antichrist only got 340,000 views.

While fighting for more clicks may be a losing battle, we must stop infantilizing conspiracy theorists and other adherents to fake news and alternative facts, as it is precisely the promise of freedom conveyed by conspiracy theories that is attractive to such individuals. We would be better off attempting to redefine the basis of shared knowledge regarding conspiracy theories, which always have two targets: lies and injustice (Peltier, 2016). Web videographers who fight against the proliferation of alternative truths wish to promote the art of doubt rather than the art of suspicion, thus allowing for the development of complex thought as a possible antidote to the rise of conspiracy theories. In order to encourage the reappropriation of critical tools that can help individuals deal with an increasingly complex and often incomprehensible reality, it is necessary but not sufficient to teach individuals how to debunk conspiracy theories. First of all, critical thinking skills must be reappropriated (analyzing facts, checking sources, comparing different viewpoints), while elaborating an inclusive political project that renews public trust in institutions. This means offering shared narratives to compensate for ideological decline and the consumerist reification of the individual as object.

---

15   A mirror site (on-te-manipule.com) popped up in response to this initiative, condemning the State's manipulation and decrying the government's attempt to establish itself as "the thought police".

3.3 Neo-democracy or Democracy Threatened by Technoculture

The technocultural modalities of public action also take root in physical spaces, thanks to the emergence of protest movements that seek to occupy public space. These movements are largely organized and publicized online, but also mobilize cultural contents and civic participation, encouraging the repoliticization of both public spaces and cultural tools, as well as culture itself. The modalities of action of these neo-political movements have been described at length in other scholarly works: the spontaneous erection of campsites, the (re)occupation of public spaces with important symbolic connotations (the Puerta del Sol in Madrid, Wall Street in New York, the Place de la République in Paris, etc.), the co-organization of debates, the combination of debate and cultural products, horizontal culture ("the process is the message!"), etc. These new political forms create an ecosystem imbued with the teachings and uses of technoculture. The modalities of action often borrow from youth culture more broadly. The demand, if it can be called that, is for visibility and recognition, as signified by the hashtag #OnVautMieuxQueCa (or similar hashtags like #WeAreBetterThanThis). In movements like Occupy Wall Street, debate takes a new form: everyone can express themselves, everyone has the same amount of time to speak so no one can monopolize the debate, votes must be passed with a special majority (80% for the *Nuit Debout* movement in France, for example) to mitigate for any errors in counting the number of hands raised. But content and output are also different with these new political movements: far from being substitutes or surrogates for democracy, new political movements are trying to achieve "real democracy," based on consensus in multiple miniature agoras that pop up as subjects need to be debated. Yves Sintomer reminds us that these movements all share a similar genesis, emerging from a spontaneous rejection of institutions and the social status quo (Sintomer, 2011), from a creative idealism prompted by an emotional reaction to current events that translates into a desire to get involved. These movements contradict many of the contemporary claims that individualism is on the rise and young people are globally disinterested in politics.

The recent *Gilets jaunes* [Yellow Vests] movement which rose to prominence in 2018–19 is an excellent illustration of the transformation of democratic functioning as a result of demands for technocultural participation. The *Gilets jaunes* had broad grassroots support, as evidenced by the fact that the movement's demonstrations lasted for over 10 months; they grew out of a call to protest rising fuel costs due to a hike in the domestic consumption tax on energy products (TICPE, *taxe intérieure de consommation sur les produits énergétiques*) which formed part of the French government's new environmental policy. Very quickly, however, demands expanded to the social and political sectors as the movement gained traction (Balibar, Bantigny, Chauvel, Graeber, Piketty, and Zancarini-Fournel, 2019) and began to shine a light on important cleavages in French society (Fourquet and Manternach, 2018; Maillard, 2019). On 17 November 2018, the *Gilets jaunes* started to organize barricades on public roads and roundabouts, as well as weekly protests on Saturdays. These protests mainly drew individuals from rural and peri-urban areas at first, but eventually grew to include major cities as well, giving rise to violent clashes with law and order (Gwiazdzinski and Floris, 2019). Capitulating to the demands of the movement, the executive branch finally abandoned its plan to increase the TICPE. Emmanuel Macron, the president of the French Republic, then announced a number of new measures and initiated a nationwide debate,[16] at the culmination of which new reforms were proposed. However, this response did not put an end to the movement: protests have continued under different guises and for different reasons.

For our purposes here, however, the uniqueness of the *Gilets jaunes* movement lies elsewhere: in its modalities of action. Unlike traditional protests, coordinated by unions and community organizations, the *Gilets jaunes* movement was created and developed online, on social media platforms (Facebook, Twitter, YouTube) and dedicated websites. Confused and threatened by this new development, the major French unions initially did not support the *Gilets jaunes*. The movement did not replicate the traditional vertical political structure of parties and unions. On the contrary, it adopted a whole new way of operating: the groups formed on social networks touted their horizontal nature and constituted new forms of media (Peltier and Saltariano, 2018) with a new relationship to power (Amaret and Graziani, 2019). In addition, this rebellion did not stem from the working or lower classes, but rather the middle-class (Noiriel, 2019), whose digital importance has only grown with the rise of technoculture.

---

16   This was a public debate launched on 15 January 2019 by the President of the Republic, Emmanuel Macron, in the context of the *Gilets jaunes* movement and designed to respond to democratic demands. The *Grand Débat*, as it was called, outlined several main themes for discussion: energy transition (responding to the general rejection of increases in energy taxes coupled with decreases in the speed limit), taxation and public spending (in response to general frustration with France's fiscal policies), democracy and citizenship, and the State and public services (in response to the claim that certain areas were abandoned by the State in terms of public services). In addition to "complaint books" made available in town halls, local debates organized by regional communities, national conferences with trade unions and regional stakeholders as well as randomly selected citizen assemblies, the *Grand Débat* provided a web page for all citizens to share their opinions and make proposals that could then be disseminated to the wider public, who could vote on such proposals.

Although the *Gilets jaunes* movement remains officially apolitical and operates on the outskirts of established political parties — this despite attempts by *La France Insoumise* and the *Front national* to co-opt its message — in reality its ambitions are highly political. While Facebook administrators for *Gilets jaunes* groups, such as Éric Drouet and Maxime Nicolle, claim to work for political renewal as managers of the social movement, with a view to instituting a "public democracy" — especially given that Facebook's algorithms overrepresent the content published by groups, to the detriment of that posted on pages and thus traditional media outlets — the movement nonetheless has its own political leanings. According to an analysis by *Décodeurs*,[17] the movement's organization on Facebook heavily relied on groups called "Colère" (followed by a *département*[18] number), that popped up in January and February 2018 in various French *départements* primarily as a reaction to another legislative proposal to lower the speed limit on side roads to 80 kilometers/hour (from 90 kilometers/hour). *Décodeurs* also noted that the movement gained important traction in the *patriosphere* composed of far right-wing sovereigntists and including militant Facebook groups such as *Debout la France* (a conservative Gaullist and Eurosceptic political party), *Rassemblement national HBM* (associated with the far-right party led Marine Le Pen) and *La nébuleuse des anti-Macron* (Senecat, 2019). In addition, the protestors designated as spokespersons for the *Gilets jaunes* and thus in the media spotlight are very often controversial political figures. Éric Drouet, one of the movement's founders and the one who called for a protest on 17 November 2018, is a vocal proponent of the movement's horizontal nature, often touted on his website "La France en Colère!!!,"[19] but he also agreed to act as the movement's representative to meet with the Minister of Transport at the time, François de Rugy. Similarly, Priscilla Ludosky, who launched an online petition in May 2018 to call for a reduction in fuel prices which obtained over a million signatures, is an environmental activist who has pivoted to organic cosmetics. Jacline Mouraud, who addressed a video to Emmanuel Macron that went viral, is a pseudoscience enthusiast with

---

17   Les *Décodeurs* is a column in the French newspaper *Le Monde* created on 10 March 2014. Its goal is to fact-check information on a wide variety of topics, calling on the work of a specialized and multidisciplinary team of about ten people. This fact-checking column was one of the first of its kind in France.
18   It is one of the three level of administrative division in France under the national level, between the regions (that are bigger units) and the communes (the smallest administrative units).
19   With 300,000 members (as of February 2019), this group is one of the largest and is often viewed, given its wide scope of diffusion, as the main channel used by Éric Drouet for mobilization.

dreams of starting her own party. And Maxime Nicolle, who plays a central role in disseminating protest videos on social networks,[20] has ties to the *Front national* (Fondation Jean Jaurès, 2019).

According to a poll in conducted in December 2018, almost 60% of French people who reported belonging to the *Gilets jaunes* movement said that they primarily used social networks to get information and news (compared to 37% of French people as a whole), relying much less on newspapers and traditional forms of media online for such purposes. Journalists were troubled: they claimed that *Gilets jaunes* members "were learning on the internet at breakneck speed" (Delacroix, 2018) and, in breaking with traditional forms of media as rejected by the movement, were thus more susceptible to conspiracy theories (Liabot, 2019) given their penchant for instantaneous and unmediated forms of media (Israel, 2019). The sociologist Gérald Bronner argues that the *Gilets jaunes* movement is a continuation of the internet into the physical world (Bronner, 2018). Consequently, the *Gilets jaunes* often exist side-by-side with all sorts of fake news, in particular concerning the alleged presence of anti-Yellow Vest "mercenaries" on the ground, rumors about the disappearance of the French Constitution or a total opening of borders to immigration,[21] "news" items that were viewed more than 100 million times. Rudy Reichstadt, the founder of the French site Conspiracy Watch, argues that while we cannot definitely prove that conspiracy theories are more prevalent in the *Gilets jaunes* movement than another other movement, there is no important conspiracy theorist in the Francophone world that does *not* have ties to the movement (Mahler, 2019). In addition, Samuel Laurent, the director of *Les Décodeurs,* emphasizes the extreme permeability of the movement to all sorts of outside information that may confirm its internal biases (Laurent, 2018).

The movement's members also tend to align around the idea of direct democracy (Thiébaut, 2019). For example, the *Gilets jaunes* call for transparency with regard to taxation and fiscal policy, as well as the organization of frequent referenda on political questions of different kinds, and the adoption of proportional voting for upcoming legislative elections. Starting in December 2018, the citizens' initiative referendum became one of the movement's main demands, given that this is a system that would allow for legislation to be passed without

---

20 His Facebook group "Fly Rider Infos Blocage" had more than 174,000 subscribers at the beginning of December 2018.

21 The greatest hoax shared was the so-called "Marrakech Pact," an international migration policy. By signing this pact, "Emmanuel Macron was selling France to the United Nations," according to the online readers who shared this information, even though the real text was in no way binding.

going through parliament. The 44,576 accounts created on the website for the national *Grand débat* illustrate these tendencies, given that their primary topics were, by order of importance: 1) the economy, financial markets, labor and public accounts; 2) democracy, institutions and the citizens' initiative referendum; and finally 3) freedom of expression and social issues. Among the 25,000 proposals recorded on the website, those that garnered the most support (from the million votes cast) were precisely those that concerned direct democracy and the end of privileges for elected officials (Cortes, 2019). But the movement's horizontal principle makes it very difficult to ensure representation — which is necessary for political negotiations in the current democratic institutions of the Republic. Consequently, when on 26 November 2018 a group of eight individuals from different regions where the movement was active declared themselves "spokespersons" in order to speak with the government, many in the *Gilets jaunes* movement expressed concern about the risk of political co-optation, as well as the fact that these spokespeople were not necessarily representative of the group as a whole. In the end, a single individual would go to meet the Prime Minister on 30 November 2019, which meant that the delegation was considered as de facto dissolved and political negotiation was no longer possible.

All of these movements have a strong cultural dimension, whether we look at individual events or the longer trajectory of a movement. In the evening of 20 April 2016, a symphonic orchestra entirely composed of amateur musicians assembled on the Place de la République in Paris to play Dvorak's Symphony No. 9 (also known as the Symphony *From the New World*) as part of the *Nuit Debout*. Their performance was broadly shared online through videos, tweets, and commentaries. The same occurred with *Musée Debout,* an initiative launched by Guillaume Kientz, the curator of the Louvre. Guillaume Kientz sought to play on the interactions between individuals and institutions: "Come with an art book or the photo of a work that changed how you see the world," Kientz said as he encouraged visitors to "rethink the world" by reintegrating history and museums — art and culture more broadly — at the heart of the political debate. The same applies to the *Gilets jaunes* movement, which has also given rise to successful songs (often self-produced and publicized online),[22] a movie,[23] and other forms of cultural content.

---

22 *Gilets jaunes* [*Yellow vests*] by Kopp Johnson (2018), *Tensions sociales* [*Social tensions*] by D.ace (2018), *Débranche ta télé et enfile ton gilet* [*Turn off your TV, put on your yellow vest*] by A. Froideveaux (2018), *Le peuple saigne* [*The people are bleeding*] by Mazfa (2018), and *Les Gentils, Les Méchants* [*The good guys, the bad guys*] by Marguerite (2019).

23 *J'veux du soleil* [*I want sun*] by François Ruffin and Gilles Perret (2019). François Ruffin, a political active director, has since become an elected official.

By flipping politics on its head, by reconnecting democracy to lived experience (a "democracy of doing") and completely internalizing the value of deliberation, and finally by drawing on the civic tradition of ancient Athens (which finds its epigones in today's constituent assemblies and the functioning of Swiss cantons), contemporary youth movements are faced with one very important question: can they sustain a collective energy that will be capable of revitalizing Western societies? Moreover, is consensus, heavily touted on the internet as an ideal mode of operations, a tenable form of social and political functioning in the long term? The philosopher Chantal Mouffe does not believe that it is: according to her, the consensus of socio-digital networks, which is structurally horizontal, completely ignores the vertical systems that are at the heart of processes of institution-building and representation (Mouffe, 2016). Similarly, Loïc Blondiaux argues that the informal nature of participatory democracy is one of its greatest assets but also its greatest obstacle (Blondiaux, 2008). Whereas in traditional circumstances, debates are held with an objective in mind, now debate becomes an end in of itself, which makes democracy a kind of individual experience that will only with great difficulty be transformed into institutional action — from which young people moreover feel increasingly distant. For Alfred Ogien and Sandra Laugier, social movements that wish to go beyond the hierarchical structures of traditional political parties may, in some cases, benefit from having even *more* rules than the latter (Ogien and Laugier, 2010).

∴

In conclusion: is this technocultural and political ecosystem an echo chamber, or to answer the criticism levied at Occupy Wall Street, at risk of "falling in love with itself" (Blimenkranz *et al.,* 2011)? Or, on the contrary, does it represent the "newfound voice of the 99%," the silent majority; does it hold the promise of better days (Gitlin, 2012)? Did Occupy Wall Street have anything to offer other than the establishment of communities in the public space and its exemplary refusal to elect spokespersons (Flank, 2015)? Similar questions are raised by the transformation of the 15-M movement into the Spanish political party *Podémos,* or, on the flipside, the inability (unwillingness?) of the *Gilets jaunes* movement to translate into political and democratic stakes. How can collective intelligence and grassroots participation truly effect social change?

The new forms of political participation being invented by youth technoculture are very different from those of the traditional political landscape, as they encourage collaboration, sharing and glocalized hybridization. Youth movements today are loathe to make specific demands, because they do not seek to enter into institutional negotiations so much as they celebrate the spontaneous outpouring of energy around shared fundamental values, conveyed using the communication tools of digital culture. Youth movements do not operate through traditional channels like voting — which young people in Europe are massively abandoning. The new forms of political engagement, which deviate from long-standing forms of participation structured around a shared ideology and the existence of political hierarchies, echo a number of online behaviors, in particular the rise of the professional amateur. Such forms of participation are intense, but potentially fleeting and reversible; they tend to also exist on the margins of institutions and have a strong utopian streak.

Is this neo-democracy an empty promise, ultimately incapable of reinventing the rules of the democratic game? How long will it last? Will it fall victim to the volatility of its circumstantial forms of engagement? Or do contemporary youth movements offer a way to rebuild the social contract and propose new possibilities for political management? As we have suggested above, political and media education will play a key role in defining the future of political participation.

CONCLUSION

Resisting the Appeal of Worst-Case Scenarios

What will the men and women of tomorrow look like? Will they be hyperconnected transhumans permanently plugged into the technocultural flows? Solitary members of fragmented communities, withdrawing into their own native cultures? Although countless theories abound in contemporary novels, movies and television shows, no one truly knows. However, the future is a subject of evident trepidation, as illustrated by current productions as well as long-ranging predictions. When we reread Jules Verne, we see that science fiction is not just fiction. So what should we believe? That the world of tomorrow will look like today's, but at a greatly accelerated technological pace, as suggested by Isaac Asimov in his *Foundation* series?[1] That the world will be dehumanized as in George Orwell's *1984*,[2] or post-humanist as in Michel Houellebecq's *La possibilité d'une île*?[3] Or, on the contrary, will the next great shift in our hyper technological society be — out of necessity — a cultural and even perhaps spiritual one, as suggested by Pierre Bordage[4] and a spate of contemporary films, including *Gattaca*[5] and *A.I.*[6]? It is very difficult to predict which technologies will

1 The *Foundation* series includes *Foundation* (1951), *Foundation and Empire* (1952), and *Second Foundation* (1952); many years later, the author added *Foundation's Edge* (1982), *Foundation and Earth* (1986), *Prelude to Foundation* (1988), and *Forward the Foundation* (1993).
2 Published in 1949, the book was later turned into a box office success by Michael Radford in 1984.
3 Michel Houellebecq. *La possibilité d'une île*. Fayard: 2005.
4 Pierre Bordage is one of the most prolific French science fiction authors (he received the Cosmos 2000 prize in 1996 for his novel *La Citadelle Hyponéros* and the *Cezam Prix Littéraire Inter* CE in 2008 for *Porteur d'âmes*). His work tends to examine the spiritual aspects of a future society.
5 *Gattaca* was a film released in 1998. In a world ruled by eugenics where potential children are genetically selected to embody the "best" hereditary traits, Jerome, an ideal candidate, sees his life destroyed by an accident while Vincent, a naturally born child and thus an imperfect human, dreams of being able to travel to space. Vincent ultimately does go to space, thanks to his tenacity and the help of those who believe, like him, that this predetermined world is not good enough.
6 *A.I.* was released in 2001. This movie presents a 21st century ravaged by climate change, where robots have become an essential component of everyday life and perform most basic tasks. One scientist tries to create the first sentient android: a child that he calls David that is capable of developing a vast repertoire of emotions and memoirs. David is placed with a couple whose young son was cryogenized until a cure could be found for his serious illness; David is then rejected by his adoptive mother. The film shows the journey that David then undertakes to understand his identity and his (perhaps secret) source of humanity.

completely change our lives, in the process altering our cultural desires and passions. It seems likely that nanotechnology and biotechnology will come to supplement our natural abilities. The customization of equipment, the segmentation of cultural products and an ever-greater ability to interact with content will also likely continue to foster the aestheticization and culturalization of our identities; at the same time, the identity-based use of cultural resources (namely, to establish and (re)present one's self) is unlikely to diminish.

Beyond technology, however, what shape will humanity take? Of particular interest is humanity's changing ability to create culture, either as a centripetal force shaping a shared core, or as a centrifugal force engendering psychological tension and conflict between groups. It is important to note that the accelerating spread of globalization that is associated with the internet produces simultaneous and contradictory movements of cultural contraction and identitarian closure at both the local and national levels, movements that can be quite conservative, even xenophobic. A marked interest in cultural diversity and openness, especially among young people, exists alongside attitudes of withdrawal and intolerance (Mayer, 2014). All around the world, conservative nationalist movements have sprung up, while significant swathes of public discourse have adopted a xenophobic tone (Attias-Donfut, Fine, and Achinger, 2012). This is the paradox of globalization and the technoculture it promotes: as a system that creates interdependencies, globalization highlights both integration and fragmentation, inclusion and exclusion. It provides opportunities for empowerment and openness for the more mobile individuals, but simultaneously fashions new sources of inequality, frustration, disillusionment and social uprooting for others (Cicchelli, 2018).

1 A Twofold Movement of Creativity and Diversity

As we have seen above, youth technoculture is generated by a twofold movement of creativity and diversity at its core. These two elements are central to the notion of human capital (the set of skills, knowledge and experiences accumulated by a given individual and which support his or her development).[7] Human capital partially determines individuals' ability to work or create for

---

7 The concept of "human capital" was defined by Theodore Schultz, an American economist, in 1961: "Although it is obvious that people acquire useful skills and knowledge, it is not obvious that these skills and knowledge are a form of capital, that this capital is in substantial part a product of deliberate investment." The concept was then further developed by Gary Becker in 1965; Becker received the Nobel Prize in Economics in 1992 for his theories.

themselves or others, and has consequently played a key role in Western developmental ideologies. And these are in fact ideologies, for these norms are likely disseminated much more broadly than their associated practices. In addition, the notion of human capital underpins many vast international initiatives, policies and forms of financial support, designed to further a political vision of the greater good.[8]

Creativity and diversity have become the social norms that characterize youth technoculture as it flourishes in Western societies. Youth modalities of reception illustrate high levels of creativity, as do the products young people choose to invent or modify. In fact, creativity has become a sort of dogma in today's so-called "knowledge" societies that recreate, under an informational guise, the dynamics of entrepreneurial capitalism: inventing new products or needs. The diversity of youth technocultural lies in its populations (subject to successive waves of migration), as well as various policies designed to recognize cultural diversity around the world (e.g., UNESCO, the Quebecois policy of "reasonable accommodation").[9]

And creativity leads to emulation. It seems that the "start-up" mentality may be reaching schools and universities. But what exactly is this start-up mentality? Usually, it entails innovative ideas that are formulated in a collaborative fashion, either during structured brainstorming or hit upon at random. In fact, individuals sometimes stumble upon something entirely different than what they had intended, either through chance or serendipity. The founders of Google, Larry Page and Sergey Brin, thus ended up designing a search engine when they had originally set out to create a digital library. In an interview with *Le Monde*,[10] John L. Hennessy, the tenth president of Stanford University, vehemently argued that educational systems must adapt to this new landscape. And so schools have started creating fab labs,[11] boot camps,[12] and all sorts of

---

[8] Policies designed to enhance human capital have multiplied since the OECD started using this term. See *Human Capital Investment,* OECD, 1998; *The Well-being of Nations. The Role of Human Social Capital,* OECD, 2001. These policies are especially concentrated in the education and training sectors.

[9] Reasonable accommodation is a term designating attempts by modern societies to meet the demands of their minority populations. The term was first used in Quebec in the context of various legislative measures dealing with minorities and indigenous populations.

[10] *Le Monde,* 16 April 2016.

[11] Short for "fabrication laboratory," fab labs are the third places of digital fabrication, operating according to the hacker ethos and the values of participatory culture. They are open to the public and offer the use of professional equipment so that users can create small-scale productions or rapid prototypes.

[12] Intensive sessions where students are called upon to rapidly develop skills.

contests to reward the most innovative thinkers in their midst. Degrees in "innovation management" have also appeared at many schools and universities, alongside courses in creativity — including Stanford's famous *d.school* which claims to promote design thinking.[13] All of these programs and courses take into account artistic, aesthetic, and cultural elements. In these new pedagogical models, the expert takes a back seat to the apprentice, whose fresh pair of eyes can spark innovation. Design thinking — variously depicted by scattered Post-its stuck on a board as ideas fly, the invention of the 3D printer and prototyping workshops, or individual playlists, mash-ups[14] and musical sampling — relies on breaking down silos and on promoting interdisciplinarity (or perhaps even a *lack* of discipline-based thinking), which in turn fosters creativity. All of these dimensions are widely exploited by young people in their diverse forms of cultural consumption, as well as the exchanges that are both the fuel and product of such behaviors.

Diversity has become an imperative: both consuming diversity (eclecticism, as discussed above), producing and preserving diversity (the French "cultural exception," as well as the wide variety of policies designed to protect endangered cultures and modelled on environmental and conservation policies). The diversity imperative relies on a standard of tolerance and the suspension of judgment which stems from the art world (philosophically speaking, this suspension of judgment forms the basis of taste preferences) but which is gradually spreading to all sectors of social life: tolerance with regard to sexual orientation, religious and political beliefs, dietary restrictions, etc. At the same time, however, the tribalism of individual generations — and perhaps of society as a whole — is broadly lamented. But there are no tribes. The segmentation of different lifestyles and living conditions among young people means that we cannot identify a single category called "youth" that overrides all previous socio-demographic affinity groups, including class, race, and gender. These characteristics combine and intersect to create highly complex embedded profiles, especially as the *mythos* of youth makes "the self" (identities, affiliations, trajectories, tastes, likes and dislikes, etc.) into an individual responsibility, as if social constraints were suddenly lifted thanks to the miracle of personal will and technological potential.

---

13   Design thinking is an approach to innovation and its management that seeks to combine analytical thought (which promotes a linear process with a clear beginning and end) and intuitive thoughts (which relies on co-creativity with feedback from end users).
14   A mash-up is a creation that combines elements from pre-existing content. Mash-ups exist in all different media: music, video, internet applications, literature, etc.

Creativity and diversity thus operate as social injunctions that produce their own share of inequalities and tensions: not all young people are creative, and the call to diversity conceals various problems and contradictions at its core. Creativity and openness to others requires a certain training — informal most of the time, and made invisible by the naturalizing effect of progress, which means that civilization and its processes come to be seen as "inherently" creative and open. Educational creativity and its policies do not target all young people equally, as they are focused on the major arts and certain forms of creativity only (very) rarely find their place in the sun (mods, for example). In addition, the imperative for openness does not apply to all individuals equally: individuals who are endowed with the greatest academic, social and economic skills are more likely to transform the latter into capital than those who are the victims of academic selection, economic competition, and social gentrification.

As universal as these standards may seem, they remain unequal in scope and application. Creativity and openness are more easily embraced by employed and highly educated young urban dwellers; it is likely this applies more to men than women, and more in certain geographical regions than others. If human development occurs through the diffusion of these standards of creativity and diversity, and if the human capital touted by our post-modern societies is indeed based on these two pillars, then the question of equal access for all returns to the fore. Education can no longer be limited to art: education must take into account culture, including scientific and technological culture.

2 Reconfiguring Public Space

A second transformation has taken place in youth technoculture: the reconfiguration of public space. The virtual public space of the internet has highlighted a new regime of opinions and amateurs that contrasts with traditional reliance on experts and debate. The internet encourages spontaneous self-expression, in relation to the collectives and events it engenders; it also bolsters the creation of new political stances that do not exploit the classic modalities of political expression (parties, unions, institutions, voting, etc.). There are many examples of this reappropriation of public space through opinion and emotion. In the political realm, we can cite *Occupy Wall Street* in the U.S., the Spanish *Indignados*, the French *Nuit debout* — but also international responses to 9/11 and the terrorist attacks in Paris (January and November 2015). Many of these reactions translated into movements of shared creativity, spawning hashtags and artists alongside a call to arms. We can also look at the proliferation of various "leaks" and increasing calls for transparency in public governance, which had led to a number of scandals (with the Panama Papers, for example).

Between the "broadcast yourself" mentality of social networks and the "do it yourself" ethos of internet democracy, there are many meaningful parallels to be drawn. While several thousand people got together on the Place de la République in Paris in the context of the *Nuit debout*, more than 80,000 people watched the reporting done by Rémy Buisine, a 25-year-old who participated in the debates and broadcast hours of footage on Periscope, Twitter's video service. Seeing these images, some people decided to rally to the movement on the Parisian square. This was similar to what happened in the 2000s, when the journalist Tim Pool used the U-stream platform to disseminate content live from *Occupy Wall Street*, thus alerting the public to police actions and abuses. This observation contradicts the common narrative that young people have resigned themselves to slacktivism, only being motivated to press "like" or sign petitions online. On the contrary, it corroborates the idea that, while such movements are social and political, they are also — and primarily — laboratories for experiments in cultural and political participation. Changing the world without seizing power is the goal of these collectives, in which we can see the legacy of anti-globalization and green movements when they seek new urban solutions, develop gender policies, fight against discrimination and build communities in the hopes of creating a society of solidarity. But we can also see the results of the ever more widespread standard of cultural diversity (which includes not just accepting diversity and living with it, but also attempting to enhance and engender it).

The various modalities of action used by such groups are mutually reinforcing when combined. In fact, grassroots political movements are gaining more and more traction among pro-ams, given that the latter are themselves the product of diverse and sometimes contradictory local breeding grounds. The objectives of pro-ams help to give new and expanded scope to grassroots collectives, although this does not occur without its share of internal tensions. Cultural diversity is sometimes accused of fomenting identity politics, which have deep roots on the internet; it also can give rise to culturalist explanations that challenge various forms of national or even international unity.

Perhaps we should view these various manifestations of groundswell as so many attempts to revisit — and revise — the social contract. Young people today are confronted with the limits and the human costs of capitalism (which they are all too familiar with, if we look at their skepticism with regard to major corporations and the workplace more generally).[15] They are witnessing

---

15   Conducted within the context of a European program, the study (titled *Changing Social Patterns of Relation to Work* — SPreW) was designed to shed light on how people view

democracy under attack, whether because of terrorism (Rousselin, 2014) or the resurgence of authoritarianism. Promised progress by Western societies, today's youth has instead experienced a series of setbacks: stalled educational improvements, difficulties on the labor market, a healthcare system mortgaged to the hilt and threatening to crumble, the gradual disappearance of intergenerational solidarity through redistribution, growing awareness of the climate crisis (Dolique, 2012). All of these elements have naturally influenced the political and social agenda of youth today.

3 Rejecting Pessimism

As we have seen, the contemporary context poses a number of issues with regard to which the younger generations have the potential to play a major role: the rise of populism, which finds its roots in the technoculture of self-expression, almost without contradiction; the appearance of threats to representative democracy on account of the uniqueness of individual voices (which representation necessarily betrays, as was argued by the *Gilets jaunes* in France); the proliferation of illiberal democracies (Chopin, 2019); the transformation of our relationship to truth, the gold standard of reality slowly being replaced by what seems "probable" and the legitimacy of individual opinions, etc. Elements that helped to shape yesterday's world are often accused of being tools for domination invented by the elites under the guise of "objectivity," a vestige of the past which must be discarded to pave the way towards a freer, more creative and more equal world.

In this context, the scientific method — to which this volume attempts to adhere — is only seen as one method among others, to be used when its conclusions are useful but to be discarded when the science contradicts what we want to say. Given the challenges of tomorrow, however, who can argue for only following one's individual intuition (no matter how good), emotions or experiences? While everyone may be free to believe what they want, not all thoughts are created equally. As a result, the key challenge of technoculture lies in the value attributed to combinatory and assumption-based thinking, which would ostensibly come to replace theory-based deductive reasoning. The danger then is not a lack of critical thinking, but the overabundance of

---

work and workplace relations across Europe, by generation and by country. The countries that participated were: Belgium, France, Germany, Hungary, Italy and Portugal. See www.ftu-namur.org/sprew.

its simulacra, of what Piper calls "pseudorationality" (Piper, 1998). Pseudorationality is a mental resource that constantly seeks to limit internal contradictions, cognitive dissonance and the impression of fragmentation, as well as a lack of continuity in our opinions (we must avoid contradicting ourselves, and most importantly, to be seen doing so). It thus gives us the illusion of epistemological solidity at the cost of true epistemological bravery — the ability to admit error, to contradict oneself, to go beyond one's modalities and patterns of thinking, etc. — which requires genuine creativity and reflection. While the contemporary imperative to think, create and exist on one's own is commendable, it cannot be satisfied in the absence of substantial education and skill development.

Transliteracy education with regard to technocultural skills is thus more than necessary to avoid cultural tribalism and fragmentation. One final example to prove this point. Researchers from the University of Pennsylvania (UPenn) analyzed the brain activity of subjects while they were reading *New York Times* articles, and linked this activity to the popularity of those same articles online (in other words, the number of times they were clicked on or shared). The results were conclusive: the success or "virality" of given articles can be predicted by the activity in certain regions of the brain — areas that are involved in self-representation and social cognition. That is to say: in the technocultural world, the choice to share an article depends more on what we expect the reaction of others will be (will my "friends" like it and is it consistent with my image and what they know of me? will it increase my personal prestige or improve my reputation?) than on any analysis of the text in question (Scholz, Baek, O'Donnell, Kim, Cappella, and Falk, 2017).

Focusing on these risks should not completely overshadow the benefits and possibilities of the technocultural future, however. Creativity and innovation can be developed, so long as cross-cutting educational policies come to support the myriad ad hoc and fragmented forms of learning that young people are currently assembling for themselves in the technocultural wilds. While this volume has presented the risks of technoculture in great detail, it has also endeavored to remain optimistic, rejecting pessimism and declinist arguments more specifically. The meandering paths that young people follow when they are led by their curiosity can shed light on what an ideal society might look like. From these youth trajectories, we may be able to develop number of educational proposals that are not predominantly based on enhancing technological skills (which are, as we have demonstrated, largely secondary compared to their strictly cultural counterparts), but rather on fostering a comprehensive political program of harmonious co-existence in which cultural citizenship will be able to truly flourish.

Bibliography

Reports

AFUTT-ANSA. 2001. *L'accès de tous aux télécommunications.* https://www.cnle.gouv.fr/IMG/pdf/ANSA_AFUTT_etude_sur_Tarif_social_NTIC_juin2011.pdf.

ARCEP. 2012. *Annual report.* https://www.arcep.fr/actualites/les-communiques-de-presse/detail/n/larcep-publie-son-rapport-annuel-2012.html.

Centre d'analyse stratégique. 2009. *La société et l'économie à l'aune de la révolution numérique.* http://archives.strategie.gouv.fr/cas/content/la-societe-et-l'economie-l'aune-de-la-revolution-numerique.html.

CIBER group. 2008. "Information behavior of the researcher of the future". University College London (UCL). http://citeseerx.ist.psu.edu/viewdoc/download?doi=10.1.1.643.8970&rep=rep1&type=pdf.

Conseil d'Analyse Économique. 2013. "L'emploi des jeunes peu qualifiés en France," *Les notes du conseil d'analyse économique,* no. 4: http://www.cae-eco.fr/L-emploi-des-jeunes-peu-qualifies-en-France-Note-du-CAE-n04-avril-2013,205. English translation available: "The employment of the low-skilled youth in France": http://www.cae-eco.fr/IMG/pdf/cae-note004-en.pdf.

France Stratégie. 2013. *Internet Prospective 2030.* https://www.strategie.gouv.fr/publications/internet-prospective-2030.

UNESCO. 2005. *Vers les sociétés du savoir.* http://www.unesdoc.unesco.org/images/0014/001419/141907f.pdf. English translation available: "Towards knowledge societies," https://unesdoc.unesco.org/ark:/48223/pf0000141843.

Prime Minister and State Secretary for Prospectives and Evaluation of Public Policies. 2008. *France numérique 2012.* https://www.vie-publique.fr/rapport/30143-france-numerique-2012-plan-de-developpement-economie-numerique.

Prime Minister and State Secretary for Prospectives and Evaluation of Public Policies. 2011. *France numérique 2012–2021. Bilan et Perspectives.* https://www.vie-publique.fr/rapport/30144-france-numerique-2012-2020-bilan-et-perspectives.

Books and articles

Acland, C. R. 2003. *Screen traffic: Movies, Multiplexes, and Global Culture.* Durham: Duke University Press.

Aguiton, C. and Cardon, D. 2012. "Expression de soi et créations identitaires sur le Web 2.0". *Lectures jeunesse* September: 10–15.

Afsa Essafi, C. and Buffeteau, S. 2006. "L'activité féminine en France : quelles évolutions récentes, quelles tendances pour l'avenir ?". *Économie et Statistique* 398–399: 85–97.

Aillerie, K. 2012. "Pratiques juvéniles d'information : de l'incertitude à la sérendipité". *Revue Documentaliste-Sciences de l'Information* 6: 62–69.

Alix, C. 2017. "La monnaie qui rend fou". *Libération*, 30 November 2017.

Allard, L. 2002. "Pluraliser l'espace public : esthétique et médias". *Quaderni* 18: 141–159.

Allard, L., and Vandenberghe, F. 2003. "Express yourself! Les pages perso. Entre légitimation technopolitique de l'individualisme expressif et authenticité réflexive peer to peer". *Réseaux* 117: 191–219.

Allison-Bunnell, S., and Thomson, S. 2007. 16–45. "Débutants et experts dans la science citoyenne nord-américaine". In *Des sciences citoyennes?*, edited by F. Charvolin, A. Micoud and L. Nyhart. La Tour d'Aigues: Éditions de l'Aube.

Amaret, C. and Graziani, C. 2019. *Le Peuple et le Président*. Paris: Michel Lafont.

Amselle, J.-L. 2001. *Branchements : anthropologie de l'universalité des cultures*. Paris: Flammarion.

Anderson, B. 1983. *Imagined Communities. Reflections on the Origin and Spread of Nationalism*. London: Verso.

Anderson, C. 2008. "The End of Theory: The Data Deluge Makes the Scientific Method Obsolete". *Wired Magazine:* https://www.wired.com/2008/06/pb-theory/.

Anderson, E. 2011. *The Cosmopolitan Canopy: Race and Civility in Everyday Life*. New York: W. W. Norton & Company.

Ang, I. 1985. *Watching Dallas: Soap Opera and the Melodramatic Imagination*. London: Methuen Publishing.

Appadurai, A. 2006. *Fear of Small Numbers: An Essay on the Geography of Anger*. Durham (North Carolina): Duke University Press.

Appadurai, A. 2000. "Glassroots globalization and the research imagination". *Public Culture* 12 (1): 1–19.

Appadurai, A. 1996. *Modernity At Large: Cultural Dimensions of Globalization*. Minnesota: University of Minnesota Press.

Appiah, K. A. 2006. "The case for contamination". *The New York Times Magazine*, 1 January 2006.

Arleo, A. and Delalande, J. (eds). 2011. *Cultures enfantines: universalité et diversité*. Rennes: Presses universitaires de Rennes.

Arnold, G. B. 2008. *Conspiracy Theory in Film, Television and Politics*. Westport: Praeger Publishers.

Assouline, D. 2008. "Les nouveaux médias : des jeunes libérés ou abandonnés?". *Rapport d'information fait au nom de la Commission des Affaires Culturelles,* Senate, no. 46.

Arnold, G. B. 2008. *Conspiracy Theory in Film, Television and Politics*. Westport: Praeger Publishers.

BIBLIOGRAPHY   181

Attias-Donfut, C., Lapierre, N. and Ségalen, M. 2002. *Le nouvel esprit de famille.* Paris: Odile Jacob.

Attias-Donfut, C., Fine, R. and Achinger, C. 2012. "Introduction to the Special Issue on Antisemitism, Racism, and Islamophobia". *European Societies* 14 (3): 467–469.

Aufray, N. and Georges, F. 2012. "Les productions audiovisuelles des joueurs de jeux vidéo : entre formation des professionnels et apprentissages esthétiques autodidactes". *Réseaux* 175: 56–75.

Autret, M., 2002. "La bouillotique nous gagne". *Écrire et Éditer,* no. 39.

Bach, J.-F., Houdé, O., Léna, P., and Tisseron, S. 2013. *L'Enfant et les écrans,* Avis de l'Académie des Sciences: https://www.academie-sciences.fr/pdf/rapport/avis0113.pdf.

Bajoit, G. and Franssen, A. 1995. *Les jeunes dans la compétition culturelle.* Paris: Presses universitaires de France.

Balibar, E., Bantigny, L., Chauvel, L., Graeber, D., Piketty, T., and Zancarini-Fournel, M. 2019. *Le fond de l'air est jaune.* Paris: Seuil.

Bandura, A. 1986. *Social Foundations of Thought and Action. A Social Cognitive Theory.* Englewood Cliffs (New Jersey): Prentice Hall.

Bandura, A. 1980. *L'apprentissage social.* Brussels: Mardaga.

Barlow, J. P. 1996. *A Declaration of the Independence of Cyberspace:* https://www.eff.org/cyberspace-independence.

Bartmanski, D. and Woodward, I. 2015. *Vinyl: The Analogue Record in the Digital Age.* London: Bloomsbury Academic.

Barrère, A. 2011. *L'Éducation buissonnière.* Paris: Éditions Armand Colin.

Barrot, A. 2000. *L'enseignement mis à mort.* Paris: Éditions 84.

Baudelot, C., Gollac, M., Bessière, C., Coutant, I., Godechot, O., Serre, D., and Viguier, F. 2003. *Travailler pour être heureux?* Paris: Fayard.

Baudrillard, J. 1998 [1970]. *The Consumer Society. Myths and Structures.* London: Sage.

Bauman, Z. 2005. *Liquid Life.* Cambridge: Polity.

Beaudoin, V. 2012. "Trajectoires et réseau des écrivains sur le Web : construction de la notoriété et du marché". *Réseaux* 175: 107–144.

Beaudoin, V. and Pasquier, D. 2014. "Organisation et hiérarchisation des mondes de la critique amateur cinephile". *Réseaux* 183: 125–159.

Beaudoin, V. and Velvoska, J. 1999. "Constitution d'un espace de communication sur Internet". *Réseaux* 99: 121–179.

Beck, U. 1998. *World Risk Society.* Cambridge: Polity Press.

Beneton, P. and Touchard, J. 1970. "Les interprétations de la crise de mai–juin 1968". *Revue Française de Sciences Politiques* 3: 7–18.

Bergé, A. and Granjon, F. 2005. "Réseaux relationnels et éclectisme culturel". *Revue LISA/LISA e-journal (online), Media, culture, history/Culture and society,* January: http://lisa.revues.org/909; DOI: 10.4000/lisa.909).

Berthomier, N. and Octobre, S. 2019a. "Enfants et écrans de 0 à 2 ans". *Culture Etudes* 1: https://www.culture.gouv.fr/Sites-thematiques/Etudes-et-statistiques/Publications/Collections-de-synthese/Culture-etudes-2007–2019/Enfants-et-ecrans-de-0-a-2-ans-CE-2019-1.

Berthomier, N. and Octobre, S. 2019b. "Primo-socialisation culturelle par les climats familiaux". *Culture Etudes* 2: https://www.culture.gouv.fr/Sites-thematiques/Etudes-et-statistiques/Publications/Collections-de-synthese/Culture-etudes-2007–2019/Primo-socialisation-culturelle-par-les-climats-familiaux-CE-2019-2.

Beuscart, J.-S., 2008. "Sociabilité en ligne, notoriété virtuelle et carrière artistique". *Réseaux* 152: 139–168.

Beuscart, J.-S. and Crepel, M. 2014. "Les plates formes d'auto-publication artistique en ligne : quatre figures de l'engagement des amateurs dans le web 2.0". In *Les stratèges de la notoriété. Intermédiaires et consécration dans les univers artistiques*, edited by W. Lizé, D. Naudier and S. Sofio, 113–123. Paris: Archives Contemporaines.

Bigot, R., Croutte, P. and Daudey, E. 2013. *La diffusion des technologies de l'information et de la communication dans la société française*. Paris: CREDOC.

Birch, H. 2016. "Feedback in Online Writing Forums: Effects on Adolescents Writer". *Teaching/Writing: The Journal of Teacher Education* 5 (1). http://scholarworks.wmich.edu/wte/vol5/iss1/5.

Blimenkranz C., Gressen K., Greif M., Leonard S., Resnick S., Saval N., Schmitt E., and Taylor A. (eds), 2011. *Occupy! Scenes from Occupied America*. London: Verso.

Blondeau, O. 2007. *Devenir Média. L'activisme sur Internet, entre défection et expérimentation*. Paris: Éditions Amsterdam.

Blondiaux, L. 2008. *Le nouvel esprit de la démocratie. Actualité de la démocratie participative*. Paris: Seuil.

Boltanski, L. 2012. *Énigmes et complots. Une enquête à propos d'enquêtes*. Paris: Gallimard.

Boltanski, L. and Chiapello, E. 1999. *Le nouvel esprit du capitalisme*. Paris: Gallimard.

Bonnet, D., Rollet, C., and de Suremain, C.-E. (eds). 2012. *Modèles d'enfances : successions, transformations, croisements*. Paris: Éditions des archives contemporaines.

Boubée, N. 2011. "Caractériser les pratiques informationnelles des jeunes: les problèmes laissés ouverts par les deux conceptions 'natifs' et 'naïfs' numériques". *Communication Rencontres Savoirs CDI*, 24 October.

Bouchayer, F. 1986. "Les usagers des médecines alternatives : itinéraires thérapeutiques, culturels, existentiels". *Revue Française des Affaires Sociales* 5: 105–115.

Bougnoux, D. 2001. *Introduction aux sciences de la communication*. Paris: La Découverte.

Bourdieu, P. 1996. *Raisons pratiques*. Paris: Seuil.

Boyadjian, J. 2016. *Analyser les opinions politiques sur Internet. Enjeux théoriques et défis méthodologiques*. Paris: Dalloz.

boyd, d. 2014. *It's Complicated: The Social Lives of Networked Teens*. New Haven/London: Yale University Press.

Brandy, G. 2020. "Des fans de K-pop ont perturbé un meeting de Donald Trump : comment ont-ils atteint ce degré d'influence en ligne ?". *Le Monde,* 24 June: https://www.lemonde.fr/pixels/article/2020/06/24/black-lives-matter-meeting-de-trump-comment-expliquer-le-pouvoir-en-ligne-des-fans-de-k-pop_6043954_4408996.html.

Bréchon, P. 2013. "L'individualisation des valeurs européennes". *Futuribles* 395: 119–136.

Breton, P. 2008. *Convaincre sans manipuler. Apprendre à argumenter.* Paris: La Découverte.

Brice, L., Croutte, P., Jauneau-Cottet, P., and Lautié, S. 2015. *La diffusion des technologies de l'information et de la communication dans la société française — édition 2015.* Paris: CREDOC.

Bromberger, C. 1998. *Passions ordinaires.* Paris: Bayard.

Bronner, G. 2018. *Cabinet de curiosités sociales.* Paris: Presses universitaires de France.

Bronner, G. 2016 [2009]. *La pensée extrême. Comment des hommes ordinaires deviennent des fanatiques.* Paris: Presses universitaires de France.

Bronner, G. 2013. *La démocratie des crédules.* Paris: Presses universitaires de France.

Bronner, S. E., 2004, "Human rights, religion and the cosmopolitan sensibility". *Human Rights Review* 5: 33–49.

Brotcorne, P., Mertens, L., and Valenduc, G. 2009. *Les jeunes off-line et la fracture numérique. Les risques d'inégalités dans la génération des « natifs numériques »,* étude réalisée à la demande du Service public de programmation Intégration sociale et de son Ministre de tutelle. Namur: Centre de recherche Travail & Technologies de l'ASBL Fondation Travail-Université.

Brougère, G. and Ulmann, A. L. 2009. *Apprendre de la vie quotidienne.* Paris: Presses universitaires de France.

Bryson, B. 1996. "What about the univores? Musical dislikes and group-based identity construction among Americans with low levels of education". *Poetics* 25 (2–3): 141–156.

Buckingham, D. 2000. *After the death of childhood.* London: Wiley.

Buckingham, D. and Sefton-Green, J. 2004a. "Structure, Agency and Pedagogy in Children's Media Culture". 125–136. In *Pikachu's Global Adventure: The Rise and Fall of Pokémon,* edited by J. Tobin. Durham (North Carolina): Duke University Press.

Buckingham, D. and Sefton-Green, J. 2004b. "Gotta Catch 'Em All: Structure, Agency and Pedagogy in Children's Media Culture". *Media Culture & Society* 25 (3): 379–399.

Buckingham, D., and Sefton-Green, J. 1994. *Cultural Studies Goes to School: Reading and Teaching Popular Culture.* London: Taylor and Francis.

Casati, R. 2013a. *Contre le colonialisme numérique : manifeste pour continuer de lire.* Paris: Albin Michel.

Casati, R. 2013b. *An Annotated Glossary for Dealing with the Digital Migration*: http://roberto.casati.free.fr/Glossary_For_Negotiating_Digital_Migrations%28Casati 2013%29.pdf.

Castells, M. 2013. *Communication et pouvoir*. Paris, MSH.castekls.
Cardon, D. 2015. *A quoi rêvent les algorithmes, nos vies à l'heure des big data*. Paris: Seuil.
Cardon, D. 2012. "Dans l'esprit du PageRank. Une enquête sur l'algorithme de Google". *Réseaux* 177: 63–95.
Cardon, D. 2010 a. *La démocratie Internet : promesses et limites*. Paris: Seuil.
Cardon, D. 2010 b. "Confiner le clair-obscur: réflexions sur la protection de la vie personnelle sur le web 2.0". 315–328. In *Web social. Mutation de la communication*, edited by F. Millerand, S. Proulx, and J. Rueff. Québec: Presses de l'université du Québec.
Cardon, D. 2008. "Le design de la visibilité. Un essai de cartographie du web 2.0". *Réseaux* 152: 93–137.
Cardon, D. and Levrel, J. 2009. "La vigilance participative. Une interprétation de la gouvernance des Wikipédia". *Réseaux* 154: 51–89.
Carpentier, L. 2013. "YouTube machine à tubes". *Cahiers du Monde*, 2–3 November 2013.
Carr, N. 2008. *The Big Switch: Rewiring the World from Edison to Google.* New York: W. W. Norton & Company.
Carr N., 2010. *The Shallows: What the Internet is Doing to Our Brains*. New York: W.W. Norton & Company.
Casilli, A. 2010. *Les liaisons numériques. Vers une nouvelle sociabilité?* Paris: Éditions du Seuil.
Castells, M. 2013. *Communication et pouvoir*. Paris, MSH.
Castell, L., Portela, M. and Rivalin, R. 2016. "Les principales ressources des 18–24 ans". *Insee Première* no. 1604.
Castronovo, R. 2007. *Beautiful Democracy: Aesthetics and Anarchy in a Global Era.* Chicago: University of Chicago Press.
Chaillan, M. 2016. *Game of Thrones. Une métaphysique des meurtres.* Paris: Le Passeur.
Chaillan, M. 2015. *Harry Potter à l'école de la philosophie.* Paris: Ellipses.
Charlier, B. and Henri, F. (eds). 2010. *Apprendre avec les technologies.* Paris: Presses universitaires de France.
Chopin, T. 2019. "Démocratie illibérale ou autoritarisme majoritaire. Contribution à l'analyse des populismes en Europe". *Institut Jacques Delors. Policy Paper* 235: https://institutdelors.eu/wp-content/uploads/2019/02/Democratieilliberaleou autoritarismemajoritaire-Chopin-fevrier2019.pdf.
Cicchelli, V. 2018. *Plural and Shared. The Sociology of a Cosmopolitan World.* Leiden/Boston: Brill.
Cicchelli, V. 2013. *L'autonomie des jeunes, questions politiques et sociologiques sur les mondes étudiants.* Paris: La Documentation française.
Cicchelli, V. 2012. *L'esprit cosmopolite, Voyages de formation des jeunes en Europe.* Paris: Presses de Sciences Po.
Cicchelli, V. and Octobre, S. 2018a. *Aesthetico-cultural cosmopolitanism among French youth.* London: Palgrave.

Cicchelli, V. and Octobre, S. 2018b. "La radicalité informationnelle: prolifération des vérités alternatives, défiance à l'égard des médias et adhésion aux théories du complot". 319–364. In *La tentation radicale : enquête auprès des lycéens,* edited by O. Galland and A. Muxel. Paris: Presses universitaires de France.

Cicchelli, V. and Octobre, S. 2018c. "Fictionnalisation des attentats et théorie du complot chez les adolescents". *Quaderni* 95: 53–64.

Cicchelli, V. and Octobre, S. 2017a. "Aesthetico-cultural cosmopolitanism: a new kind of "good taste" among French youth". 69–95. In *Cosmopolitanism, Markets, and Consumption. A Critical Global Perspective,* edited by J. Emonstpool and I. Woodward. London: Palgrave.

Cicchelli, V. and Octobre, S. 2017b. "Aesthetico-Cultural Cosmopolitanism Among French Young People: Beyond Social Stratification. The Role of Aspirations and Competences". *Cultural Sociology* 11 (4): 416–437.

Cicchelli, V. and Octobre, S. 2015. "Sur le cosmopolitisme esthétique chez les jeunes". *Le Débat* 183: 101–109.

Cicchelli, V. and Octobre, S. 2013. "A cosmopolitan perspective of globalization: Cultural and aesthetic consumption among young people". *Studies of Changing Societies* 3 (7): 3–23.

Cicchelli, V., Octobre, S. and Riegel, V. 2016. "After the Omnivore, the Cosmopolitan Amateur". *Global Studies Journal* 9 (1): 55–70.

Cicchelli, V., Octobre, S., Riegel, V., Katz-Gerro, T., and Handy, F. 2018. "A tale of three cities: Aesthetico-cultural cosmopolitanism as a new capital among youth in Paris, São Paulo, and Seoul". *Journal of Consumer Culture:* https://doi.org/10.1177/1469540518818629.

Citton, Y. 2017. *The Ecology of Attention.* London: Polity.

Citton, Y. 2010. *L'avenir des humanités. Économie de la connaissance ou cultures de l'interprétation ?* Paris: La Découverte.

Clark, C. and Foster, A. 2005. *Children's and Young People's Reading Habits and Preferences: The Who, What, Why, Where and When.* London: National Literacy Trust.

Coale, S. C. 2005. *Paradigms of Paranoia: The Culture of Conspiracy in Contemporary American Fiction.* Tuscaloosa: University Alabama Press.

Cocquebert, V. 2019. *Millenium Burn-Out: X, Y, Z ... comment l'arnaque des « générations » consume la jeunesse.* Paris: Arkhé.

Cohen, G. 2013. "Deeper into Bullshit". 321–339. In *The Contours of Agency: Essays on Themes from Harry Franckfurt,* edited by S. Buss and L. Overton. Cambridge: MIT Press.

Coit, Murphy P. 2003. "Books Are Dead, Long Live Books". 52–65. In *Rethinking Media Change: The Aesthetic of Transition,* edited by D. Thornton and H. Jenkins. Cambridge: MIT Press.

Colonna, V. 2010. *L'art des séries télé.* Paris: Payot.

Comarmond, (de) L. xxx. 2018. "Les syndicats bousculés par le phénomène des Gilets jaunes", *Les echos.fr.* 14 November: https://www.lesechos.fr/economie-france/social/les-syndicats-bouscules-par-le-phenomene-des-gilets-jaunes-147328#Xtor=AD-6000.

Combes, B. 2010. *How much do traditional literacy skills count? Literacy in the 21st century & reading from the screen*: http://www.slideshare.net/IASLonline/literacy-skills-challenged.

Cook, D. T. 2004. *The Commodification of Childhood: The Children's Clothing Industry and the Rise of the Child Consumer.* Durham (North Carolina): Duke University Press.

Cordier, A. 2015. *Grandir connectés. Les adolescents et la recherche d'information.* Paris: C&F Éditions.

Cortes, A. 2019. "Les résultats du « vrai débat » des Gilets Jaunes". *Marianne,* 21 March: https://www.marianne.net/societe/exclusif-les-premiers-resulats-du-vrai-debat-des-gilets-jaunes.

Corsaro, W. 2011 [3rd edition]. *The Sociology of Childhood.* London: Sage.

Corsaro, W. 2003. *We're Friends, Right?: Inside Kids' Culture.* Washington DC: Joseph Henry Press.

Coulangeon P. 2013. "Class and Culture in Contemporary France". 46–57. In *Language and Social Structure in Urban France,* edited by M. Jones and C.D. Hornsby. Jones M. Oxford: Legenda.

Coulangeon, P. 2011. *Les métamorphoses de la distinction, inégalités culturelles dans la France d'aujourd'hui.* Paris: Grasset.

Coulangeon, P. 2007. "Lecture et télévision: les transformations du rôle culturel de l'école à l'épreuve de la massification scolaire". *Revue française de sociologie* 48 (4): 657–691.

Coulangeon, P. 2003. "Quel est le rôle de l'école dans la démocratisation de l'accès aux équipements culturels?". 245–262. In *Les publics de la culture,* edited by O. Donnat and P. Tolila. Paris: Presses de Sciences Po.

Coulangeon, P. and Duval, J. 2013. *Trente ans après la Distinction.* Paris: La Découverte.

Crary, J. 2000. *Suspensions of Perception: Attention, Spectacle and Modern Culture.* Cambridge: M.I.T. Press.

Croutte, P., Lautié, S., and Hoibian, S. 2016. *Baromètre du numérique.* CREDOC: https://www.credoc.fr/publications/barometre-du-numerique-edition-2016.

Dagiral, E. and Tessier, L. 2008. "24 heures! Le sous-titrage des nouvelles séries télévisées". 107–123. In *Les arts moyens aujourd'hui,* edited by F. Gaudez. Paris: L'Harmattan.

Dagnaud, M. 2013. *Génération Y : Les jeunes et les réseaux sociaux de la dérision à la subversion.* Paris: Presses de Sciences Po.

Dajez, F. and Roucous, N. 2010. "Le jeux vidéo, une affaire d'enfants. Enquête sur le parc à jouets numérique d'enfants de 6 à 11 ans". 85–102. In *Enfance et culture.*

Transmission, appropriation et representation, edited by S. Octobre. Paris: La Documentation Française.

Damon, J. 2013. "Les métamorphoses de la famille : rétrospective, tendances et perspectives en France". *Futuribles* 396: 5–21.

Daniels J, Gregory, K and McMillan Cottom, T. (eds). 2017. *Digital Sociologies.* Bristol: Policy Press.

Davenel, Y.-M. 2014. *Les pratiques numériques des jeunes en insertion socioprofessionnelle. Étude de cas: Les usagers des missions locales face aux technologies de l'information et de la communication.* Paris: Emmaüs Connect.

Davidson, C. N. 2011. *Now You See It: How Technology and Brain Science Will Transform Schools and Business for the 21st Century.* New York: Penguin.

Dawson S. and McWilliam, E. L. 2008. "Teaching for Creativity: Towards Sustainable and Replicable Pedagogical Practice". *Higher Education* 56 (6): 633–643.

Certeau (de), M. 1980. *L'invention du quotidien I, Les arts de faire.* Paris: UGE.

Debord, G. 1967. *La société du spectacle.* Paris: Buchet/Chastel.

Delacroix, G. 2018. "Sur le web, les gilets jaunes apprennent à vitesse grand V". *Médiapart.* 7 December: https://www.mediapart.fr/journal/france/071218/sur-le-web-les-gilets-jaunes-apprennent-vitesse-grand-v?onglet=full.

Delalande, J. 2014. "Comment des enfants et des adolescents voient-ils les âges de la vie?". *Le Télémaque* 37: 71–81.

Delamotte, E., Liquète, V., and Frau-Meigs, D. 2014. "La translittératie, à la convergence des cultures de l'information : supports, contexte et modalités". *Spirale* 53: 145–146.

Delaunay-Teterel, H. and Cardon, D. 2006. "La production de soi comme technique relationnelle. Un essai de typologie des blogs par leurs publics". *Réseaux* 138: 15–71.

Deleuze, G. 1981. *Logique de la sensation* (2 vols). Paris: Éditions de la Différence.

Denouël, J. and Granjon, F. 2010. "Exposition de soi et reconnaissance de singularités subjectives sur les sites de réseaux sociaux". *Sociologie* 1: 25–43.

Descombes, V. 2004. *Le complément de sujet. Enquête sur le fait d'être soi-même.* Paris: Gallimard.

Desmurget, M. 2019. *La fabrique du crétin digital. Les dangers des écrans pour nos enfants.* Paris: Le Seuil.

Détrez, C. 2015. *Quel genre ?* Paris: Thierry Magnier Éditions.

Détrez, C. and Octobre, S. 2011. "De Titeuf aux séries à succès : trajectoires de lecteurs de la fin de l'enfance à la grande adolescence". 61–92. In *Lectures et lecteurs à l'heure d'Internet : livre, presse et bibliothèques,* edited by C. Evans. Paris: Édition du Cercle de la Librairie.

Détrez, C. and Vanhée, O. 2012. *Les mangados, lire des mangas à l'adolescence.* Paris: Centre Georges Pompidou.

Dewey, J. 1934. *Art as experience.* New York: Perigree Books/Penguin.

Dieguez, S. 2018. *Total Bullshit ! Au cœur de la post-vérité.* Paris: Presses universitaires de France.

Didier, E. 2013. "Histoire de la représentativité statistique: quand le politique refait toujours surface". 15–30. In *La Représentativité en statistique.* Paris: Presses universitaires de France/INED.

DiMaggio, P. 1992. "Cultural boundaries and structural change: the extension of the high culture model to theater, opera and the dance, 1900–1940". 21–57. In *Cultivating Differences: Symbolic Boundaries and the Making of Inequality,* edited by M. Lamont and M. Fournier. Chicago: The University of Chicago Press.

DiMaggio, P. 1987. "Classification in art". *American Sociological Review* 52 (4): 440–445.

DiMaggio, P. 1982. "Cultural capital and school success: the impact of status culture participation on the grades of US high school students". *American Sociological Review* 47 (2): 189–201.

Dolique, L. 2012. *Risques globaux et développement durable : fausses pistes et vraies solutions.* Paris: L'Harmattan.

Donnat, O. 2013. "Les connaissances artistiques des Français. Éléments de comparaison, 1988–2008". *Culture Études* 5: 1–16.

Donnat, O. 2009a. *Les pratiques culturelles des Français à l'ère du numérique.* Paris: La Découverte.

Donnat, O. 2009b. "Les passions culturelles, entre engagement total et jardin secret". *Réseaux* 153: 79–127.

Donnat, O. 1994. *Les Français face à la culture, de l'exclusion à l'éclectisme.* Paris: La Découverte.

Donnat, O. and Lévy, F. 2007. "Approche générationnelle des pratiques culturelles et médiatiques". *Culture prospective* 3: 1–31.

Drew, R. 2001. *Karaoke Nights: An Ethnographic Rhapsody.* Lanham: Altamira Press.

Duch, H., Fisher, E. M., Ensari, I., and Harrington, A. 2013. "Screen time use in children under 3 years old: a systematic review of correlates". *International Journal of Behavioral Nutrition and Physical Activity* 10 (1): 102: http://www.ijbnpa.org/content/10/1/102.

Dumazedier, J. 1988. *Révolution culturelle du temps libre, 1968–1988.* Paris: Méridiens Klincksieck.

Dunbar, R. 1997. *Grooming, Gossip and the Evolution of Language.* Harvard: Harvard University Press.

Dupeyron, J.-F. 2012. "L'enfance de l'hypermodernité : le problème de l'autorité". 13–31. In *Repenser l'enfance,* edited by A. Kerlan and L. Loeffel. Paris: Hermann éditeurs.

Durand, E. 2016. *L'attaque des clones, La diversité culturelle à l'ère de l'hyperchoix.* Paris: Presses de Sciences Po.

Ehrenberg, A. 2010. *La société du malaise.* Paris: Odile Jacob.

Esquenazi, J.-P. 2011. *Les séries télévisées? L'avenir du cinéma*. Paris: Armand Colin.
Featherstone, M. 1987. "Lifestyle and Consumer Culture". *Theory, Culture & Society* 4 (1): 55–70.
Feixa, C. and Nofre, J. (eds). 2013. *#Generación Indignada, Topías y Utopías del 15M*. Lleida: Milenio.
Fiske, S. and Taylor, S. 1984. *Social Cognition*. New York: Random House.
Fize, M. 2006. *L'adolescent est une personne … normale*. Paris: Seuil.
Fize, M. 1990. *La démocratie familiale. Évolution des relations parents-enfants*. Paris: Presses de la Renaissance.
Flank, L. 2011. *Voices From the 99 Percent: An Oral History of the Occupy Wall Street Movement*. St. Petersburg: Red Black & Publishers.
Flichy, P. 2010. *Le sacre de l'amateur, sociologie des passions ordinaires à l'ère numérique*. Paris: Seuil.
Foa Roberto, S. and Mounk, Y. 2016. "The Danger of Deconsolidation: The Democratic Disconnect". *Journal of Democracy* 3: 5–17.
Fondation Jean Jaurès. 2019. "Éric Drouet et Maxime Nicolle: que nous apprennent leurs pages Facebook?". *L'Obs*. 14 January: https://www.nouvelobs.com/politique/20190114.OBS8414/eric-drouet-et-maxime-nicolle-que-nous-apprennent-leurs-pages-facebook.html.
Fourquet, J. and Manternach, S. 2018. *Les « Gilets jaunes » : révélateur fluorescent des fractures françaises*. Paris: Fondation Jean-Jaurès.
Frank, T. 2015. "Occuper Wall Street, un mouvement tombé amoureux de lui-même". *Le Monde Diplomatique*. 3 January: 3–4.
François, S. 2009. "Fanf(r)ictions". *Réseaux* 153: 157–181.
Franguiadakis, S., Ion, J. and Viot, P. 2005. *Militer aujourd'hui*. Paris: Autrement.
Friedman, T. L. 2005. *The World is Flat: A Brief History of the Twenty-First Century*. New York: Farrar, Straus and Giroux.
Frith, S. 1989. "Towards an Aesthetic of Popular Music". 257–275. In *Music and Society: The Politics of Composition, Performance and Reception*, edited by R. Leppert and S. McClary. Cambridge: Cambridge University Press.
Galland, O. 2011. *Sociologie de la jeunesse*. Paris: Armand Colin.
Galland, O. 2001. "Adolescence, post-adolescence, jeunesse: retour sur quelques interprétations". *Revue française de sociologie* 42 (4): 611–640.
Galland, O. 1999. *Les Jeunes*. Paris: La Découverte.
Galland, O. and Roudet, B. 2012. *Une jeunesse différente? Les valeurs des jeunes Français depuis 30 ans*. Paris: INJEP/La Documentation Française.
Galland, O. and Roudet, B (eds). 2005. *Les jeunes européens et leurs valeurs. Europe occidentale, Europe centrale et orientale*. Paris: La Découverte.
Gambetta, D. 1994. "Godfather's gossip*". *European Journal of Sociology* 35 (2): 199–223.

Garcia Canclini, N., 2013. "Les enfants : entre la ville et les réseaux". 159–178. In *L'enfant et ses cultures : approches internationals,* edited by S. Octobre and R. Sirota. Paris: La Documentation Française.

Garcia Canclini, N. 2004. *Diferentes, desiguales y desconectados: mapas de la interculturalidad.* Barcelona: Gedisa.

Gardner, H. and Davis, K. 2014. *The App Generation: How Today's Youth Navigate Identity, Intimacy and Imagination in a Digital World.* New Haven/London: Yale University Press.

Gauchet, M. 2010. "Trois figures de l'individu". *Le Débat* 160: 45–62.

Gauvrit, N. and Delouvée, S. 2019. *Des têtes bien faites. Défense de l'esprit critique.* Paris: Presses universitaires de France.

Gee, J.-P. 2005. *Language, Learning and Gaming: A Critique of Traditional Schooling.* New York: Routledge.

Gee, J.-P. 2004. *Situated Language and Learning. A Critique of Traditional Schooling.* London: Routledge.

Gershuny, J. 2000. *Changing Times: Work and Leisure in Postindustrial Society.* Oxford: Oxford University Press.

Giddens, A. 1984. *The Constitution of Society. Outline of the Theory of Structuration.* Cambridge: Polity.

Giry, J. 2017. "Le complotisme 2.0, une étude de cas de vidéo recombinante : Alain Soral sauve Glenn et Tara dans *The Walking Dead*". *Quaderni* 94: 41–52.

Gitlin, T. 2012. *Occupy Nation: The Roots, the Spirit, and the Promise of Occupy Wall Street.* New York: It Books.

Glévarec, H. 2012. *La sériephilie : sociologie d'un attachement culturel et place de la fiction dans la vie des jeunes adultes.* Paris: Ellipses.

Glévarec, H. 2009. *La culture de la chambre : préadolescence et culture contemporaine dans l'espace familial.* Paris: La Documentation Française.

Glévarec, H. and Pinet, M. 2009. "Tablature et structuration des goûts musicaux : un modèle de structuration des préférences et des jugements". *Revue Française de sociologie* 50 (3): 599–640.

Goffman, E. 1973. *La mise en scène de la vie quotidienne : 1 la présentation de soi.* Paris: Éditions de Minuit.

Goldhaber, M. H. 1996. "Principles of the new economy": https://people.well.com/user/mgoldh/principles.html.

Granovetter, M. 1983. "The Strength of Weak Ties: A Network Theory Revisited". *Sociological Theory* 1: 201–233.

Grignon, C., and Passeron, J.-C. 1989. *Le Savant et le populaire. Misérabilisme et populisme en sociologie et en littérature.* Paris: Seuil/Gallimard.

Guibert, G.-C. 2004. *Le Mythe Madonna.* Paris: Nouveau Monde Éditions.

Guthrie, J. T. and Anderson, E. 1999. "Engagement in reading: processes of motivated, strategic, knowledgeable, social readers". 17–45. In *Engagement in Reading. Processes, Practices and Policy Implications*, edited by J. T. Guthrie and D. E. Alvermann. New York/London: Teachers College Press.

Gwiazdzinski, L. and Floris, B. 2019. *Sur la vague jaune : L'utopie d'un rond-point*. Paris: Éditeur Elyascop.

Habib, A. 2014. "Archives, modes de réemploi. Pour une archéologie du *found footage*". *Cinémas* 242–243: 97–122.

Hanson, K. and Nieuwensberg, O. (eds). 2013. *Reconceptualizing Children's Rights in International Development: Living Rights, Social Justice, Translations.* Cambridge: Cambridge University Press.

Hargittai, E. and Hinnant, A. 2008. "Digital Inequality: Differences in Young Adults' Use of the Internet". *Communication Research* 35 (5): 602–621.

Harrel, A. 2010. "Political tolerance, racist speech and the influence of social network". *Social Science Quarterly* 92: 724–740.

Hayles, K. 2012. *How We Think: Digital Media and Contemporary Technogenesis.* Chicago: The University of Chicago Press.

Heinich, N. 2012. *De la visibilité. Excellence et singularité en régime médiatique.* Paris: Gallimard.

Héran, F. 2013. "L'anglais hors la loi ? Enquête sur les langues de recherche et d'enseignement en France". *Population et sociétés* 501: 1–4.

Héran, F. 1988. "La sociabilité, une pratique culturelle". *Économie et statistiques* 216: 3–22.

Hindman, M. 2009. *The Myth of Digital Democracy.* Princeton: Princeton University Press.

Hobbs, R. 2010. "Digital and Media Literacy: A Plan of Action". *The Aspen Institute Communications and Society Program*: http://www.knightcomm.org/wp-content/uploads/2010/12/Digital_and_Media_Literacy_A_Plan_of_Action.pdf.

Hondeberie, I.,2017, "Le fabuleux secret de la grande muraille de Chine", *Le Journal de Montréal*, 17th February. https://www.journaldemontreal.com/2017/02/18/le-fabuleux-secret-de-la-grande-muraille-de-chine-1.

Houzel, D. 1998. "Attention consciente, attention inconsciente". *Spirale* 9: 24–36.

Inchley, J., Currie, D, Young, T., Samdal, O., Torsheim,T., Augustson, L., Mathison, F., Aleman-Diaz, A., Molcho, M., Weber, M., and Barnekow, V., 2016, "Growing up unequal. HBSC 2016 study (2013/2014 survey)", *Health Policy for Children and Adolescents*, No. 7. https://www.euro.who.int/en/health-topics/Life-stages/child-and-adolescent-health/health-behaviour-in-school-aged-children-hbsc/hbsc-international-reports/growing-up-unequal.-hbsc-2016-study-20132014-survey.

Illouz, E., 2006. *Les sentiments du capitalisme.* Paris: Seuil.

Ion, I. 1997. *La fin des militants.* Paris: L'Atelier.

Israel, D. 2019. "Gilets jaunes et médias, deux mondes qui se regardent sans se comprendre". *Médiapart*. 11 January: https://www.mediapart.fr/journal/france/110119/gilets-jaunes-et-medias-deux-mondes-qui-se-regardent-sans-se-comprendre?onglet=full.

Ito, M. 2008. *Hanging Out, Messing Around and Geeking Out: Kids Living and Learning with New Media.* Chicago: John D. and Catherine T. MacArthur Foundation.

Iwabuchi, K. 2002. "From Western Gaze to Global Gaze: Japanese Cultural Presence in Asia". 256–273. In *Global Culture: Media, Arts, Policy and Globalization,* edited by D. Crane, N. Kawashima and K. Kawasaki. New York: Routledge.

Jackson, N. and Shaw, M. 2005. *Subject perspectives on creativity: A preliminary synthesis.* York, UK: An Imaginative Curriculum Study for The Higher Education Academy.

Janssen, S., Verboord, M., and Kuipers, G. 2011. "Comparing cultural classification: high and popular arts in European and US newspapers". *Kölner Zeitschrift für Soziologie und Sozialpsychologie Special Issue* 51: 139–169.

Jameson, F. 2007. *La totalité comme complot : conspiration et paranoïa dans l'imaginaire contemporain.* Paris: Les Prairies Ordinaires.

Jamous, H. 1968. "Eléments pour une théorie sociologique des décisions politiques". *Revue française de sociologie* 9(1): 71–88.

Jehel, S. 2011. *Parents ou médias, qui éduque les préadolescents?* Paris: Ères.

Jenkins, H. 2007. *The Wow Climax: Tracing the Emotional Impact of Popular Culture.* New York: New York University Press.

Jenkins, H. 2006. *Convergence Culture: Where Old and New Media Collide.* New York: New York University Press.

Jenkins, H. 1992. *Textual Poachers.* New York: Routledge.

Jenkins, H. Ford, S. and Green, J. 2013. *Spreadable Media: Creating Value.* New York: New York University Press.

Jenkins, H., Clinton, K., Purushotma, R., Robison, A. J., and Weigel, M. 2006. *Confronting the Challenges of Participatory Culture: Media Education for the 21st Century.* Chicago: MacArthur.

Joerges, B. 1999. "Do Politics Have Artefacts?". *Social Studies of Science* 29 (3): 411–431.

Johnson, S., 2005. *Everything Bad is Good for You: How Today's Popular Culture Is Actually Making Us Smarter.* New York: Penguin.

Jost, F. 2018. *La méchanceté en actes à l'ère numérique.* Paris: CNRS Éditions.

Jost, F. 2015. *Les nouveaux méchants. Quand les séries américaines font bouger les lignes du Bien et du Mal.* Paris: Bayard.

Jost, F. 2011. *De quoi les séries américaines sont-elles le symptôme ?* Paris: CNRS Éditions.

Jost, F. 2001. *La télévision du quotidien. Entre réalité et fiction.* Brussels: De Boeck-INA.

Jouet, J. 2004. "Les dispositifs de construction de l'internaute par les mesures d'audience". *Le temps des médias* 3 (2): 160–174.

Kahnman, D. 1973. *Attention and Effort.* Englewood Cliffs (New Jersey): Prentice Hall.

Karbovnik, D. 2017. "De l'alterscience au conspirationnisme : l'exemple de la diffusion et de la réception du documentaire *La révélation des Pyramides* sur l'Internet". *Quaderni* 94: 63–74.

Karbovnik, D. 2015. "Théorie du complot et OVNIS". *Diogène* 249–250: 240–251.

Katz-Gerro, T. 2017. "Cross-National Differences in the Consumption of Non-National Culture in Europe". *Cultural Sociology* 11 (4): 438–467.

Keen, A. 2008. *Le culte de l'amateur, comment Internet détruit notre culture.* Paris: Scali.

Kimbrough, S. 2006. "On letting it slide". 3–18. In *Bullshit and Philosophy,* edited by G. Hardcastle and G. Reisch. Chicago: Open Court.

Kirschner, P. A. and De Bruyckere, P. 2017. "The Myth of the Digital Native and the Multitasker". *Teaching and Teacher Education* 67: 135–142.

Kniht, P. 2000. *Conspiracy Culture. From Kennedy to the X-Files.* New York: Routledge.

Koops, L. 2014. "Songs from the Car Seat: Exploring the Early Childhood Music-Making Place of the Family Vehicle". *Journal of Research in Music Education* 62 (1): 52–65.

Kotras, B. 2018. *La voix du Web : nouveaux régimes de l'opinion sur Internet.* Paris: Seuil.

Kredens, E., and Fontar, B. 2010. *Comprendre le comportement des enfants sur Internet pour les prévenir des dangers.* Paris: Fondation pour l'enfance.

Lahire, B. 2006. *L'homme pluriel : les ressorts de l'action.* Paris: Fayard.

Lahire, B. 2000. "Héritages sexués et incorporation des habitudes et des croyances". 9–25. In *La dialectique des rapports hommes-femmes,* edited by T. Blöss. Paris: Presses universitaires de France.

Lahire, B. 1995. *Tableaux de famille.* Paris: Gallimard.

Lamont, M. and Molnar, V. 2002. "The study of boundaries in the social sciences". *Annual Review of Sociology* 28: 167–195.

Lamont, M., Pendergrass, S., and Pachucki, M. C. 2015. "Symbolic boundaries". 850–855. In *International Encyclopedia of Social and Behavioral Sciences,* edited by J. Wright. Oxford: Elsevier.

Lamont, M. and Thevenot, L. 2000. *Rethinking comparative cultural sociology. Repertoires of evaluation in France and United States.* Cambridge: Cambridge University Press.

Lapalissade, G. 1963. *L'entrée dans la vie. Essai sur l'inachèvement de l'homme.* Paris: Éditions de Minuit.

Lasch, C. 1981. "Mass Culture Reconsidered". *Democracy* 1 (4): 7–22.

Laurent, S. 2018. "Gilets jaunes et complotisme". *France Inter. L'Instant M.* 10 December: https://www.franceinter.fr/emissions/l-instant-m/l-instant-m-10-decembre-2018.

Lavocat, F. 2016. *Fait et fiction. Pour une frontière.* Paris: Seuil.

Le Breton, D. 2005. "Rites personnels de passage. Jeunes générations et sens de la vie". *Hermès* 43: 101–108.

Le Guern, P. 2002. *Les cultes médiatiques. Cultures fans et œuvres cultes.* Rennes: Presses universitaires de Rennes.

Le Pape, C. 2005. "Le couple et ses lignées. Mémoire et enjeux de filiation en milieux populaires". *Dossiers d'études de la CNAF* 64: 17–32.

Leadbeater, C. and Miller, P. 2004. *The Pro-Am Revolution: How Enthusiasts Are Changing Our Economy And Society.* London: DEMOS.

Leccardi, C. 2012, "Changing time experience, changing biographies and new youth values". 225–238. In *Youth Policy in a Changing World. From Theory to Practice,* edited by M. Hahn-Bleibtreu and M. Molgat. Leverkusen: Barbara Budrich Publishers.

Lee, F. L. F. 2008. "Hollywood movies in East Asia: Examining cultural discount and performance predictability at the box office". *Asian Journal of Communication* 18 (2): 117–136.

Lehrer, J. 2012. *Imagine: How creativity works.* New York: Houghton Mifflin Harcourt Publishing.

Legon, T. 2011. "La force des liens forts : culture et sociabilité en milieu lycéen". *Réseaux* 165: 215–248.

Léridon, H. 1998. *Les enfants du désir.* Paris: Hachette.

Lévy, P. 1997. *L'intelligence collective. Pour une anthropologie du cyberespace.* Paris: La Découverte.

Liabot, T. 2019. "Sondage : les Gilets jaunes sont plus sensibles aux théories du complot". *Journal du Dimanche.* 11 February: https://www.lejdd.fr/Societe/sondage-les-gilets-jaunes-sont-plus-sensibles-aux-theories-du-complot-3855563.

Liebes, T. and Katz, E. 1990. *The export of meaning: cross national readings of Dallas.* New York: Oxford University Press.

Lin, N. 2000. "Inequality in social capital". *Contemporary Sociology* 29 (6): 785–895.

Lindell, J. and Danielsson, M. 2017. "Moulding cultural capital into cosmopolitan capital. Media practices as reconversion work in a globalizing world". *Nordicom Review* 38 (2): 51–64.

Lipovetsky, G., and Serroy, J. 2013. *L'esthétisation du monde. Vivre à l'âge du capitalisme artiste.* Paris: Gallimard.

Livingstone, S. M. 2007. "From family television to bedroom culture: young people's media at home". 302–321. In *Media Studies: Key Issues and Debates,* edited by E. Devereux. London: Sage.

Livingstone, S. M. and Lunt, P. K. 1994. *Talk on television: Audience participation and public debate.* London: Routledge.

Loveluck, B. 2008. "Internet, vers la démocratie radicale". *Le Débat* 4: 150–166.

Lussault, M. 2017. *Hyper Lieux. Les nouvelles géographies de la mondialisation.* Paris: Seuil.

Madrigal, A. 2014. "How Netflix Reverse Engineered Hollywood". *The Atlantic.* 2 January.

Macé, E. and Maigret, E. 2005. *Penser les médiacultures.* Paris: Armand Colin.

Manin, B. 1995. *Principes du gouvernement représentatif.* Paris: Calman-Lévy.

Mahler, T. 2018, "Chaque événement marquant est dorénavant accompagné de sa version complotiste". *Le Point*. 25 December: https://www.lepoint.fr/societe/les-gilets-jaunes-sont-ils-complotistes-05-12-2018-2276879_23.php.

Maillard, D. 2019. *Une colère française : ce qui a rendu possible les Gilets jaunes*. Paris: Éditions de l'Observatoire.

Mannheim, K. 1952 [1928]. "The problem of generation". 276–322. In *Essays on the Sociology of Knowledge: Collected Works*, Volume 5, edited by P. Kecskemeter. New York: Routledge.

Martel, F. 2010. *Mainstream. Enquête sur cette culture qui plait à tout le monde*. Paris: Flammarion.

Martin, O. 2004. "L'Internet des 10–20 ans. Une ressource pour une communication autonome". *Réseaux* 123: 25–58.

Martuccelli, D. 2010. *La société singulariste*. Paris: Armand Colin.

Math, F., Desor, D. and Witkowski, P. 2015. *Comprendre la violence des enfants : L'apport des neurosciences*. Paris: Dunod.

Maurin, E. 2009. *La peur du déclassement*. Paris: Seuil.

Mayard, A. 2020. "BlackLivesMatter: comment les fans de K-pop ont aidé la révolte", *l'ADN*. 11 June: https://www.ladn.eu/nouveaux-usages/usages-par-generation/blacklivesmatter-comment-fans-k-pop-aident-revolte/.

Mayer, N., Michelat, G., Tiberj, V., and Vitale, T. 2014. "Un refus croissant de l'autre". 157–208. In *La lutte contre le racisme, l'antisémitisme et la xénophobie. Année 2013*, edited by la Commission nationale consultative des droits de l'homme. Paris: La Documentation Française.

Mazin, C., 2017, "Les garçons lisent plus ces dernières années, et voudraient lire plus encore", *ActuaLitté*, 30th January. https://www.actualitte.com/article/monde-edition/les-garcons-lisent-plus-ces-dernieres-annees-et-voudraient-lire-plus-encore/69389.

McCram, R. 2012. "L'art du plagiat". *Courrier International* 25–31 March: 42–43.

McGuigan, J. 2009. *Cool Capitalism*. London: Pluto Press.

McRobbie, A. 1990. *Feminism and Youth Culture: From "Jackie" to "Just Seventeen"*. London: Palgrave.

McWilliam, E. 2009. "Teaching for creativity: From sage to guide to meddler". *Asia Pacific Journal of Education* 29 (3): 281–293.

Mehl, D. 1996. *La télévision de l'intimité*. Paris: Seuil.

Mémeteau, R. 2014. *Pop Culture: réflexions sur les industries du rêve et l'invention des identités*. Paris: La Découverte.

Metton-Gayon, C. 2009. *Les adolescents, leur téléphone et Internet. « Tu viens sur MSN? »*. Paris: L'Harmattan.

Meyers, E. M., Fisher, K. E. and Marcoux, E. 2009. "Making Sense of an Information World: The Everyday-Life Information Behavior of Preteens". *The Library Quarterly* 79 (3): 301–341.

Milner, J.-C. 2014. *Harry Potter. A l'école des sciences morales et politiques.* Paris: Presses universitaires de France.

Modlelski, T. 1982. "The rhythms of reception: daytime television and women's work". 67–75. In *Regarding Television. Critical Approaches. An Anthology,* edited by A. E. Kaplan. Berkeley: California University Publications of America.

Molloy, D. and Tidy, J. 2020. "George Floyd: Anonymous hackers re-emerge amid US unrest." *BBC News.* 1 June: https://www.bbc.com/news/technology-52879000.

Monnot, C. 2009. *Petites filles d'aujourd'hui. L'apprentissage de la féminité.* Paris: Autrement.

Morch, S. and Andersen, H. 2006. "Individualisation and the changing youth life". 63–84. In *A new Youth? Young People, Generations and Family Life,* edited by C. Leccardi and E. Ruspini. Aldershot: Ashgate.

Moreno, R. and Mayer, R. 2000. "A coherence effect in multimedia learning: The case for minimizing irrelevant sounds in the design of multimedia instructional message". *Journal of Educational Psychology* 92 (1): 117–125.

Mouffe, C. 2016. *L'illusion du consensus.* Paris: Albin Michel.

Moulier-Boutang, Y. 2007. *Le capitalisme cognitif : La nouvelle grande transformation.* Paris: Éditions Amsterdam.

Mounk, Y. 2018. *The People vs. Democracy: Why Our Freedom is in Danger and How to Save It,* Harvard: Harvard University Press.

Mullan, K. 2010. "Families that read: A time-diary analysis of young people's and parents' reading". *Journal of Research in Reading* 33: 414–430.

Muxel, A. 2010. *Avoir 20 ans en politique.* Le Seuil: Paris.

Muxel, A. 2008. *Toi, moi et la politique. Amours et convictions.* Paris: Seuil.

Muxel, A. 1984. "Mémoire familiale et projet de socialisation de l'enfant : des obstinations durables". *Dialogue* 84: 46–56.

Nagel, I. 2010. "Cultural participation between the ages of 14 and 24: Intergenerational transmission or cultural mobility?". *European Sociological Review* 26: 541–556.

Noiriel, G. 2019. *Les Gilets jaunes à la lumière de l'histoire : dialogue avec Nicolas Truong.* La Tour-d'Aigues: Éditions de l'Aube.

North, P. 2012. *The Problem of Distraction.* Palo Alto: Stanford University Press.

Notten, N., and Kraaykamp, G. 2009. "Parents and the media study of social differentiation in parental media socialization". *Poetics* 37 (3): 188–200.

Octobre, S. 2017. "Les temporalités du métier de consommateur culturel". 91–112. In *Jeunes et generation,* edited by G. Pronovost and M.-C. Lapointe. Québec: Presses de l'Université du Québec.

Octobre, S. 2014a. *Deux pouces et des neurones, les cultures juvéniles de l'ère médiatique à l'ère numérique.* Paris: La Documentation Française.

Octobre, S. (ed.). 2014b. *Question de genre, questions de culture.* Paris: La Documentation Française.

Octobre, S. 2011. "Du féminin et du masculin : genre et trajectoires culturelles". *Réseaux* 168–169: 23–57.

Octobre, S. 2010. "Les transmissions culturelles chez les adolescents : influences et stratégies individuelles". 205–221. In *Enfance et culture. Transmission, appropriation et representation,* edited by S. Octobre. Paris: La Documentation Française.

Octobre, S. 2004. *Les loisirs culturels des 6–14 ans.* Paris: La Documentation Française.

Octobre, S., and Dallaire, C. (eds). 2017. *Jeunes et cultures. Dialogue franco-québécois.* Laval: Presses universitaires de Laval.

Octobre, S., Détrez, C., Mercklé, P., and Berthomier, N. 2010. *L'enfance des loisirs, trajectoires communes et parcours individuels de la fin de l'enfance à la grande adolescence.* Paris: La Documentation Française.

Octobre, S. and Jauneau, Y. 2008. "Tels parents, tels enfants? Une approche de la transmission culturelle". *Revue française de sociologie* 49 (4): 695–722.

Octobre, S. and Pasquier, D. (ed.). 2011. "Pratiques culturelles et enfance sous le regard du genre". *Réseaux* special issue, 168–169.

Octobre, S. and Patureau, F. 2020. *Sexe et genre des mondes culturels.* Paris: ENS Éditions.

Octobre, S. and Patureau, F. 2018. *Normes de genre dans les institutions culturelles.* Paris: Presses de Sciences Po.

Octobre, S. and Sirota, R. 2013. *L'enfant et ses cultures : approches.* Paris: La Documentation Française.

Ogien, A., and Laugier, S. 2010. *Pourquoi désobéir en démocratie ?* Paris: La Découverte.

Olmsted, K. S. 2011. "The Truth is Out There: Citizen Sleuths from the Kennedy Assassination to the 9/11 Truth Movement". *Diplomatic History* 35 (4): 671–693.

Ophir, E., Nass, C., and Wagner, A. D. 2009. "Cognitive control in media multitaskers". *PNAS* 106 (37): 15583–15587.

Orfeuil, J.-P. 2013. *Mobilités urbaines, l'âge des possibles.* Paris: Scrinéo.

Orfeuil, J.-P. 2012. *Grand Paris. Sortir des illusions, approfondir les ambitions.* Paris: Scrinéo.

Orfeuil, J.-P. 2008. *Une approche laïque de la mobilité.* Paris: Descartes et Cie.

Origgi, G. 2013. "Un certain regard. Pour une épistémologie de la réputation". *Communication* 93 (1): 101–120.

Ottavi, D. 2012. "L'enfant autonome et l'expérimentation démocratique". 33–48. In *Repenser l'enfance,* edited by A. Kerlan and L. Loeffel. Paris: Hermann éditeurs.

Ostashewski, N., Howell, J. and Cleveland-Innes, M. (eds). 2016. *Optimizing K-12 Education Through Online and Blended Learning.* Hershey: IGI Global.

Palfrey, J., and Gasser, U. 2008. *Born Digital. How Children Grow Up in a Digital Age.* New York: Basic Books.

Pariser, E. 2011. *The Filter Bubble. What the Internet is Hiding from You.* New York: The Penguin Press.

Pasquier, D. 2005. *Cultures lycéennes. La tyrannie de la majorité.* Paris: Autrement.

Pasquier, D. 2002. "Les « savoirs minuscules. Le rôle des médias dans l'exploration des identités de sexe". *Éducation et sociétés* 2: 35–44.

Pasquier, D. 1999. *La culture des sentiments. L'expérience télévisuelle des adolescents.* Paris: Éditions de la Maison des Sciences de l'Homme.

Pasquier, D., Beaudoin, V., and Legon, T. 2014. *"Moi je lui donne 5/5", Paradoxe de la critique amateur en ligne.* Paris: Presses des Mines.

Passeron, J.C. 1991. *Le raisonnement sociologique. L'espace non-poppérien du raisonnement naturel.* Paris: Nathan.

Pennycook, G., Cheyne, J., Koehler, D., and Fugelsang, J. 2015. "On the reception and detection of pseudo-profound bullshit". *Judgment and Decision Making* 10: 549–563.

Peltier, M. 2016. *L'ère du complotisme. La maladie d'une société fracturée.* Paris: Les Petits Matins.

Peltier, E., and Satariano, A. 2018. "After Yellow Vests Come Off, Activists in France Use Facebook to Protest and Plan". *New York Times.* 14 December.

Percheron, A. 1991. "La transmission des valeurs". 123–139. In *La Famille, l'état des saviors,* edited by F. de Singly. Paris: La Découverte.

Peterson, R. A. 1991. "Understanding audience segmentation, from elite to omnivore and univore". *Poetics* 21: 243–258.

Peterson, R. A. and Kern, R. 1996. "Changing highbrow taste: From snob to omnivore". *American Sociological Review* 61: 900–907.

Peterson, R. A. and Simkus. A. 1992. "How musical tastes mark occupational status groups". 152–168. In *Cultivating Differences,* edited by M. Lamont and M. Fournier. Chicago: University of Chicago Press.

Pierru, E., and Spire, A. 2008. "Le crépuscule des catégories socio-professionnelles". Revue Française de Sciences Politiques 58 (3): 457–481.

Pieterse, J. N. 2009. *Globalization and Culture. Global mélange.* New York: Rowan & Littlefield Publisher.

Piketti, T. 2013. *Le Capital au XXIe siècle.* Paris: Seuil.

Piper, A. 1998. "Pseudorationality". 173–197. In *Perspectives on Self-Deception,* edited by B. McLaughlin and A. Rorty. Berkeley: University of California Press.

Poyntz, S., and Hoechsmann, M. 2008. "Learning and Teaching Media Literacy in Canada: Embracing and Transcending Eclecticism". *Taboo: The Journal of Culture and Education* 12 (1): https://doi.org/10.31390/taboo.12.1.04.

Pourtier-Tilinac, H. 2011. "La fin du réalisme dans les séries télévisées: la narration à portée généralisante, un tournant télévisuel?". *Réseaux* 165: 21–51.

Prensky, M. 2001. "Digital Natives, Digital Immigrants". *On the Horizon* 9 (5):1–6.

Quemin, A. 2013. *Les stars de l'art contemporain. Notoriété et consécration artistiques dans les arts visuels.* Paris: CNRS Éditions.

Ramdarshan Bold, M. 2016. "The Return of the Social Author: Negotiating Authority and Influence on Wattpad". *Convergence* 24 (2): 117–136.

Regev, M. 2013. *Pop-Rock Music: Aesthetic Cosmopolitanism in Late Modernity.* Cambridge: Polity Press.

Renard, J.-B. 2010. "Croyances fantastiques et rationalité". *L'Année sociologique* 60 (1): 115–135.

Renard, J.-B. 2011. *Le merveilleux.* Paris: CNRS Éditions.

Retière, J.-N. 2003. "Autour de l'autochtone: réflexions sur la notion de capital social populaire". *Politix* 16 (63): 121–143.

Ricœur, P. 1980. *Soi-même comme un autre.* Paris: Seuil.

Ritzer, G. 1993. *The McDonaldization of Society: An Investigation into the Changing Character of Contemporary Social Life.* Newbury Park: Pine Forge Press.

Robertson, R. 1995. "Glocalisation: Time-Space and Homogeneity-Heterogeneity". 23–44. In *Global Modernities,* edited by M. Featherstone, S. Lash, and R. Robertson. London: Sage.

Rosa, H. 2010. *Accélération. Une critique sociale du temps.* Paris: La Découverte.

Rosanvallon, P. 2006. *La contre-démocratie. La politique à l'âge de la défiance.* Paris: Seuil.

Rosling, H., Rosling Rönnlund, A. and Rosling, O. 2018. *Factfulness. Ten Reason We Are Wrong About The World and Why Things are Better Than You Think.* New York: Flatiron Books.

Roudet, B. 2014. "Les jeunes, la politique et la démocratie". 115–143. In *Une jeunesse différente ?,* edited by O. Galland and B. Roudet. Paris: La Documentation Française.

Rousselin, P. 2014. *Les démocraties en danger.* Paris: First éditions.

Saint-Maurice (de), T. 2009. *Philosophie en séries.* Paris: Ellipses.

Salmon, C. 2019. *L'ère du Clash.* Paris: Fayard.

Sauvayre, R. 2012. *Croire à l'incroyable. Anciens et nouveaux adeptes.* Paris: Presses universitaires de France.

Schaeffer, J.-M. 2016. "Pour une approche esthétique de la lecture". *Lecture Jeune* 157: 25–29.

Schaeffer, J.-M. 2011. *Petite écologie des études littéraires : pourquoi et comment étudier la littérature.* Vincennes: Éditions Thierry Marchaisse.

Schaeffer, J.-M. 1995. *L'expérience esthétique.* Paris: Gallimard.

Scholz, C., Baek, E., O'Donnell, M., Kim, H., Cappella, J., and Falk, E. 2017. "A Neural Model of Valuation and Information Virality". *Proceedings of the National Academy of Sciences* 114: 2281–2886.

Schön, E. 1993. "La fabrication du lecteur". 17–44. In *Identité, lecture, écriture,* edited by F. de Singly. Paris: Centre Georges Pompidou/BPI.

Schwartz, B. 2004. *The Paradox of Choice. Why More is Less.* New York: HarperCollins Publishers.

Ségalen, M. 2011. *A qui appartiennent les enfants ?* Paris: Taillandier.

Segatti, P., Gavalli, A., Biorcio, R., and Lescure, N. 1998. "Changement culturel et orientations politiques chez les jeunes européens". *Agora/Débats jeunesse* 12 (1): 81–97.

Sénecat, A. 2019. "Enquête sur les usines à fausses informations qui fleurissent sur Facebook". *Le Monde.* 5 July: http://www.lemonde.fr/les-decodeurs/article/2017/07/05/enquete-sur-les-usines-a-fausses-informations-qui-fleurissent-sur-facebook_5156313_4355770.html.

Sénecat, A. 2019. "Derrière la percée des Gilets Jaunes, des réseaux pas si « spontanés » et « apolitiques »". *Le Monde.* 17 April: https://www.lemonde.fr/les-decodeurs/article/2019/04/17/derriere-la-percee-des-gilets-jaunes-des-reseaux-pas-si-spontanes-et-apolitiques_5451242_4355770.html.

Serain, F., Vaysse, F., Chazottes, P., and Caillet, E. (eds). 2016. *La médiation culturelle, la cinquième roue du carrosse?* Paris: L'Harmattan.

Serres, M. 2012. *Petite Poucette.* Paris: Le Pommier.

Shusterman, R. 2007. *Conscience du corps. Pour une soma-esthétique.* Paris: Éclat.

Signoret, P. 2018. "Face aux théories du complot sur YouTube, les « anticonspis » veulent « occuper le terrain »". *Le Monde.* 14 February: https://www.lemonde.fr/pixels/article/2018/02/13/face-aux-theories-du-complot-sur-youtube-les-anticonspis-veulent-occuper-le-terrain_5255963_4408996.html.

Simon, H. 1971. "Designing organizations for an information-rich world". 37–72. In *Computers, Communication and the Public Interest,* edited by M. Greenberger. Baltimore: John Hopkins Press.

Simondon, G. 2005. *L'Individuation à la lumière des notions de forme et d'information.* Grenoble: Million.

Singly (de), F. 2006. *Les Adonaissants.* Paris: Armand Colin.

Singly (de), F. (ed.). 2004. *Enfants-Adultes. Vers une égalité des statuts ?* Paris: Universalis.

Singly (de), F. 1995. "Elias et le romantisme éducatif. Sur les tensions de l'éducation contemporaine". *Cahiers internationaux de sociologie* 99: 279–287.

Singly (de), F. 1993, "Les habits neufs de la domination masculine". *Esprit* November: 54–66.

Sintomer, Y. 2011. *Petite histoire de l'expérimentation démocratique.* Paris: La Découverte.

Sirota, R. (ed). 2006. *Éléments pour une sociologie de l'enfance.* Rennes: Presses universitaires de Rennes.

Sola Pool, I. 1990. *Technologies Without Boundaries: On Telecommunication in a Global Age.* Cambridge: Harvard University Press.

Speber, D. and Wilson, D. 1989. *La pertinence, communication et cognition.* Paris: Éditions de Minuit.

Speber, D. 2010. "The Guru Effect". *Review of Philosophy and Psychology* 1: 583–592.

Stiegler, B. (ed). 2014. *Digital studies: organologie des savoirs et technologies de la connaissance.* Paris: FYP Éditions.

Stora, M. 2012. "L'adolescence à l'épreuve du virtuel : entre construction identitaire et excès". *Lecture Jeunesse* September: 44–47.

Strathern, M. 1997. " 'Improving ratings': Audit in the British University System". *European Review* 5 (3): 305–321.

Surowiecki, J.,2004. *La sagesse des foules.* Paris: Jean Claude Lattes.

Swire, B., Berinsky, A., Lewandowsky, S., and Ecker, U. 2017. "Processing political misinformation: comprehending the Trump phenomenon". *Royal Society Open Science* 4: https://doi.org/10.1098/rsos.160802.

Szendy, P. 2009. *Listen: A History of Our Ears.* New York: Fordham University Press.

Taguieff, P.-A. 2006. *Le sens du progrès.* Paris: Champs Flammarion.

Tarde, G., 1902. *Psychologie économique.* Paris: Alcan.

Tarde, G. 1903 [1895]. *The Laws of Imitation.* New York: H. Holt.

Tardif, J., and Farchy, J. 2006. *Les enjeux de la mondialisation culturelle.* Paris: Éditions Hors Commerce.

Taylor, C. 1989. *Sources of the Self.* Cambridge: Harvard University Press.

Thiébaut, M. 2019. *Gilets jaunes : vers une démocratie réelle ?* Versailles: VA Press.

Tiffany, K. 2020. "Why K-pop Fans Are No Longer Posting About K-pop". *The Atlantic.* 6 June: https://www.theatlantic.com/technology/archive/2020/06/twitter-k-pop-protest-black-lives-matter/612742/.

Tisseron, S. 2016. "L'âge du strip-tease numérique". *Sciences Humaines* 278: 30–31.

Tisseron, S. 2013. "Faut-il avoir peur des MMORPG? Que disent les recherches à propos des jeux de rôle massivement multijoueurs (MMORPG)?". *Sciences Humaines* 252: 11–15.

Tisseron, S. 2003. *L'intimité surexposée.* Paris: Hachette.

Toffle, A. 1974 [1970]. *Le choc du futur.* Paris: Denoël.

Tomlinson, J. 2003. "Globalization and Cultural Identity". 269–278. In *The Global Transformations Reader: An Introduction to the Globalization Debate,* edited by D. Held and A. McGrew. Cambridge: Polity Press.

Tomlinson, J. 1999. *Globalization and culture.* Chicago: University of Chicago Press.

Trudy, J. 2010. *Anatomie du scénario.* Paris: Nouveau Monde.

Turner, F. 2006. *From Counterculture to Cyberculture: Stewart Brand, the Whole Earth Network, and the Rise of Digital Utopianism.* Chicago: University of Chicago Press.

Urfalino, P. 2007. "La décision par consensus apparent. Nature et propriétés". *Revue européenne des sciences sociales* 136: 47–70.

Veltz, P. 2005. *Mondialisation, villes et territoires.* Paris: Presses universitaires de France.

Von Schiller, F., 2004 [1794]. *On the aesthetic education of Man.* London: Dover Publications.

Wagner, A.-C. 2010. "Le jeu de la mobilité et de l'autochtonie au sein des classes supérieures". *Regards sociologiques* 40: 89–98.

Ward, K. J. 1999. "Cyber-ethnography and the emergence of the virtually new community". *Journal of information and technology* 14 (1): 95–105.

Wilde, O. 1891. *Intentions*. London: Methuen and Co.
Williams, B. 2002. *Truth and Truthfulness*. Princeton: Princeton University Press.
Winckler, M. 2012. *Petit éloge des séries télé*. Paris: Gallimard.
Winner, L., 1980. "Do Artifacts Have Politics?". *Daedalus* 109 (1): 120–146.
Wollscheid, S. 2014. "The impact of the leisure reading behaviors of both parents on children's reading behavior: investigating differences between sons and daughters". *Poetics* 45: 36–54.
Yonnet, P. 1999. *Travail, loisir. Temps libre et lien social*. Paris: Gallimard.
Zaffran, J. 2010. *Le temps de l'adolescence, entre contrainte et liberté*. Rennes: Presses universitaires de Rennes.
Zegai, M. 2010. "Trente ans de catalogues de jouets : mouvances et permanences des catégories de genre". In *Actes du colloque Enfance et cultures : regards des sciences humaines et sociales,* edited by S. Octobre and R. Sirota: http://www.enfanceetcultures.culture.gouv.fr/actes/zegai.pdf.

Index

Activism
   Cultural activism 42
   Media activism 152, 157
   Political activism 152
Additive comprehension 59, 74–75, 78
Aesthetization 35
Aesthetic
   Aesthetico (cultural) experience 56, 104, 106
   Aestheticism 49
Amateur 5–7, 22, 24, 36, 37, 50, 128, 174
   Amateurism/amateur expertise 45, 56, 61–64, 97, 105, 108, 116
   Pro-amateur/professional amateur 37–42, 47, 158
   Amateur communities 46, 76, 94, 109, 116
Appropriation/reappropriation 18, 48, 51, 65, 68, 73, 95, 102, 122, 162, 174
   Recycling 20, 51
Attachment 8, 16, 48, 72
Attention 3, 33, 35, 51, 54–58
Attention blindness 55
   Attention span 20, 51–53
   Collective/joint attention 52
   Hyper attention 55–58
   Partial/suspended/distracted attention 54–55
Attraction 64, 65, 89, 106
Audience/digital audience 27, 29, 30, 39, 50–51, 56, 59, 64, 70, 91, 97, 104, 116, 129, 143, 149, 162
Autonomy 4, 10, 40, 42, 81, 89, 91–93, 102, 145
   Cultural autonomy/digital autonomy 81–83, 86–89, 96, 99, 137
   Private/Public autonomy 84–85
   Political autonomy 141
Authentic/authenticity 6, 10, 18, 23, 40, 51, 64, 66, 71–73, 82–88, 108, 140, 147, 158

Big data 15, 31, 34, 45, 149
Bullshit 112–113
Buzz/Media Buzz 34, 55, 61, 66, 77, 114

Capitalism/ artistic/creative/cognitive/ emotional capitalism 15, 16, 46, 77, 87, 88, 145, 172, 175

Choice/cultural choice/hyper-choice 4, 10, 21, 29, 32–35, 47, 59, 75–77, 81, 86, 88–91, 95, 102, 115, 128, 133, 140, 177
Citizenship/Cultural citizenship 73, 84, 100, 103, 111–113, 116, 139, 164–165, 177
Cognitive/ cognitive skills or abilities 30, 52, 54–57, 60–61, 65, 83, 100, 104–105, 108, 113–115, 125, 150
   Cognitive bubbles 160–162
   Cognitive effects or costs 146, 161
   Cognitive dissonance 177
Collaborative 15, 43, 45, 48, 74, 156, 172
Collective intelligence 42–47, 49, 51, 144, 168
   experience 33, 107
Community/communities 16, 28, 38, 46, 85, 148, 164
   Online/digital community 22, 25, 39–43, 94, 103, 107, 109, 143
   Imagined community 149
Conformity 86, 102, 151
Convergence 15–16, 28, 43, 51, 66, 110
Conversation 1, 5, 13, 64, 85, 92, 98–99, 130, 133, 144–148
Cosmopolitanism/cosmopolopitanization/ cosmopolitan 7, 27, 68–70, 73
Creation/Co-creation 2, 4, 14, 28, 37, 39–42, 47, 52, 61, 73, 111, 114, 130, 153
Creativity 3, 6, 11, 37, 47, 48–51, 60, 94, 98, 102, 108, 113–114, 140, 171–174, 177
Credibility 76, 146, 149
Crowds 147–149
Culture
   mass culture 2, 21–23, 49, 57
   popular culture 21, 26, 43, 49, 56, 94, 103
Cultural
   autonomy 81, 86–88, 96, 99
   behavior 1, 2, 8, 35
   capital 33, 42, 72, 86, 103, 107, 125, 135
   citizenship 73, 84, 101, 103, 111, 116, 139
   consumer 4, 6, 61, 87, 89
   contents 4, 8, 15, 19–21, 75, 92, 100–103, 110, 121, 125, 128, 133, 142, 157, 159, 163, 167
   engagement 36, 37, 86, 90, 95
   expertise 45–47
   globalization 5, 18, 42, 69

Cultural (*cont.*)
  industries/technocultural industries   4, 6, 8, 12, 18–21, 33, 35, 39, 42, 58, 69, 82, 84, 94, 101, 106, 108, 116, 139
  institutions   7, 13, 19, 22, 45–46, 65, 115
  inequality   13, 42, 47, 119, 131, 137
  legitimacy   21, 47, 97, 108, 137
  participation   6, 47, 73, 139, 143, 165
  popular culture / low-brow   21, 26, 43, 47, 49, 50, 56, 94, 96, 103, 137
  poaching   37
  repertoire   6, 47, 73, 84, 93, 96, 116
  remix/remixing   49–51, 93, 152

Democracy   13, 31, 67, 107, 140, 142, 144, 146, 148, 151, 153, 156–159
  Neo-democracy   163–169
Digital
  computational device   30
  media   4, 19, 51, 83, 86, 102, 117, 140
  sociability   91
  natives   1, 3, 24, 117, 110, 122, 136
Digitalization   16, 26, 29, 163
Divide
  access divide   120
  transferability divide   123
  usage divide   121

Eclecticism/omnivorism   21, 25, 96–98, 116, 135, 140, 173
Education
  cultural education   11, 25, 100, 102, 117, 157
  educators   9, 48, 90, 124
  informal education   102, 124
  self-education   100–118
Emotion/emotional   16, 25, 27, 29, 30, 39, 46, 48, 50, 53, 59, 62, 63–65, 79, 96, 107, 127–128, 146–149, 158, 163, 176
  emotion economy   65
  emotional capitalism   16
Empowerment/ self-empowerment   11, 63, 82, 90, 115, 128, 131–132, 140, 171
Engagement/cultural or techno-cultural engagement   9, 38, 43, 46, 62, 73, 81, 86, 89–95, 114, 122, 140–141, 143
  civic engagement   56, 152, 157, 160, 169
Ethics/ethical   27, 48, 60, 73, 79, 84, 85, 100, 112, 117, 120, 140, 144, 154

Experience/consumption experience   5, 16, 24, 49, 55, 63, 65, 75, 78, 90, 97, 124
  aesthetic/cultural experience   56, 61
  collective experience   33, 40, 64, 76, 107
  learning experience   46, 101
  virtual experience   62, 77
Experimentation   59, 61–63, 95, 97
Expertise   32, 38–39, 42, 45–46, 61, 78, 94, 109, 116, 150, 159
Expression   23, 34, 47, 65, 84, 102, 140–141, 167
  self-expression   41, 60, 63, 73, 129, 145, 157, 161, 174, 176
  expressivity   95
Extimacy   85, 160

Fan/fandomism   2, 21, 24, 28, 37, 41, 47, 53, 61, 82, 91, 95, 142–143
  fan community   38, 48, 63, 76, 102, 108, 113
Fears   5, 9–10, 14–18, 25, 29, 35, 53, 72, 81, 147, 151
Fiction/ fictional/fictionalization   62, 70, 106, 112, 154, 159
Filter   112, 149, 160
  reputation filter   76
  filtering   85

Gender   6, 11, 13, 61, 69, 89, 102, 107, 109, 129, 132–134, 157, 173, 175
Globalization   16–18, 42, 46, 50, 66, 68–69, 71, 95, 144, 166, 171, 175

Hacktivism   154, 157
Hoax   28, 126, 127, 147, 158
Homogeneity/ homogenization   18, 23, 32, 36, 50, 69, 132, 137
Hyper-choice   4, 29

Identity   18, 35, 36, 42, 60, 61, 80, 85, 86, 91, 93, 95–96, 114, 126–127, 129, 146, 157, 159, 160, 171, 175
  Identity marker   1, 6, 35
Identification   97, 106, 156
Imagination   49, 50, 97
Inclusion/inclusive   51, 97–99, 103, 120, 123–124, 153, 155–157, 162, 171
Individualism/individualization   14–15, 26, 59–60, 82, 85, 88, 90, 97, 128, 144, 163
Inequality/inequalities   13, 42, 119–120, 123, 125, 129–130, 132–133, 135–137, 171, 174

INDEX

Information   4, 7, 18, 29–30, 33, 36, 43, 45, 48, 52–55, 64–65, 74, 76–78, 83, 85, 89, 98–99, 102–103, 109–113, 122, 125–129, 144, 146, 150, 153–154, 158–161, 166, 172
   Information technology   34
   Information overload   52
Innovation   6, 14, 27, 41, 49–51, 98, 104, 131, 135, 156, 173, 177
Intimacy   64, 87, 105, 108

Knowledge   8, 11, 17, 22, 25, 39, 40, 42–46, 58, 62, 64–65, 71–72, 75–76, 86, 101–104, 108–109, 114–116, 128–129, 140, 150, 153, 161–163, 172
   miniscule knowledge,   8, 89
   reflexive knowledge   24

Language   17, 29, 38, 68–71, 73–75, 109, 116, 143, 158
Learning   1, 11, 45–46, 48, 62, 74, 83–84, 90, 96, 100, 106, 108–110, 117, 128, 166, 177
Leisure   6–8, 11, 38, 47, 49, 63–64, 71, 78, 82–83, 87, 90, 116, 120, 123–124, 127, 130, 132–133, 141, 146
Legitimacy   4, 24, 33, 44, 87, 97, 104, 108, 114, 137, 144, 176
Literacy/transliteracy   100, 101, 110–112, 115, 117, 124, 177
Local/localism   5, 16–18, 23, 28, 30, 40, 44, 46, 50, 65, 69, 72–73, 97, 99, 103, 106, 114, 136, 146, 171, 175

Mediaculture   1–9
Mediatization   63
Mediation/remediation   2, 15, 22, 28, 38, 47, 74, 83, 108, 115–118, 128, 138, 149
Mobility   39, 45–46, 60, 66–67, 71–74, 143
Moral panic   1, 9, 10, 12, 14, 26
Multitasking   53–54, 106, 128
Mythos   43, 73, 174

Networks   6
   digital networks   21, 66, 67, 77, 78, 92, 168
   social networks   16, 17–19, 21, 28, 30, 34, 36, 60, 61, 67, 70, 87, 92, 109, 113, 116, 120, 126, 130, 132, 142, 147, 149, 153, 158, 160, 164–166, 175
Neutrality   6, 66, 101, 140

Norm   67, 81–82, 86, 90, 98, 99
   social norm   67, 172
   collective norm   86

Omnivore/Omnivorism   21, 96, 99, 135

Participation   6, 36, 38–41, 45–51, 64, 73, 75, 81, 86, 89, 90, 94, 05, 105, 109, 111, 116, 139–140, 141, 143, 154, 156, 157, 163, 168, 169, 175
Passion   8, 25, 38, 39, 41, 47, 83, 124, 171
Pleasure   23, 47, 57, 104, 106, 127, 128, 159
Political   9, 13, 23, 31, 34, 45, 48, 60, 63, 94–95, 103, 110–113, 120, 126–128, 131–132, 137, 140, 143, 144
   political space   142–144
   politics   27, 46–47, 95, 144–145, 147–148, 151, 155, 164, 168, 176
Power   2, 3, 22, 27, 44–45, 49, 69, 78, 85, 110, 119, 137, 141, 143, 145, 147, 148, 150, 153, 154, 155, 159, 164, 175
   empowerment   3, 11, 38, 63, 68, 82, 90, 115, 128, 131, 171
Presentification   65–66
Pro-am/pro amateur   37–43, 58, 144, 175
   -sumer   37
Protest   155–157, 163–166
Public   31, 32, 36, 39, 42, 48, 50, 60, 62, 85, 104, 107, 108, 115, 130, 149, 152
   digital public   151
   emotional public   64
   imagined publics   144
   public opinion   46, 127, 147–149, 151
   public space   126, 138, 144, 152–153, 163, 168, 174–176
   public sphere   85, 108, 146

Recommendation   2, 29, 31, 32, 33, 35, 74, 77–79, 87, 91, 97, 112
Recycling   20, 51
Regime
   additive regime   76, 78
   emotional regime   68
   techno-cultural regime   6, 14, 20, 21, 37, 101, 113, 119, 140, 145–146
   regime of truth/of opinion   158, 162, 174
Reputation/reputational   4, 30–33, 40, 76–79

Resources 8, 42, 44, 52, 71, 72, 73, 81, 88, 98, 103, 112, 122, 125, 129, 156
  cultural/technocultural resources 4, 6, 33, 42, 58, 119, 171
Rumor 77, 127, 145, 146, 166

Scapes 8
Self
  self–construction 63, 96, 103
  self-expression 41, 59, 73, 129, 145, 158, 161, 174
Skills 4, 5, 6, 10, 13, 23, 40, 48, 52, 56, 66, 71, 82, 85, 87, 93, 96, 100, 105, 117, 128, 134, 138, 145, 171
  cognitive skills 56, 57, 153, 161–162
  digital skills 119, 122, 123–124, 151
  language/linguistic skills 71–72, 75, 132
  political skills 140
  social skills 8
  technical skills 47, 100, 143
  technocultural skills 39, 102, 108, 110–115, 128, 155, 177
Sociability 60, 91, 93, 105
Social capital 74, 76, 86, 102
Space 73, 74, 76, 80, 81, 84, 85, 87, 88, 92, 105, 129
  affinity space 108–109
  cyberspace 94
  hyperspace 71
  political space 142
  public space 126, 138, 144, 152–153, 163, 168, 174–176
  private space 64, 84, 85, 140, 144
  space segregation 85

Speech 130, 131, 144, 152, 153
Spreadable/spreadable media 70
Symbol/symbols/symbolic 7, 17, 27, 34, 46, 61, 67, 73, 84, 88–89, 135, 163

Taste 10–11, 15, 24, 30, 32–33, 35, 64–65, 71, 75, 78, 82, 84, 87, 89–93, 97–99, 108, 128, 135, 173
Television shows 12, 17–19, 56, 62, 68, 75, 105, 108, 171
Ties
  Strong ties 91–93
  Weak ties 28, 73, 93, 145
Time/cultural time 1, 4–5, 10, 16, 19–20, 24, 29, 44, 56, 58, 82, 84, 86
  Free time/leisure time 4, 7, 11, 82, 87, 119, 123–124
Transmedia 25, 66, 74–75, 94, 105–106, 130, 151
Transmission 1, 6, 10–12, 14, 22, 42, 45, 62, 86–88, 134
Truth 31, 85, 108, 112, 114, 129, 146–148, 150–153, 158
  Post-truth/alternative truth 112–113, 158

Video game/gaming 5, 7, 9, 11–12, 25, 28, 36, 39–41, 43, 47, 50, 56, 62–64, 67, 76, 87, 96, 104, 106, 109–110, 115, 134, 152
  Serious game 83–84
Visibility 7, 19, 22, 51–52, 61, 66, 73, 78, 85, 94, 113, 129, 144, 148, 163
  Victory of the visible 79
Visual 49, 61, 65–66, 69, 74–75, 104, 109, 111, 125, 128, 130, 151